IN SEA
OF THE BLUES

Marybeth Hamilton was born in California and teaches American History at Birkbeck College, University of London. She is the author of *When I'm Bad, I'm Better: Mae West, Sex and American Entertainment.*

By the same author

When I'm Bad, I'm Better: Mae West, Sex and American Entertainment

MARYBETH HAMILTON

IN SEARCH
OF THE BLUES

Black Voices, White Visions

JONATHAN CAPE
LONDON

Published by Jonathan Cape 2007

2 4 6 8 10 9 7 5 3 1

Copyright © Marybeth Hamilton 2007

Marybeth Hamilton has asserted her right under the Copyright, Designs
and Patents Act 1988 to be identified as the author of this work

The author is grateful for permission to use the following images: 'Howard Odum
outside log cabin' from Howard Washington Odum Papers, courtesy of Southern
Historical Collection, Wilson Library, the University of North Carolina at Chapel Hill.
'Frances Densmore records Blackfoot' courtesy of the Library of Congress.
'Dorothy Scarborough' courtesy of The Texas Collection, Baylor University, Waco, Texas.
'John Lomax's recording machine' courtesy of the Archive of Folk Culture, the Library
of Congress. 'Alan Lomax' courtesy of the Alan Lomax Archive. 'Charles Edward Smith,
William Russell and Frederic Ramsey' courtesy of the Historic New Orleans
Collection. 'Fred and Amelia Ramsey' courtesy of Martha Ramsey. 'James McKune'
courtesy of Pete Whelan. Every effort has been made to obtain necessary permissions
with reference to copyright material. The publishers apologise if inadvertently any
sources remain unacknowledged.

First published in Great Britain in 2007 by
Jonathan Cape
Random House, 20 Vauxhall Bridge Road,
London SW1V 2SA

www.randomhouse.co.uk

Addresses for companies within The Random House Group Limited can be found at:
www.randomhouse.co.uk/offices.htm

The Random House Group Limited Reg. No. 954009

A CIP catalogue record for this book is available from the British Library

ISBN 9780224060189

The Random House Group Limited makes every effort to ensure that the papers used
in its books are made from trees that have been legally sourced from well-managed
and credibly certified forests. Our paper procurement policy can be found at
www.randomhouse.co.uk/paper.htm

Typeset in Bodoni by Palimpsest Book Production Limited,
Grangemouth, Stirlingshire

Printed and bound in Great Britain by
Mackays of Chatham plc, Chatham, Kent

For Jackson and Lukas

CONTENTS

The ruins of a bridge, Mississippi Delta

Chapter One

The Delta Revisited

On Old Highway 61 in Mississippi, between Lula and Robinsonville in the heart of the Delta, stand the remains of a wooden railroad bridge partially submerged in a murky swamp. The air enveloping the bridge is sticky and fetid, thick with the smell of decayed vegetation, and the dark, stagnant water stretches far into the distance, flooding the banks, engulfing the trees. To look at the scene is to peer at an eerie, apparently timeless landscape, primordial and untouched by history, the world Noah might have glimpsed after the flood.

I photographed this bridge in May 1999 while driving south through the Mississippi Delta, aware all the while of following a well worn and cliché-ridden trail. The trek through the Delta in search of the roots of the blues has been a trope of music writing since the early 1960s, the opening years of the blues revival, when white Americans and Europeans rediscovered a music that African Americans had long left behind. My aim in coming to the Delta was, I thought, more sophisticated: to get a handle on the pilgrim experience, to reconstruct the breathless hunt for the blues's authentic origins. And yet here I was, slamming to a halt on a desolate highway, bewitched by the sight of that decaying bridge, transported into what felt like a mystical landscape, a world frozen outside the passage of time.

The tale of the Delta as a land outside history was told by the area's earliest boosters: turn-of-the-century railroad entrepreneurs, who seized upon a region that had only just been opened for agriculture – as late as 1860, ninety per cent of the Delta was covered in swamps – and wrapped it in the romantic imagery of the Old South. 'Nowhere in Mississippi have antebellum conditions of landholding been so nearly preserved as in the Delta,' rhapsodised the Illinois Central Railroad in 1910. 'The Negro is naturally gregarious in instinct, and is never so happy as when massed together in large numbers, as on the Delta plantations.' That tale – framing the Delta as 'the Old South reincarnate', with its unspoken assurances of subservient darkies – was given a more sinister cast by the anthropologists who flocked to the region in the mid-1930s. Those observers – John Dollard, Hortense Powdermaker, Allison Davis, all of them Northern and, in Davis's case, black – painted a stark, vivid portrait of a land of unparalleled brutality, marked by naked extremes of wealth and destitution and by caste domination in its most blatant forms.

Yet none of those descriptions of the Delta landscape was as luminous as that set out in the blues revival. The 1960s saw a flood of record collectors and folk-music enthusiasts head south from Memphis and north from Vicksburg armed with tape recorder, camera and notepad, determined to cut through the dross churned out by the commercial record companies and capture the sound of the real thing. The real thing was the Delta blues, the name they devised for the intense voices they found on scratchy 78s and newly issued LP compilations: singers like Son House, Skip James, Charley Patton and Robert Johnson. What distinguished the music, above all, was the arresting character of the singing. 'Rough, spontaneous, crude and unfinished', dominated by 'stark, unrelieved emotion', this was an intense distillation of the music of slavery, 'only a step from the wordless field cries and hollers of an older generation'. In those recordings these new listeners heard the birth of the blues: impassioned voices echoing with pain and privation, emanating from a flat, waterlogged, primitive landscape seemingly untouched by the modern world.

As I made my way south – past the bridge to Clarksdale, Tutwiler, Itta Bena, Parchman, all the places whose names resonate in accounts of blues history – I found myself wholly caught up in that story. Everywhere seemed to demand to be photographed, as my trek was punctuated by enchanted moments when the Delta looked as it was supposed to: trees submerged in water, crumbling sharecroppers' cabins, arid fields under a moonlit sky. At some level I knew that these photos were hackneyed, that they had been taken by every blues pilgrim before me. But the power of the tale was too strong to resist, that sense of stepping out of history, and entering a mythic, primordial world.

It took several months for the spell to be broken. Over time, once I'd returned to a frenetically urban, post-industrial London, that railway bridge began to tell a new tale and I came to see the hand of modernity in my photograph. In the swamp's stagnant water, I saw commercial land clearance: the process, which had absorbed the efforts of thousands of black workers in the late nineteenth century, of draining some areas and engulfing others to open the Delta for cotton crops. And in the submerged bridge I saw remnants of the rail network that had connected the Delta to Chicago in the early twentieth century. If every landscape is a work of the mind, shaped by the memories, the obsessions, of its observers, these were memories that had been pushed to the margins: a Delta determinedly touched by history, manipulated by commerce and machines.

I first heard of the Delta blues sometime around 1977, when I was going to high school in San Diego, about as far south-west as you can get in America without crossing the Mexican border. The school was dominated, in ways more and less tangible, by the presence of the Pacific Ocean. If you sat high enough in the football bleachers you could see the breaking waves. I did not surf or spend much time on the beach or go on dates or to parties or dances. As a child I had thrown myself into fleeting, solitary obsessions (Scout Finch, Eleanor Roosevelt, Anne Frank, Pauline Kael), and in my early teens I discovered music. My initial passion was for the New York Dolls, whose songs sounded rough and unfinished, partly because they could just about manage their instruments, and who appeared on the cover of their first album in drag, their faces slathered in pancake make-up, the band's name scrawled across the top in lipstick.

At first this obsession was solitary too, but eventually I found friends who shared it, some my age and some a bit older, who had dropped out of college or never bothered to go. On Saturday nights five or six of us would cram into a Volkswagen Beetle and drive to Los Angeles to the Whiskey a Go Go to see and hear whoever was playing: Patti Smith, Talking Heads, the Ramones, Blondie, the Germs, the Screamers, the Dickies, X. We were a cohort who considered ourselves an avant-garde. Our bible was *Creem*, an iconoclastic compendium of salacious party gossip and flamboyantly articulate record reviews published monthly out of a commune in Detroit. Like most of the *Creem* writers, we took pride in the fact that the stuff we listened to was too edgy and raw for the radio to handle (though once, en route to LA, we heard a local AM radio station play 'Pretty Vacant' by the Sex Pistols, and in the shock and exhilaration that followed we almost careened off the road).

One day at the library I saw that a writer whose name I knew from *Creem*, Greil Marcus, had published a book called *Mystery Train: Images of America in Rock 'n' Roll Music*. I took it home and spent a week reading it. Though his subjects were, by and large, musicians I didn't particularly care about, the book made surprising connections – between Randy Newman and Herman Melville, or Elvis Presley and the Puritan Jonathan Edwards, who left his mark on American history with a fire-and-brimstone sermon called 'Sinners in the Hands of an Angry God'. Marcus explored the ways in which the greatest rock artists, like the greatest writers, reworked enduring American stories. At their best and most risky, they contested 'the very idea of America', teasing out its dark undercurrents and exposing something 'complicated, dangerous, and alive'.

Most dangerous of all was a musician Marcus profiled early on, a Mississippi blues singer named Robert Johnson. I had never heard his name before, and even Marcus knew only the barest facts of his life: that he was born in 1911 and died violently and mysteriously in 1938. But it was his music that mattered: the twenty-nine songs he recorded in 1936 and 1937, songs that loomed over every blues singer and every rock and roller that followed, because they went further than any artist had dared into the underside of the American dream. Johnson sang of 'a world without salvation, redemption, or rest', of anguished, incessant wandering, of being pursued by baying hellhounds, of Satan knocking at his door. While blues in general 'made the terrors of the world . . . more real', Johnson's made them more real than anyone else's. His greatest recording, 'Stones In My Passway', was 'a two-minute image of doom that has the power to make doom a fact'.

This was serious, weighty stuff. Whatever unvarnished truth I was hearing in punk, it seemed Robert Johnson had got there first, and in his shadow everything else became play-acting, flimsy, trifling, inconsequential and fake. Reading about him left me feeling challenged and, in some obscure way, affronted. Marcus's rhapsodic praise of the tormented drifter seemed somehow to exclude me, as a woman if nothing else. Perhaps that was why it took me fifteen years to get around to listening to Johnson's recordings, and why, when I did, I heard very little, just a guitar, a keening vocal and a lot of surface noise. I certainly did not hear the tale of existential anguish that Marcus and others discerned within them. I wondered if this revealed some defect in me, or if there might be another blues story to tell.

As it is ordinarily told, the story of the Delta blues has a prelude of sorts in August 1920, with the release of 'Crazy Blues' by Mamie Smith and her Hot Jazz Titans, the first blues recording by an African American singer. Though sold almost exclusively in black areas and steeply priced at one dollar (by contrast, admission to the motion pictures cost ten cents), 'Crazy Blues' stunned virtually everyone by selling hundreds of thousands of copies, 75,000 in its first month of release. Its success revealed the scale of a musical market that the recording industry had long refused to believe could exist. That African Americans would buy phonograph records in disproportionate numbers became startlingly audible in those last weeks of summer: people said that you could hear Mamie Smith's recording playing in every black neighbourhood in the US.

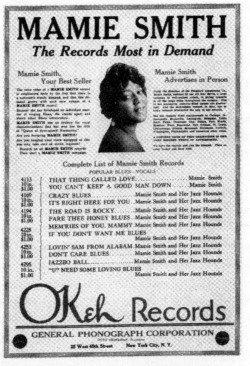

Okeh's advertisement for Mamie Smith

What followed were recordings by Ma Rainey, Ida Cox, Victoria Spivey, Alberta Hunter and a host of performers with the surname Smith, an outpouring that is described in identical terms in nearly every work of blues history. These women, so we are told, were popularisers, not folk singers: trained on the black vaudeville and tent-show circuits, their gift was for glitz and titillation, not the raw truth-telling that was the blues at its most intense. That kind of music would not be recorded until the end of the decade – and this is when the story really heats up, when the phonograph records acquire integrity, when (to quote a chapter title in Giles Oakley's *The Devil's Music*) 'The Men Start Recording'. Suddenly, unaccountably, record companies began sending mobile recording units across the South, auditioning singers and musicians with local reputations who might appeal to regional markets. The talent scouts had dubious credentials: technicians and salesmen, nearly all of them white, with scant familiarity with African American music. So it was largely by a stroke of luck that they happened into the Mississippi Delta and captured the searing voices of a few wandering minstrels who expressed blues anguish in its purest form: Charley Patton, Son House, Skip James and Robert Johnson, itinerant loners bred in the land where racial oppression hit hardest, the land where the blues began.

From that point on, those voices take over the story. The mournful drifter roaming the Delta, pouring his desolation into his music: for chroniclers of black song since the 1960s this is African American song-making stripped down to its essence, exuding the despair bred by Jim Crow and slavery, the alienation from which the authentic blues sprang. The tale has proven especially bewitching to scholars of black American experience, for whom blues recordings have become a form of historical documentation, compelling, even mystical in their power. From Lawrence Levine's monumental *Black Culture, Black Consciousness: Afro-American Folk Thought from Slavery to Freedom*, published in 1977, to Leon Litwack's *Trouble in Mind: Black Southerners in the Age of Jim Crow*, published in 1998, the Delta blues has provided a luminous focus for a rewriting of African American history, attentive to the experience of the faceless black masses, to voices that mainstream historians had too long ignored. As historical evidence, its value appears to lie in its sheer direct-ness. To listen to Robert Johnson, Litwack argues, 'is to feel – more vividly and more intensely than any mere poet, novelist, or historian

could convey – the despair, the thoughts, the passions, the aspir-
ations, the anxieties, the deferred dreams, the frightening honesty of
a new generation of black Southerners and their efforts to grapple
with day-to-day life, to make it somehow more bearable, perhaps even
to transcend it.' What Johnson's blues provides, in other words, is a
kind of audio snapshot of the innermost truths of the past. As Litwack
writes, quoting the Delta blues chronicler Robert Palmer: 'How much
history can be transmitted by pressure on a guitar string? The thought
of generations, the history of every human being who's ever felt the
blues come down like showers of rain.'

It is enormously seductive, this idea of the Delta blues as history
transmitted by a guitar string. In a virtual-reality world of replicas,
pastiches and hybrids, one cannot but crave that direct connection,
the opportunity, as the critic Hillel Schwartz puts it, 'to touch what
the Folk naively touched, to feel what they felt'. Yet there is something unsettling about it too. Historians ordinarily pride themselves
on their methodological rigour, the unsparing eye with which they
scrutinise evidence. Why is it, then, that when they turn to the blues
that pose of critical distance evaporates and their writing takes on
the hues of romance? It is, I think, curious to find an historian as
sophisticated as Litwack framing the blues in this populist way as
the voice of the folk, the pure and unmediated cry of the masses.
That reverence for the music's evidentiary powers recalls nothing so
much as the claims made, decades ago, for oral history: that it allows
us to bypass the dangers of historical interpretation by removing the
need for an historian, that it enables us to communicate with the past
directly by presenting past experience in its purest form.

Enraptured with the purity of the Delta blues, the resonant truth
of the voices within it, historians have neglected some basic questions, foremost among them the question of audience. The awkward
fact is that as newly minted 78s, Charley Patton's recordings sold
only moderately in the 1920s and 1930s; those of Son House, Skip
James and Robert Johnson sold barely at all. Even in the heart of
the Mississippi Delta, the so-called Delta bluesman had limited

appeal. A Fisk University sociologist who surveyed the black bars of Clarksdale late in the Depression found not a single local performer upon the jukeboxes. Top sellers were the same as they were in black areas across the United States: Louis Jordan, Lil Green, Count Basie, Fats Waller, all patently urban and unabashedly sexual, their songs laden with double (and sometimes single) entendres, backed by a jazz-inflected sound that pulsed with the rhythms of city life.

The voices of Johnson, House, Patton and James were pushed to the foreground not by black record buyers, but by more elusive mediators and shapers of taste. Underpinning the rapturous acclaim for the music's 'almost archaeological purity', its 'rough, spontaneous, crude and unfinished' voices, is the legacy of those mediations, an unspoken conviction that what we are hearing is uncorrupted black singing, the African American voice as it sounded before the record companies got to it. At the core of the idea of the Delta blues is a sense that some forms of black music are more real than others, an investment in purity with a tangled history that blues chroniclers, in the main, have neither perceived nor explored.

The realness of the Delta blues, its much-heralded purity, lies in those raw, archaic, supposedly uncompromised voices. Yet those voices were originally disseminated via the commercial race records industry and, decades later, recycled, recontexualised and given new meanings on LP anthologies and compact discs. Blues enthusiasts, in the main, have ignored those technological trappings, the phonograph, the disc, the electrical current; only the voices remain, fierce and immediate, communicating 'so directly', writes Greil Marcus, 'any distance between the singer and the listener is smashed'. What makes the Delta blues singular, and paradoxical, is its magical capacity to transcend that technology, to be conveyed mechanically and yet be perceived as pristinely untouched by the modern world.

This book aims to unravel that paradox by offering a different sort of Delta blues history. It argues that the Delta blues was 'discovered' – or, if you like, invented – as the culmination of a quest that began in the early twentieth century, as white men and women unsettled by the phenomenal success of race records set out in search of black voices that they heard as uncorrupted and pure. In an age of mechanical reproduction, they set themselves up as cultural arbiters, connoisseurs whose authority rested on their powers of discernment, their ability to distinguish the ersatz from the real.

Some of these enthusiasts are well known in the annals of blues history. I explore, for example, the renowned journeys of the father-and-son folklorists John and Alan Lomax, who combed the Depression-era South in search of black song and found authenticity in a Louisiana convict named Leadbelly, whose rough, ragged, melancholy vocals evoked the anguish of the chain gang. But I also examine more obscure searches by individuals who may seem unlikely characters in a blues context: the Southern sociologist Howard Odum; the Texas novelist Dorothy Scarborough; the jazz historians Frederic Ramsey, Charles Edward Smith and William Russell; and a reclusive record collector named James McKune. In tracking their involvement with African American music, I am interested less in their 'discoveries' than in their fears and obsessions. All were captivated by the idea of (in John Lomax's term) 'uncontaminated' black singing, all embarked on quests to unearth it, and all, in different ways, addressed the same question: how do you capture and preserve the real black voice in the age of mechanical reproduction? Answering that question meant engaging with the very technology whose impact they feared, ferreting out singers with portable phonographs and, eventually, rifling through bins in used-record stores, searching for voices that sounded archaic, willing themselves to hear past the machine.

For the first generation of American intellectuals to encounter race records, hearing past the machine rarely came easily. Even in a business that cut every corner, the so-called 'race record' manufacturers of the 1920s and 1930s were notorious for their shoddy materials, with the biggest race label, Paramount, determined to drive its production costs below the $1.50 per hundred that the industry considered the bottom line. Skimping on shellac, the most expensive ingredient, it packed out the 'dough' with low-quality filler. The result was a 'tin-pan tone', as one retailer put it, a disc that sounded worn and scratchy before it was ever put on a turntable. 'You couldn't get anything on Paramount,' talent scout Harry Charles lamented years later. 'I put some good songs on there; you'd never know it.'

All the more startling, then, was the sheer zeal with which America's black population embraced them. It made a sharp contrast to what the Edison Corporation had found a few years before, when it marketed its state-of-the-art Diamond Disc phonograph to white middle-class consumers and had to hide the machinery inside decorative cabinets and unveil demonstration models in concert halls to dispel a persistent scepticism of recorded music, a widespread unwillingness to accept it as 'real'. None of those techniques of persuasion were needed when it came to African Americans. All they required was for someone to put their music on phonograph records, and even men like songwriter Perry Bradford, who had spent years promoting black singers, were unprepared for the sheer volume of discs they purchased, the vast sums of money they were ready to spend. The African American folklorist Zora Neale Hurston was astonished at the end of the 1920s by the extent to which 'the mechanical, nickel phonograph' had come to dominate the turpentine, logging and phosphate camps of rural Florida where home-made songs had once reigned supreme. 'No, ma'am, they don't make up many songs,' one foreman told her. 'The boys used to be pretty bad about making up songs but they don't do that now.' Instead, such 'made-up songs' with their roots in the region gave way to 'Pinetop's Boogie-Woogie' and other songs learned from recordings. Seemingly overnight, an oral culture was inundated with mechanical reproductions, as a people long celebrated for spontaneous singing immersed themselves in the sound of recorded discs.

Hurston, for her part, viewed this development with undisguised dismay. On the road in the South in the late 1920s she searched for a black voice that she was convinced was disappearing, a vocal majesty and creativity that were in the process of being drowned out. 'Enclosed find all of the material that I have transcribed into ink,' she wrote to the anthropologist Franz Boas in 1927. 'It is fortunate that it is being collected now, for a great many people say, "I used to know some of that old stuff, but I done forgot it all." You see, the Negro is not living his lore to the extent of the Indian. He is not on a reservation, being kept pure. His Negroness is being rubbed off by close contact with white culture.' Her report concluded: 'The bulk of the population spends its leisure in motion picture theatres, or with the phonograph and its blues.'

Preserving 'Negroness' was Hurston's concern, and endangering that purity was the race record. That fear was echoed by other African American intellectuals who, like Hurston, were entranced with the power of black folk song and speech. The writer Jean Toomer, a native of Washington, DC, moved to a 'crude . . . but strangely rich and beautiful' part of rural Georgia in 1921 and was distressed by what he encountered, only one year after 'Crazy Blues' had burst in upon the African American soundscape:

> There was a valley . . . with smoke-wreaths during the day and mist at night. A family of back-country Negroes had only recently moved into a shack not too far away. They sang. And this was the first time I'd ever heard the folk-songs and spirituals. They were very rich and sad and joyous and beautiful. But I learned that the Negroes of the town objected to them. They called them 'shouting'. They had Victrolas and player-pianos. So, I realised with deep regret, that the spirituals, meeting ridicule, would be certain to die out. With Negroes also the trend was towards the small town and then towards the city – and industry and commerce and machines.

Machines were the problem: like the city, like industry, like commerce, they corrupted whatever fell in their path. 'The supreme fact of mechanical civilisation is that you become part of it, or get sloughed off,' Toomer wrote to his friend Waldo Frank in 1922. 'Negroes have no culture to resist it with (and if they had, their position would be identical to the Indians), hence industrialism the more readily transforms them.' Even Hurston, more sanguine than Toomer about the persistence of folk song in some black rural areas, felt that this survival could only be temporary, that the 'lush glades of primitive imagination' would inevitably be 'drained by mechanical invention'.

In part, this suspicion of the machine and mass-produced culture echoed a longstanding lament among intellectuals across the industrial West at the loss of what Walter Benjamin described in 1936 as the 'aura' of the work of art. By 'aura', Benjamin meant its authenticity, its uniqueness as a hand-made object, or, in the words of historian Miles Orvell, the 'quality of intensity [that makes it stand] out against the featureless background that constitutes the main hum of experience'. Central to that featureless background were the standardised products of commercial amusement. Even before the recording industry developed, many feared that authentic folk songs were being drowned out by assembly-line replicas. That no piece of sheet music could be an authentic folk song was accepted virtually without debate. Folk music was composed anonymously, transmitted orally, and suffused with the spirit of the peasantry, and since that unspoiled people was fast disappearing, genuine folk song was fading fast. Its gentle tones could not compete with the strident strains of commercial popular music. 'There is an enemy at the doors of folk-music which is driving it out, namely the common popular songs of the day, and this enemy is one of the most repulsive and most insidious,' noted the British composer Hubert Parry in 1899. 'In true folk songs there is no sham, no got-up glitter, and no vulgarity. [T]hese treasures of humanity are getting rare, for they are written in characters the most evanescent you can imagine, upon the sensitive brain fibres of those who learn them, and have but little idea of their value.'

Yet if Hurston and Toomer's distaste for commercial recordings in some ways simply extended a longstanding elegy, it also had meanings that were specifically racial. Since the mid-nineteenth century African American intellectuals had stressed the importance of song as communication, a critical source of expression for a people otherwise forced into silence. The slave-turned-abolitionist Frederick Douglass wrote in 1845 of the significance to be found in music that genteel whites dismissed as childlike gaiety or primitive noise. 'Rude and apparently incoherent' though the slave songs might be, beneath the surface they contained unfathomable depths of suffering: 'They were tones loud, long, and deep, they breathed the prayer and complaint of souls boiling over with the bitterest anguish. Every tone was testimony against slavery, and a prayer to God for deliverance from chains.'

In the wake of emancipation, African American writers and activists built on Douglass's reflections. The black sociologist W. E. B. DuBois, writing in *The Souls of Black Folk* in 1903, stressed the spirituals' importance as testimony, a powerful refutation of historians' claims 'that life was joyous to the black slave, careless and happy'. However guarded their language, the sorrow songs confronted the listener with 'death and suffering and unvoiced longing toward a truer world', a yearning for deliverance to a place and time where 'men will judge men by their souls and not by their skins'. And in an era of rampaging commerce and industry, they offered a simplicity and purity of spirit unparalleled in a nation effectively born in modernity, a nation that lacked a peasant past. 'There is no true American music but the wild sweet melodies of the Negro slave,' he concluded. 'All in all, we black men seem the sole oasis of simple faith and reverence in a dusty desert of dollars and smartness.'

But what if 'we black men' abandoned that role? That was what Hurston and Toomer perceived in the pell-mell embrace of race records: a mechanisation of the song-making process, a standardisation of that transcendent voice. With World War One had come an intensification of urbanisation, of black people's movement from field to factory, and the explosive growth of urban enclaves like Harlem. Even black intellectuals like the writers Langston Hughes and Sterling

Brown, who saw the blues as a modern folk music, shared something of Hurston's apprehension about what this embrace of the modern world meant. Though devoted consumers of race records, they kept that enthusiasm to their private letters; their published writings celebrating the blues as an expression of black memory and community (like Hughes's 1929 novel *Not Without Laughter* and Brown's 1930 poem 'Ma Rainey') effaced the recorded disc and depicted the music in live performance. It would not be until 1952, when the nameless protagonist of Ralph Ellison's *Invisible Man* burrows into his hidden basement in Harlem, lights up a joint, drops a 1929 Louis Armstrong disc upon the turntable, and finds 'a new analytical way of listening to music', that an African American novelist reflected on the possibilities opened up by the phonograph record. In those three decades of silence, it would seem, lay unspoken tensions about the impact of mechanical reproduction and of this strange process of hearing music by putting a platter on a recording machine.

If even black intellectuals found the emergence of race records unsettling, it was all the more jarring for white men and women enchanted by African American singing, whose numbers were greater than one might suppose. That enchantment stretched back at least to the mid-nineteenth century with the development of minstrel shows, whose racism thinly disguised a fascination with the vitality of black music, yet it reached a new peak during and after the Civil War when the South was flooded with white Northerners, veterans of anti-slavery efforts, who travelled among the emancipated slaves and were riveted by the music they heard. The spirituals, the work songs, the 'long, lonely sing-song of the fields': such music was beautiful, haunting, somehow unearthly – it strained the white listener's capacity to describe it, to fix it on paper in musical notes. Those who tried became obsessed by the impossibility of the task before them. 'It is difficult to express the entire character of these negro ballads by mere musical notes and signs,' wrote the abolitionist campaigner Lucy McKim in 1862. 'The odd turns made in the throat; and that curious rhythmic effect produced by single voices chiming in at different irregular intervals seem almost as impossible to place on score as the singing of birds, or the tones of an Aeolian Harp'. The anti-slavery activist William Allen felt the same sense of awe at the sheer *difference* of the black voice. 'The best we can do . . . with paper and types, or even with voices, will convey but a faint shadow of the original. The voices of the colored people have a peculiar quality that nothing can imitate; and the intonations and delicate variations of even one singer cannot be reproduced on paper.'

In the years that followed, the elusiveness of the black voice, its resistance to reproduction, became an indispensable axiom, the eye of the needle through which any discussion of African American song had to pass. As the cult of the spirituals grew in the 1870s and 1880s with the international success of the Fisk Jubilee Singers, white intellectuals in America and Europe lauded what they saw as a wholly untutored artistry that owed its power to racial difference, to the 'remarkable musical capacity' of a 'half-barbarous' race that remained tied to the natural world. In that indescribable, unreproduceable voice, enthusiasts heard a purity of spirit and a wild, untamed longing, a mournfulness that spoke not just of slavery but of something universal in the human soul. As one-time Union commander Thomas Wentworth Higginson put it, 'Never, it seems to me, since man first lived and suffered, was his infinite longing and suffering uttered more plaintively.' Deepened by suffering, honed by anguish, the black voice could reach peaks of emotion that white voices could not; through rapt attention, white listeners could absorb it and experience something of the sublime.

All the more unsettling, then, to hear that fierce, untutored, primitive voice captured by this most modern of technologies and to see America's black population shelling out millions to buy up those discs. The titles of the records were bad enough – hit releases like 'Black Snake Moan', 'Meat Cutter Blues', 'I Got The Best Jelly Roll In

Town' – but more fundamentally, the very act of fusing the black voice and modern technology made for a kind of mongrel amalgamation that left connoisseurs of the spirituals distinctly uneasy. Few were as blunt as the song collector Robert Gordon, who stated that in preserving black folk song he aimed to help 'the whites of the South to keep *one* bunch of Negroes from becoming utterly worthless and *modern* in the city coon sense'. Yet many shared the feeling underlying Gordon's pronouncement: that the cultural value of African Americans lay in their remaining rural and primitive, and that as they abandoned that role something essential was being lost. 'When black takes on the prowlings and pratings of the white race and becomes a strutting chrysalis in silk shirts and Ford cars, the mystery is gone forever,' wrote one journalist. That lament went hand in hand with a yearning for 'real' black music charged with the mystery of racial difference, emanating from African American singers who resisted the pull of the modern world.

What follows are the stories of a few white men and women who went in search of those magical voices, who set out to stem the tide of mass-produced replicas by uncovering the sound of the real thing. In writing this history of exploration and connoisseurship, inevitably, I have been selective. For many enthusiasts of African American singing, the recording machine posed grave dangers even as it opened up new possibilities: at once the prime destroyer of authenticity and an unparalleled tool of authentication. I have looked for people whose experience seemed to shed light on that contradiction, whose passions and vulnerabilities I felt for, and whose struggles I thought I could bring alive.

Out of those struggles, over time, emerged the idea of the Delta blues. By now it should be obvious that mine is not a conventional Delta blues history. I make no attempt to cover the ground mapped in Robert Palmer's canonical *Deep Blues*, with its focus on the development of a musical style and lines of artistic transmission (Charley Patton begets Son House begets Robert Johnson begets Muddy Waters). In such a history, the protagonists are black, quite rightly. My central characters are white. At the core of the idea of a Delta blues, of an undiluted and primal black music, is an emotional attachment to racial difference that extends back at least to the mid-nineteenth century, to abolitionists' enchantment with the peculiar power of black singers, their uncanny ability to allow their white listeners to experience an unimagined transcendence, a level of emotional intensity otherwise out of their reach.

The folklorists, critics and collectors I've written about were all searching for that vicarious ecstasy. All were born in the era of segregation; in different ways, all felt imaginatively tied to the South. Throughout their lives, they made racial assumptions that were hackneyed, condescending and often offensive. Yet as I read their words, tracked their obsessions, and revisited their journeys, I came to appreciate what they have left us, the reservoir of recovered music, the chain of knowledge and expertise. In time, I learned to admire the sheer fortitude it took to engage with an art form that few whites of their generation respected. Even as they feared black modernity, they struggled to cope with it, and some-times to transcend their racist beginnings. We are their debtors, even if we cannot avoid being their critics.

In the end, theirs is not a straightforward history with a discernible chronology. To excavate the idea of the Delta blues is to describe something more amorphous and intangible: a history of voices and responses to voices, of the memories and emotions they generate, of how those associations change over time. What emerges from their stories is a genealogy of feeling and sensibility. The idea of a genuine, uncorrupted black voice has long had a potency that goes far beyond music. The Delta blues, in essence, was the end product of a journey of the imagination, in which the search for authentic black voices came to focus on commercial blues race records – and remade the blues itself in the process.

Chapter Two

Impartial Testimony

In the midst of the vast, flat expanse of swamp and field that is the Mississippi Delta is a small, deteriorating hamlet called Tutwiler. Getting there means heading out of Clarksdale south on Highway 49. Fifteen miles down on the roadside are two wooden signs built in the shape of a railway depot, one displaying a large replica of a harmonica, the other an outsized guitar. 'Tutwiler,' they announce, 'Where "Blues" was born.'

There were few signs of blues, or indeed of much else, on the day I drove into Tutwiler. A few wooden buildings, some boarded up, lined the main street, along with a larger building bearing the words 'US Post Office, Tutwiler, Mississipp'. It took only minutes to reach what must have been, in earlier days, the town centre: a dirt square abutting a small patch of grass. When I got out of the car the air was humid and stagnant, the only sound the occasional rush of a truck on the distant highway, and I crossed a grass verge alongside a railroad track and looked at what I had come there to see.

On the near side of the track is a brass plaque mounted upon a stone pillar that had been placed there in 1976. 'A Landmark of American Music' it reads. 'In his autobiography *Father of the Blues*, W. C. Handy stated that he first heard the blues, a native Negro ballad form, in the railroad station of Tutwiler in 1895. Presented by the National Music Council, Mississippi Music Educators Association and Exxon.' On the far side of the track, painted on the back wall of a long brick building, is a mural in the form of a triptych, the left panel showing a steam locomotive and the right showing bluesman and native son Sonny Boy Williamson, who is buried nearby. The middle panel depicts two black men sitting on a wooden bench, one stiff and rigid in a dark suit, the other in ragged jeans and workshirt and holding a guitar. Between the first and second panels is a painted sign.

> In 1903 while touring the Delta and playing musical engagements, W. C. Handy was waiting for a train in Tutwiler. At the train depot an unknown musician was singing, while sliding a knife blade down the strings of his guitar. The sound and effect were unforgettable to Handy and became the music known worldwide as 'The Blues'.

It is hard to know what to make of these monuments. As memorials of the blues they are remarkably feeble, not least in the fact that the memorialisers could not agree amongst themselves about the year in which this encounter was meant to take place. Yet that very uncertainty points to a truth. Though in the wake of the blues revival historians have routinely rooted the blues in the Mississippi Delta, in point of fact they have had little hard evidence to back that claim up. As a music of a denigrated, impoverished class, the early blues left the barest traces behind it. While scholars agree that the AAB verse form first appeared in the early twentieth century, even that is less fact than inference: nothing resembling that form appears in nineteenth-century ballad-hunters' reports. Otherwise, all comes down to guesswork. No one knows who sang the first blues, or where they sang it, or when.

Lacking sound evidence, historians have relied upon stories, tales told retrospectively by well-placed observers about encountering the blues for the first time. By far the most frequently told of those tales is W. C. Handy's 1941 description of his late-night encounter in the Mississippi Delta, when 'one night in Tutwiler, as I nodded in the railroad station while waiting for a train that had been delayed nine hours, life suddenly took me by the shoulder and wakened me with a start.'

A lean, loose-jointed Negro had commenced plunking a guitar beside me as I slept. His clothes were rags; his feet peeped out of his shoes. His face had on it some of the sadness of the ages. As he played, he pressed a knife on the strings of the guitar in a manner popularised by Hawaiian guitarists who used steel bars. The effect was unforgettable. His song, too, struck me instantly.

'Goin' where the Southern cross the Dog.'

The singer repeated the line three times, accompanying himself on the guitar with the weirdest music I had ever heard. The tune stayed in my mind.

Over the past forty years, Handy's story of the ragged man at the Delta train station has become a blues legend, repeated by chroniclers from Robert Palmer to Greil Marcus, all eager to assert the primacy of the Delta in blues history with little hard evidence to back up that claim. In their hands Handy's Delta vagrant has been transformed into the archetypal bluesman: drifting aimlessly, owning nothing, singing, but not to any purpose, singing simply to while away the time. In the process of singing, he gives voice to melancholy, the emotion that Handy says powered the blues. 'Suffering and hard luck were the midwives that birthed these songs,' wrote Handy. 'The blues were conceived in aching hearts.'

At its simplest, Handy's drifter has drawn blues scholars because he so closely resembles the musicians whose recordings they venerate, Delta drifters like Charley Patton (David Evans even speculates that Handy's minstrel may have *been* Patton), Son House and, above all, Robert Johnson, self-accompanied acoustic bluesmen whom chroniclers champion as the real thing. Yet the story's importance, as they use it, runs deeper. By spotlighting Handy's luminous tale, they suggest what they cannot prove: the blues in a state of nature, as it were, as it sounded before recording companies got hold of it. In their hands the story has become a foundation myth, seeming to convey something essential and incontrovertible about the origins of the blues tradition. To its enthusiasts, the blues expresses fundamental emotions, universal echoes of black – indeed, human – suffering. It makes sense that it would enter history not through its invention but through its discovery, encountered as Handy encountered it, in the form of a sorrowful wanderer adrift in the timeless landscape of the Mississippi Delta, appearing before him as if from a dream.

There is, however, one account of the early blues that is not retro-spective, an account that historians, by and large, have ignored. It takes place not in the Delta, but forty miles east in Lafayette County, and what it tells us is skewed by its narrator, a young white Southerner with no ear for music and scant knowledge of African American culture who was deeply unsettled by what he heard.

A decade and a half before the advent of race records, one unknow-able day in 1907, a bespectacled twenty-three-year-old, Howard Odum, saddled his horse and set out on a journey to find the truth of black song. He had just turned his back on the study of classics that had earned him an MA at the University of Mississippi and thrown himself into social science, a revolutionary new field that applied to the study of man and society the rigorous empiricism of a laboratory experiment. Social scientists disdained texts and libraries in favour of the real world, people and places observed at close range. That zeal for fact gave it limitless potential to shape public policy, to arbitrate conflict – ultimately, Odum thought, to remake the South. And it offered its practitioner the chance to be a leader, even while dedicating himself to higher things, to the service of man, truth, and God.

The South needed leaders: of that Odum was certain. Looking beyond the university at the bare hills and rolling fields of Lafayette County, he saw white families edging steadily into poverty, as more and more of them lost control of their farms and fell into tenancy and sharecropping. Schooling was minimal, even for whites, outside the university town of Oxford, and lives were shaped by superstition: tales of the shrieking ghosts haunting Cassidy's Bayou and of the spectral panthers to be glimpsed by the swamps, their fur gleaming black, their eyes burning yellow, their jaws dripping with blood. There was a more palpable ghost as well: the spirit presence of the Old South. Not for nothing did its native son William Faulkner name the region 'Yoknapatawpha', a Chickasaw term that translates roughly as 'water runs slow through flat land' – there was something eerie, dreamlike, about the place. As a young graduate student trekking through the county on horseback, Odum would have seen the skeletal remains of country manors like Abbeville, once the pride of the county but burned in two Civil War battles and then lingering in slow decay, overgrown by weeds, engulfed by jungle, as the westernmost fringes of the Appalachian forest encroached ever further, seemingly ready to claim the land back. There were flesh-and-blood ruins too: sons and daughters of the deteriorating gentry who were tormented by the past. Once, when one of those young men, whom he knew slightly, lost his precarious hold upon sanity, Odum chased him on an unbroken colt for forty miles from Toccapola to New Albany, 'in and out across swollen streams and backwoods and pinehills, often reflecting a physical reality stranger than fiction'. In his native north Georgia, only a fraction of the antebellum population had owned any slaves and the plantocracy was a distant presence. Here, memories of plantation grandeur hung over the landscape like a malignant spirit. 'I myself have known Yoknapatawpha and it is no purely imaginary fantasy,' he remembered thirty years later. 'I have been close enough to Faulkner's quicksands to sense something of its terrors and have often imagined, behind the cedars and columned houses, that anything could happen there.'

In amongst the cedars and columned houses were the cabins of African Americans. Comprising forty-five per cent of the county's population, they had powerful ghosts of their own, slavery and, still within living memory, the betrayal that was Reconstruction. Here as in the rest of the South, hopes of forty acres and a mule gave way to the reality of the sharecropping system, in which families leased land from a planter, grew what he ordered (invariably cotton) and promised him half the yield. Inevitably, they mortgaged away even more. During the growing season, from March through August, families kept themselves alive with loans from planters and merchants who provided them with food and farming supplies. Only if the value of their crop exceeded that of their 'furnish' did they end the year with a profit. In years when cotton prices were low, families were often poorer after the harvest than they had been before the season began.

With sharecropping came systematic racial oppression and ostracism. Black Mississippians were kept from the polls by force, fraud and, after 1890, provisions in the state constitution that withheld the vote from those judged to be vicious or ignorant. The state's first 'Jim Crow' statute, mandating separation of the races on railway coaches, was passed in 1888, formalising a practice of racial exclusion that had been customary for at least fifteen years. In schools, hospitals, restaurants, hotels, railway stations, streetcars and prisons, African Americans were kept separate from whites. Those who broke the rules, who appeared sullen or uppity, or who allowed their eyes to meet a white woman's, could be harassed, beaten, jailed or lynched. Over 200 black men and women were lynched in Mississippi in the decade around the turn of the century, more than any other state in the South. 'If necessary every Negro in the state will be lynched,' stated its governor James K. Vardaman in 1907. 'It will be done to maintain white supremacy.'

Before he arrived at the University of Mississippi, Odum gave no more thought than most other white Southerners to life on the other side of the colour line. In the Civil War stories that haunted him as a boy, the principal victims were white. His mother's family had been successful slaveholders wiped out by the advance of Union troops, and both his grandfathers had served in the Confederate army and returned broken in body and spirit. He grew particularly close to his paternal grandfather, John Wesley Odum, a small farmer who had owned no slaves. The elder Odum spent much of the war sick and despondent, suffering near-fatal injuries and a nervous breakdown in battle; when his company marched a few miles from his farm, depressed and confused he 'slipped off and went home'. The young Howard Odum, at his grandfather's knee, heard the tale of his desertion over and over. At commemorations to mark the Confederate dead, he watched him burn with shame and discomfort, 'his broad forehead moist with perspiration . . . his big blue eyes peering straight ahead with the hurt look of the innocent wounded.'

In time Odum would fuse his grandfather's story with the tragedy that was Southern history. As a boy, however, he felt only humiliation, to which he added despair all his own. He was born in 1884 near the tiny village of Bethlehem, Georgia, the second son of a struggling truck-and-dairy farmer, William Pleasants Odum, and his wife Mary Ann Thomas. Odum's mother nursed painful memories of her comfortable girlhood on a plantation; fuelled by a bitter hatred of Yankees, she pushed her children to learn, to achieve, to regain something of the family's lost standing. She shaped their home as a rarefied world of books, music and spiritual devotion, and Howard, an early reader, soon became the focus of her ambitions. He wanted to please her, but it was difficult. The scrappy, arid plains around Bethlehem; the threadbare school that he attended erratically; the harsh, pious Methodism that terrorised him: it all made his every effort seem futile. He had a big nose; he lisped; he was cripplingly shy; and his early memories were shadowed by death. As a young boy, too sickly for farm chores, he had been left to look after his three younger siblings, all of whom died – one from burns suffered in a brush fire, one from a spinal injury after falling from a tree, the last from diphtheria. Though none of the deaths owed to his negligence, he felt profoundly responsible, and a sense of guilt and self-loathing would haunt him for the rest of his life.

By 1904 when he graduated from Emory College in Georgia, earning a BA in classics without making an impression on anyone, Odum's ambitions to move ahead in the world were undercut by an awareness of his own marginality. 'I [had a strong sense of being] what I designated as AIUP,' he remembered, 'awkward, ignorant, ugly and poor.' He took the only job that he could find, as a schoolteacher in Toccapola in northern Mississippi; six months into the post, he enrolled at the University of Mississippi as a graduate student in classics. His aim, now, was to become a college lecturer, teaching classics to keen undergraduates – not exactly his mother's dream that he serve God and redeem the South, but still a step up in the world. He travelled the twenty miles to Oxford on horseback, shuddering at the dense forests and swamps that he passed through, and settled into life immersed in the tragedies of Oedipus and Antigone, tales of fatalism, defeat and disaster that he sometimes merged into his own.

Then one day in 1906, Odum stumbled into a graduate seminar on the 'Psychology of the Negro Problem', led by a charismatic professor of social psychology, Thomas P. Bailey. By Mississippi standards, Bailey was cosmopolitan. Though born, raised and schooled in South Carolina, he found his first teaching posts at the University of Chicago and the University of California at Berkeley, and built a national reputation for studies that probed the making of human character, the means by which men and women mastered their instincts to become rational, disciplined, self-motivated adults. Those studies imbued him with a messianic sense of the importance of the social scientist's task. Labour unrest, urban crime, the upheavals wrought by industrialisation: these were deviant forms of human behaviour, and they needed impartial, rigorous, expert attention if they were not to spin out of control. Arriving at the University of Mississippi in 1903, he conveyed to his students that same sense of urgency. 'Science, and science alone, star-eyed science, truth-loving science, spiritually intellectual science' could help the South find its way out of its most vexing dilemmas – above all, out of the problem of race.

'Does the Negro show potentialities as a race?' Bailey's research in Mississippi was driven by the question, and it guided his seminar on Negro psychology. What could black men and women make of themselves, if genuinely given the chance? It seemed indisputable that at this moment African Americans were inferior to whites; indisputable too that segregation was wise, necessary and natural, if only to avoid racial amalgamation and keep up 'the physical stock of the higher racial types'. Yet who was to say for how long that would remain imperative? Blacks were currently 'less developed' than whites, but that did not mean that they were inherently 'lower' – no one knew what their capacities were. A full and reasoned judgement of Negro capacity awaited the verdict of science – ideally, a team of scientists, sponsored by leaders from across the country. Until then, it was up to individual researchers to ask the questions that needed answers. Was the Negro capable of reaching a mature standard of white Christian conduct, of exercising rational self-control? 'Is the Negro really adaptable, or is he parasitic? Is his slowness of development due to deep-lying anatomical and physiological causes or to environmental causes? Is the Negro deteriorating? If so, why?'

Odum was accustomed to the sight of African Americans, but not to asking questions about them. With his eyes opened by Bailey, he found it impossible to stop. Those dark faces that turned away when they saw him watching: what did the men and women behind them feel, what did they think? Surveying the bent figures in the cotton fields outside Oxford, he saw a compelling enigma, a mystery that needed unravelling. 'The Negro has a life and an environment of his own which the whites do not see, which after all may be at the bottom of his actions,' he wrote in 1910. Some way had to be found to penetrate that life, that environment, if the South were to move forward – some way of seeing beyond surface appearances deep into the heart of African American character, of reaching past the mask for a glimpse of the genuine Negro face.

In folk song, he thought, he could find the answer. In the songs he sang at home, work and leisure, the Negro revealed his true self, 'what he *is* rather than what he appears to be'. Odum took the idea from sociologist William Graham Sumner's 1906 book *Folkways*, which explored the power of tradition and custom at primitive stages of social organisation. Prise apart a traditional song or tale and you could identify the distinctive mindset of a

Howard Odum outside the log cabin he built on his farm, c. 1928

culture; primitive traditions and rituals grew out of basic desires and mental traits, and they resisted all pressure to evolve or change. With Bailey's help, Odum devised a plan to travel through Lafayette County collecting black song with a recording phonograph, transcribing the lyrics and subjecting them to social-science analysis.

The result would be 'impartial testimony', objective data revealing the truth of a bewildering race.

That impartial evidence was all the more crucial in light of the misguided notions that had long surrounded black music. Odum had read the rapturous accounts of the spirituals written just after the Civil War, and he had read W. E. B. DuBois's *The Souls of Black Folk*, and in DuBois's erudition Odum found ominous indications of where the cult of the spirituals was bound to lead. No matter that on its publication in 1903 DuBois was very much a lone voice; no matter that with popularisation the spirituals were being steadily stripped of political overtones, their grammar cleaned up, their imagery conventionalised, so the songs were fit to sing 'at all manner of occasions, from funerals to yachting parties'. To champion the sorrow songs was effectively to pose them as 'the truest representation of the Negro's real self', songs whose transcendent power gave cheering hopes for cultivation and refinement in African American life. To Odum, this was sentimental nonsense. The spirituals were beautiful, but they were hardly representative: artificially preserved by choirs and sheet-music publishers, they did not reflect what black Southerners were singing now. Though 'the religious songs of the Negro have commonly been accepted as the characteristic music of the race,' he maintained, 'observation for the most part has been made by those who have heard the Negro songs but have not studied them.' By working with a phonograph, he would change that, replacing facile hopes and rosy dreams with irrefutable, objective facts, the stark, brutal truths of Negro psychology, social and mental traits candidly revealed in song.

Though new technologies are commonly celebrated as either miracles or inevitabilities, every mechanical innovation is the material expression of an idea. In the case of the phonograph, the idea was to do for the ear what the daguerreotype had done for the eye: to freeze sensory impressions that would otherwise be evanescent, to protect them from the destruction of time. 'We will be able to preserve and hear again . . . a memorable speech . . . the last words of a dying man . . . of a distant parent, a lover, a mistress,' explained Thomas Edison in 1878, one year after inventing the talking tinfoil. The phonograph could be an aid to business, making dictation possible without a stenographer. It could uplift the blind through 'phonographic books', mechanical recordings of classic texts. And human knowledge and learning would be enriched through the machine's ability to reproduce foreign languages, to teach elocution, to record a teacher's lessons to be heard at home.

Number four on Edison's inventory of possibilities was the reproduction of music. That it did not rank higher owed partly to his priorities ('I don't want the phonograph sold for amusement purposes, it is not a toy,' he told an associate in 1894), but also to the limitations of the technology. The original tinfoil phonograph produced an indistinct sound, just about clear enough to convey human speech but nowhere near sufficiently nuanced for musical subtleties. It would take another two decades of technical innovations to produce machines that could convey resonant musical sounds. In 1886 Alexander Graham Bell and his cousin Charles Tainter devised a wax cylinder recording machine with far better sound quality than Edison's model; it was also more practical, since the wax cylinders could be removed, stored and replayed, while the tinfoil-wrapped cylinders, once removed, were destroyed. The wax cylinder recorder would be eclipsed in turn by the disc-playing gramophone introduced by Emile Berliner in 1895. The gramophone pared down the cost of the Bell cylinder phonograph by offering only half of its functions: it could play music but could not record it. Consumers liked the savings; phonograph vendors liked the guaranteed market for pre-recorded discs. Over the next ten years sales of discs and disc players grew steadily, with the manufacture of cylinder phonographs ceasing altogether by 1913.

Yet in one area the cylinder recorder was not supplanted: in the new scholarly disciplines of social science, where it had been embraced as an indispensable tool nearly from the moment of its invention. In his visionary excitement about the technology, Odum tapped into a sense of the machine's possibilities first expressed in 1890, when the ethnographer Jesse Walter Fewkes pioneered the use of a cylinder phonograph to record the language patterns of Maine's Passamaquoddy Indians. 'The apparatus proves to be a means by which the actual sound itself of which a music consists may, even in many of its more delicate characteristics, be stored up by the traveler, in a form permanently accessible to observation,' noted the psychologist Benjamin Gilman on hearing Fewkes's recordings. '[The recording] can be interrupted at any point, repeated indefinitely, and even within certain limits magnified, as it were, for more accurate appreciation of changes in pitch, by increasing the duration of notes.' The Hungarian composer Bela Bartok, who made field recordings of Eastern European folk music around 1900, found that the cylinders made audible 'notes between the notes' that 'cultured'

Westerners could not ordinarily discern. The phonograph, in other words, expanded and intensified sensory perception, just as the microscope had for the eye. By extracting the voice from its human context and reproducing it in mechanical form, the machine allowed the investigator to strip bare its workings, to probe and manipulate, to parse and dismember. What resulted were objective facts, free from the investigator's projections and sentimental effusions – not to mention the errors that were inevitable in any attempt to transcribe sound by hand.

The earliest known photograph of a graphophone in use: Frances Densmore records Blackfoot leader Mountain Chief

That capacity for verisimilitude, for capturing what sounds like truth, has shaped how the phonograph has been written into the history of African American music.

In sharp contrast to the story of recording for profit is the story of recording for knowledge: the story of what since the 1950s has been labelled 'field recording', in which the machine is put to nobler uses, as a heroic tool for unearthing 'roots'. It is a tale (as one recent account puts it) 'of high adventure and dedicated scholarship', of men and women who felt passionately that endangered music *mattered* and who set off down the backroads lugging unwieldy equipment to capture what commerce and industry threatened to drown out. Employed in this fashion, as a tool for preserving marginal cultures, the recording machine seems a progressive instrument. It seems, indeed, part of the cultural and intellectual revolution signalled by the anthropologist Franz Boas, who inveighed against scholarly racism, disputed the idea that some peoples were 'primitive' and urged his students to value all the peoples they studied by making accurate records of their words and their sounds.

Yet though they used phonographs routinely, Boasian ethnographers in 1907 did not study African American music. The purpose of fieldwork, as Boas conceived it, was to map 'culture patterns', and for that reason his students focused on Native Americans, who had elaborate, picturesque and obviously doomed expressive systems that needed to be documented, analysed and explained. But while African Americans had songs and animal tales that ethnographers noted with a fair bit of interest, no one at that stage, not even the liberal Boas, believed that those practices cohered into a distinctive and integrated whole. Bluntly put, black Americans did not have culture patterns – they had lost their African traditions in crossing the Atlantic: so believed Boas, so believed virtually every early-twentieth-century ethnographer. The fact that African Americans were renowned internationally for their resonant singing did not in itself arouse their interest. Though between 1890 and 1930 ethnographers studying Native American song made some 14,000 cylinder recordings, of African American voices they appear to have made only a handful.

Howard Odum, it seems, was the first, and he was not a Boasian. Eventually, as the South's premier sociologist, his views on race would become more liberal, and he would come to oppose segregation privately and on principle while seeking its incremental abolition in practice. But in 1907 he took up his cylinder recorder in the same spirit that physical anthropologists of the day took up callipers – to provide hard and objective proof of black inferiority.

Though Howard Odum embarked on his search out of devotion to Science, in the process he stumbled upon History. As he travelled across Lafayette County, he found something curious: songs made up of a single line, repeated two or three times. He heard them from itinerant players – 'music physicianers', 'musicianers' and 'songsters', they called themselves – who carried their songs and guitars along the backroads and sang into his phonograph in return for small change. They adapted their songs to suit their mood, and they could stretch them out for what seemed like hours, fusing lines from different tunes to take them straight from one song to another and sliding a knife or a bone along the guitar strings to make the instrument 'talk' in response. The effect was hypnotic, and the words they sang were elliptical and haunting. 'I'm po' boy long way from home,' one bedraggled man intoned. 'I got the blues, but I'm too damn mean to cry.'

What Odum found was the blues in formation. Whether the form had yet acquired the name 'blues' is debatable, since none of Odum's informants labelled it as such; they spoke of 'coon songs', 'rag times', 'knife songs', 'devil songs', 'breakdowns', and any one song could have a variety of labels depending on the context in which it was played. Odum's findings consisted, it would seem, largely of a collection of musical fragments combined and reused in song after song, barely distinguishable from the minstrel show tunes, ballads and Tin Pan Alley standards that made up the itinerant player's repertoire. As a blanket term of description, the term 'blues' seems to have materialised around 1912, with the first publication of such song titles on sheet music; ten years later, in the wake of 'Crazy Blues', that label was everywhere. To most white observers the music seemed to have materialised instantaneously, but Odum knew better. In 1925 he drew up the following list:

LINES AND TITLES OF SONGS COLLECTED TWENTY YEARS AGO	LINES AND TITLES OF RECENT POPULAR BLUES
Laid in jail, back to the wall.	Thirty days in jail with my back turned to the wall.
Jailer, won't you put 'nother man in my stall?	Look here, mister jailer, put another gal in my stall.
Baby, won't you please come home?	Baby, won't you please come home?
Wonder where my baby stay las' night?	Where did you stay last night?
I got my all-night trick, baby, and you can't git in.	I'm busy and you can't come in.
I'll see her when her trouble's like mine.	I'm gonna see you when your troubles are just like mine.
Satisfied.	I'm satisfied.
You may go, but this will bring you back.	I got what it takes to bring you back.
Joe Turner	Joe Turner blues.
Love, Kelly's love	Love, careless love
I'm on my las' go-round	Last go-round blues.

Equipped with his cylinder recorder, Odum captured what later enthusiasts would regard as a Holy Grail: the voice of the blues before record companies got to it, the sound of the music in its natural state. Yet we have no way of hearing the voices he heard, no means of recovering the sounds that he documented. Odum seems to have lost or discarded his cylinders at some point in the 1920s, after his research assistant Guy Johnson made use of them. They form no part of the voluminous collection of his papers and artefacts held at the University of North Carolina; that we know of them at all comes down largely to the recollections of family, like his daughter Mary Frances, who can locate neither cylinders nor field notebooks but (she has written me) can picture them in her 'mind's eye'. Odum himself never described the process of recording and never itemised the cylinders' contents. That the recordings themselves might become objects of interest does not seem to have crossed his mind.

What mattered to Odum was scientific truth, not the music he uncovered, yet in stumbling upon (and then losing) the blues, he discovered things that he had not foreseen. He went into the field styling himself as a hard-nosed scientific explorer, but he had not anticipated the difficulties he faced, the roiling emotions his research would call up. Most unsettling was the enforced intimacy. Odum's search for the facts of black song demanded that he act as spy and voyeur, exploring black neighbourhoods, eavesdropping on singers and coaxing them to sing into the horn. He had grown up believing in cleanliness of body and spirit, in the purity of hearth and home, in the values of self-restraint, hard work and service. 'We should all try to discharge our duty', read the maxim on the calendar Odum kept at his bedside; in the margins he scribbled a fervent 'Yes'. Face to face with black Southerners he encountered a world from which, to his eyes, such ideals were entirely absent. Nothing in his devout, driven, duty-bound upbringing prepared him for the itinerant players from whom he collected the bulk of his songs, dissolute, self-indulgent drifters guided by 'an independent ethics of vagrancy'. 'The Negro has little home conscience or love of home, no local attachment of the better sort,' he maintained.

Love amongst black people was fleeting and casual, its expression carnal and animalistic, a state of moral pollution reflected in the general dirt and disorder. 'Filth and uncleanness is everywhere predominant. One must refrain from a description of the worst phase of the Negro's personal habits.' The songs the musicians performed for him grew out of those noxious surroundings: they were 'openly descriptive of the grossest immorality', 'vicious and obscene', 'rotten with filth'. The more he heard, the more the whole enterprise of song-gathering repelled him. 'The student finds difficulty in holding himself to the persistent, sustained, and laborious effort that a searching investigation requires,' he admitted. 'Many incidents growing out of the efforts to secure his information are repulsive, not to say nauseous and gruesome. Only the hardiest scientific interest in discoverable facts can sustain the investigator.'

Given the violence of his response, it is perhaps not surprising that Odum soon abandoned the study of black music. The songs he gathered in Mississippi provided the raw material for two PhD dissertations, after which he turned to the study of white rural underdevelopment, the subject on which he would build his career. Nor should it be surprising that Odum's journey did not lead to follow-ups by other investigators. It would not be until the mid-1920s that scholars again recorded itinerant black singers, and not until the mid-1930s that they took much care to preserve the results. Field recording, Odum discovered, brought a physical proximity that could be unsettling, so much so that for the next two decades most folklorists employing phonographic technology preferred to avoid black informants outright.

Intriguingly, however, Odum did eventually return to the subject. In 1924, prompted by the race-record phenomenon, he got his research assistant Guy Johnson to pore over his findings from Mississippi and shape them into a book, published in 1925 as *The Negro and his Songs*. So much attention did the book receive that the pair went to work on a follow-up volume and began haunting construction sites and logging camps for itinerant singers to interview and record. At some point in the summer of 1925 Odum had an encounter with a labourer whose identity he never revealed but to whom he gave the name Left Wing Gordon. The man was a rambler, a guitarist and a singer – to Odum's ears he seemed to remember every song he had ever heard – and over a few days Odum plied him with whiskey, got him talking and set about writing it down.

The result, in 1928, was *Rainbow Round My Shoulder*, billed by Odum's publisher as 'the Negro's own story, the autobiography of the Negro supertramp'. The book appeared to be based on verbatim testimony, and that was how Odum had sold it to his editor, Gordon's words reproduced 'exactly as given', 'all pictures, all concreteness', an 'untouched phototype'. But Odum had only so many of Gordon's words to go on; to build a full-length account he had to draw on his memories of the drifters he encountered in Mississippi two decades before. In the end, the book took shape less through transcription or compilation than through minstrelsy or, perhaps, psychoanalysis, as Odum called up those labourers out of his imagination, dictating in his office for hours at a stretch, eyes closed, stock-still, singing and speaking in the voices he remembered, as his secretary struggled to get down every word.

What lay at the heart of the book were the songs Gordon sang, the same songs Odum had heard two decades earlier, which he now thought of as the 'folk blues'. Odum devised that term to distinguish the songs he had heard in Mississippi from the 'formal blues' now being sold on race records. Looking back on the former now, he remembered their earthy natural charm, their freshness and innocence, which were being cheapened on record by thinly veiled double entendres and a spirit of calculation and artifice. Partly this came down to the singers – the phonograph records were dominated by women, while the songsters he had recorded had all been men – but the transformation ran deeper. The tone, the sensibility, had been transformed, and in the process something precious was being lost.

Bringing that something precious to life was his purpose in writing about Left Wing Gordon. As Odum evoked him, Gordon gave his life story in speech and in song, but the text made little distinction between them. So fully did he embody the blues that speaking and singing became one and the same:

> Good Lawd, I can't be satisfied. If I been back here mo' 'n twenty times, maybe I'll come back twenty mo' an' maybe I won't. I don't stay noplace mo' 'n three weeks, leastwise never mo' 'n fo'. I'm gittin' out o' here now for Philadelphia see does my baby know right from wrong.

> O Lawd, if I feel tomorrow
> Like I feel today
> Good God, gonna pack my suitcase
> Lawd, an' walk away.

In those ceaseless wanderings that once had repulsed him, Odum now perceived something poignant and noble, a 'Black Ulysses' driven by a yearning, restless spirit untamed by the constraints of family or home. And in the blues that Gordon could never stop singing, he heard songs 'so strange and varied as to reveal a sort of superhuman evidence of the folk soul'. While he held out some hope that folk blues and formal blues could continue to exist side by side, this could only happen so long as black labourers remained uncorrupted, permeated by an essential simplicity. 'There will be the folk blues,' Odum concluded, 'as long as there are Negro toilers and adventurers whose naivete has not been worn off by what the white man calls culture'.

By 1928 Odum waxed rhapsodic about the simple, unworldly singers he had met in Mississippi, yet his cylinders, were we now able to hear them, might well have told a different story. Though he had gone into the field in 1907 with a messianic vision of science, his cylinder recorder a bit player in that larger drama, in practise the machine had proved an intrusive third party in his encounters with the guitarists whom he persuaded to sing into the horn. As travelling performers at dances and on roadsides, they were accustomed to playing to the crowd, and in their recording sessions they sought to demonstrate their up-to-date repertoires which, Odum realised the more he encountered it, was decidedly not what he was after. 'All manner of "ragtimes", "coon-songs", and the latest "hits" replace the simpler Negro melodies,' he lamented. 'Young Negroes pride themselves on the number of such songs they can sing, at the same time that they resent a request to sing the older melodies'. Far from being inhibited by Odum's cylinder recorder, they welcomed it as a means of broadcasting their music. Odum was particularly unsettled by 'the young Negro who wished to call out his name before each song which he was singing into the phonograph. "Song composed by Will Smith of Chattanooga, Tennessee," he would cry out, then begin his song; for, he maintained, these songs would be sung all over the world, and he deserved the credit for them.'

In Will Smith, Odum heard a modernity he had not expected, a welcoming of technology and a worldly ambition that the recording machine seemed not simply to capture but to provoke. Though he had seized upon the phonograph as a scientific tool, he discovered that it could propel his subjects into distinctly unfolkish behaviour. That twenty years on he discarded those cylinders should perhaps not surprise us. Faced with the voices that race records generated, he wanted to remember voices that were purer, more magical, voices that sang the 'simpler Negro melodies', the 'soft, stirring melodies of a folklife'.

Chapter Three

On the Trail of Negro Folk Songs

Near the end of her life, as she sat musing in her roof garden overlooking 113th Street, Dorothy Scarborough liked to remember the moment when her search first came to fruition, when after months of letter writing and interviews she uncovered the sound of the uncorrupted black voice. It came to her in the Manhattan town house owned by John Allan Wyeth, a seventy-six-year-old Civil War veteran and surgeon of national renown, one-time president of the American Medical Association and founder of the Polyclinic Hospital, the first postgraduate school of medicine in the US. Seven years earlier, in 1914, Wyeth had published his memoirs, *With Sabre and Scalpel*, which included accounts of slave songs and dances he had learned growing up on his family's Alabama plantation. Scarborough was desperate to meet him, and a doctor friend offered to make introductions. Letters were sent, an appointment was made, and on a spring evening in 1921 the friend brought Scarborough to Wyeth's door.

With his leonine head and stern, chiselled features, Wyeth was an imposing figure, reserved and formal and accustomed to deference, but Scarborough soon felt at ease. At forty-three, she had a calm, sweet, daughterly manner, and though she had spent the last few years in New York City teaching creative writing at Columbia University, she had an intimate knowledge of Southern patriarchs. Her father, John Bledsoe Scarborough, had been a Confederate veteran from Louisiana, like his wife a child of slaveowners, and like Wyeth he had risen in the war's aftermath to a position of power and influence. Trained as a lawyer, he worked as a judge in a series of Texas towns before settling in Waco, home to Baylor University, whose board of trustees he soon joined. Dorothy Scarborough grew up in the shadow of this pillar of the local community, which proved particularly burdensome after her mother's early death when, as the lone unmarried daughter, she was expected to serve as her father's hostess. She had ideas, and determination; in her quiet way, she rebelled. By 1899 she had earned a BA and an MA in English at Baylor, and when her father died in 1905 she instantly put her degree to work. Over the next twelve years, she would teach intermittently at Baylor while pursuing a doctorate in English literature, travelling first to the University of Chicago, then to Oxford University, only to discover to her dismay that this bastion of higher learning refused to grant women degrees. In 1915 she enrolled at Columbia University and began a PhD dissertation on the supernatural in English fiction, and almost immediately Columbia's extension division offered her a teaching post. She quit her job at Baylor, shipped up the last of her belongings, and settled in New York City for good.

Up until then, Scarborough's writing had focused on the lore and literature of distant lands, but abruptly, when she moved to New York, she began writing about the South. In 1919 she published *From a Southern Porch*, a celebration of languorous days spent on her sister's front porch in Richmond, Virginia, where she fled every summer when Manhattan's gasoline fumes became stifling and the streets grew gummy with melted tar. There she would sit from early morning until the last traces of light disappeared from the sky, with a notebook in her lap, ostensibly working, but mostly watching the procession of life. 'I can see a black woman going by on the road, a basket of clothes balanced on her head – swaying but never in danger of falling,' she wrote.

Groups of laughing gay young Negroes pass by to their work or to errands in town. Little boys, as black as the berries they have in their buckets for sale, are on their way to market. An old mule ambles restfully down the road, drawing a cart that

creaks with rheumatism and years, and that has one hind
wheel at an alarming angle with the body of the cart. But the
driver, an ebony antique, is unagitated, and the animal at ease
of mind. Not for any inducement would that mule quicken his
pace. Autos from the city whirl by with sophisticated snorts
and honk-honks, raising dust in whorls.

What Scarborough revelled in from the front porch was a South that
felt and sounded unchanging. It could not have been more different
from what she encountered on her roof garden on West 113th Street,
where her attempts to lose herself in reverie were continually foiled by
the screech of argumentative voices, the honking and roaring of cars
and buses, and the jangle and crackle of Victrolas pumping canned
music from all directions, meshing and merging with the noise of the
city, 'the hurdy-gurdy of the street beyond'. The black folk she saw
from the porch could have stepped straight out of the mid-nineteenth
century. 'Not for any inducement would that mule quicken his pace'
– nor, she might have added, would the 'ebony antique' who drove
him. On foot and in horse carts, calm and unhurried, they exuded a
placid contentment that was altogether unshakeable, that could not
be disturbed even by the passing automobiles.

So Scarborough had believed in 1919. But the next year brought
Mamie Smith's 'Crazy Blues', and with it a mass black consumption
of recorded music all across the US, including the South. Suddenly
her portrait of a people doggedly resisting technology seemed much
harder to sustain. Suddenly those mellifluous voices that she heard
from the front porch seemed in danger of falling silent, and while
she could not have said what it was exactly, she knew that something
essential was being lost. In January 1921, five months after 'Crazy
Blues' began reverberating across her roof garden, Scarborough sent
out a letter on Columbia University stationery asking for help in
collecting black songs. The spirituals, she argued, had been well
documented, but Negro folk song was a far broader category. 'I am
trying to make as complete a collection of these as possible, since

these interesting and valuable reflections of our Southern life may soon be forgotten if they are not preserved in some permanent way,' she noted. 'It is the genuine Negro songs that I wish, not those written by white people, but the ones made and sung by the colored race.'

As she came into Dr Wyeth's parlour, Scarborough would have looked round her at the evidence of his long and distinguished career: the plaques commemorating his surgical innovations (ligation of the external carotid artery, bloodless amputation at shoulder and hip joints), the medals for his Civil War service. She would have observed the long lines in his face that spoke of his sixteen months confinement in a Union prison, where he contracted pneumonia, malaria and typhoid, and watched thousands of Confederate prisoners die of starvation, an experience he later chronicled in an article for *Century* magazine that created a national furore. Not long before, he had broken his hip, and now he walked with a cane. He settled into his chair slowly and carefully and turned to her to begin the interview with the grave dignity of a venerable man who had outlived most of his critics and felt sure of his place in the world.

Yet as he began to speak, it was as though time slipped away. Scarborough asked Wyeth about his childhood in the valley of the Tennessee River, and he told her about his parents, who like 'so many of the best people in the South' had been, at heart, emancipationists. They bought slaves for house service only because white domestic servants were not an option, and they treated them with a kindness that soon turned to love, nursing them through sickness and age. The slaves, men and women 'of fine character', responded with unflagging devotion. He had been particularly close to an elderly slave, Uncle Billy, who had taught him how to sing and dance and play the banjo. 'When the boy became more proficient than the old man,' Scarborough related, 'Uncle Billy put away the banjo and never played again.' Like all the family's servants, Billy remained loyal during the war, and after the Confederate surrender, a Republican Negro cut his throat.

They were nearly all dead now, Wyeth mused, those old-time

Negroes. Faithful, patient, submissive, contented, they had a 'charm of manner' that today's 'colored citizens' utterly lacked. The trust and affection between the races had disappeared too. No white child growing up today could know what it felt like to sit at Mammy Tildy's hearth late at night listening to her 'skeery' stories, or to sit on the steps of Uncle Billy's cabin, where he had learned to play the banjo, the slave's large hands guiding his small ones as they pressed and plucked the strings.

Long ago, after Billy was murdered, he had put his old banjo away, but he brought it out for Scarborough's visit. He could still remember the songs. The scientist in him found them intriguing (the Negroes' idea of rhythm, he told her, showed their 'low order of development' – when dancing, they patted the ground, while the more evolved Indians reached away from the earth), and sometimes, if he was lucky, he could capture the grain of Billy's voice. He sang 'Jimmy Rose', a song that he believed Billy had made up, and 'Run Nigger Run', a song Scarborough remembered her mother singing, about the comic misadventures of the darkies eluding the slave patrols. He showed her the instrumental techniques that Uncle Billy had taught him, demonstrating that he had never lost the proficiency that made his slave companion set the banjo aside. 'He evoked melodies of wistful gaiety by drawing a handkerchief across the banjo strings,' Scarborough noted, 'and lively tunes by playing it with a whisk-broom.' They were 'magical tricks', she concluded. 'This is astounding to anybody who has seen him in the operating room,' her doctor friend whispered. 'The rest of us feel honored at handing him a sponge, and no one could have convinced us he would turn himself loose on a banjo like this.'

And then, in the dwindling light, the old doctor rose to his feet and tossed aside his cane. He wanted to show Scarborough some of the old breakdowns, the way the slaves themselves had danced them, so slowly, gingerly, he began moving his body as Uncle Billy had taught him to move. He clapped his hands, bent his knees, clicked his heels, and patted his thighs; he hopped and shuffled and kicked his legs skyward and hopped and shuffled and kicked again. As Scarborough watched, the surroundings faded, the tasteful decor and the expensive furniture and the roar and screech of the traffic below. Dr Wyeth jumped and twirled. 'I felt transported,' she wrote years later, 'to an old plantation of days before the war.'

To an extent that Edison could not foresee, the mechanical reproduction of music transformed human experience by freeing sound from its roots in communities, from the constraints of time and place. There may have been only one Mamie Smith, but by 1920 there were one million of her records in circulation, making it possible to hear her simultaneously from New Orleans to Chicago, from Charleston to Seattle, from London to Johannesburg. Recording and mass-producing music allowed it to transcend more than just regional moorings: to an extent never before possible, African American songs could break through the colour line. Once only encountered at house parties and barn dances, on street corners and the black showbiz circuit, the blues could be heard pouring out of speakeasies, nightclubs, houses, apartments, drug stores and barbershops, hardware stores and funeral parlours, anywhere race records were played or sold. White people in cities could not avoid hearing it, and many were frankly appalled. 'Hundreds of "race" singers have flooded the market with what is generally regarded as the worst contribution to the cause of good music ever inflicted on the public,' one aggrieved listener noted. 'The lyrics of a great many of these "blues" are worse than the lowest sort of doggerel and the melodies are lacking in originality, lilting rhythm and any semblance to musical worth.' For some, this was vulgarity pure and simple, and they gave it no more thought than that. For others, no less dismayed, but more reflective, this was something more unsettling: the clarion call of a new black urban world.

From her apartment on the fringes of Harlem, Dorothy Scarborough heard that clarion call loud and clear. Her 1921 appeal for 'genuine

A page from *On the Trail of Negro Folk Songs*

Negro songs', the appeal that took her to Dr Wyeth, resulted in her 1925 book *On the Trail of Negro Folk Songs*. Part song anthology, part history, part folklore compendium, part memoir, the book is virtually unread today, and Scarborough herself has slipped into the peculiar obscurity of Southern apologists, those white men and women who lamented the passing of the gracious days of the plantation and who were, on the face of it, utterly untroubled by what W. E. B. DuBois famously called 'the problem of the color line'. Without doubt, the book makes for difficult reading. Scarborough's prose, 'delightful' according to her original reviewers, has a studied whimsy about it that feels, today, affected and cloying. More troubling still are the assumptions she makes: that the music passed down by black Southerners reflects 'the lighter, happier side of slavery'; that the songs' syncopated rhythms and singular wordplay speak of the irrational, illogical 'colored mind'.

Yet behind the book lies an obsession that demands scrutiny. Scarborough's interview with Dr Wyeth launched a four-year search for 'genuine Negro melodies' that took her across the South, as she met up with white informants who recreated the voices of the kindly aunties and uncles who had fed them, played with them and sung them to sleep. In none of this was she unusual. At a time when ethnographers documenting Native American ritual collected from Native Americans directly, enthusiasts of black song like Newman White, Robert Gordon, Emmet Kennedy, Frank Dobie and Frank Brown preferred to rely on their own recollections or those of elderly white Southerners whose reminiscences of a childhood soundscape were shot through with 'the fairy tale of a happy slave civilisation', as W. E. B. DuBois called it.

What should we do with these recreations? It is too simplistic, obviously, to treat them as evidence of a 'slave culture'. To give just one example: 'Run Nigger Run', which Wyeth sang to Scarborough, did date back to the mid-nineteenth century, but it is unlikely that slaves themselves originated or even willingly sang it, at least not in the form of the comic ditty that Wyeth and Scarborough remembered. The slave patrols that it described were notorious for their brutality. Asked about the song in the 1930s, one ex-slave remarked, 'Sometimes I wonder iffen de white folks didn't make dat song up so us niggers would keep in line.' Wyeth's narrative of his idyllic childhood is permeated with a reactionary nostalgia that cannot help but tarnish whatever facts it might contain. The songs themselves seem almost incidental to the memories their performance evoked and (from Wyeth's side anyway) to the experience of projecting himself into an imagined blackness. While he did not don blackface, it is impossible not to see this as minstrelsy. That Wyeth inveighed against the Negro's 'low order of development' while 'turning himself loose on the banjo' is the classic blackface dynamic – revulsion mixed with fascination, disgust with desire.

Yet to dismiss these enactments as mere racist fantasy is to miss much of what they have to reveal. What passed between Wyeth and Scarborough was more than an interview – it was a ritual of belonging. Recreating the voice of the plantation Negro had been a Southern obsession since the late nineteenth century, carried out in dialect fiction, stage performances, and state and local folklore societies. Scarborough's list of her informants reads like a who's who of self-styled 'darky dialecticians', from John Trotwood Moore to Louise Clarke Pyrnelle to Thomas Nelson Page, who built careers ventriloquising the plantation Negro in stage appearances and works of fiction that brought regional, sometimes national renown.

Fearing that authentic black music was being drowned out by mass-produced replicas, Scarborough set out in search of the real thing. That the real thing turned out to be a white imitation invites us to consider the place of nostalgia, imagination and fantasy in the shaping of the African American folk canon and, indeed, the protean nature of 'authenticity' itself. Claims of discerning authenticity – in effect, assertions that some expressive forms are more 'real' than others – are, unavoidably, political and social critiques. In proclaiming her capacity to distinguish the real from the spurious, Scarborough set herself up as a cultural arbiter, endowed with superior taste and discernment, a role that gave her the authority to contest the shape of popular art.

Like DuBois in his 1903 book *The Souls of Black Folk*, Scarborough was moved by her memories of transcendent black singing, but while DuBois heard echoes of the horrors of slavery, Scarborough discerned different meanings, a different history, and a different set of emotional and political truths. That she sought those resonances in re-enactments by white Southerners raises questions about the tangled history of song-collecting in the age of mechanical reproduction, the masks employed by enthusiasts of black music swept up in the magic of their search for the real.

In the years it took her to complete her book, Dorothy Scarborough made several trips to the South, relatively brief ones in 1921 and 1922 and then a year's sabbatical beginning in the autumn of 1923. It is virtually impossible to pin down where she journeyed and when: she drew up no itinerary (or at least did not preserve one); nor did she keep a diary or field notes. The account that she published in *On the Trail* depicted less a purposeful trek than a set of meander-ings: a lazy few days in South Carolina, a languorous week in Mississippi – in her remembrance they blended into each other, one long amble through an enchanted landscape. Like her friend Emmet Kennedy, whose 1925 book *Mellows* was an ecstatic reminiscence of the black songs of his childhood, she was searching for a place that was not on the map, 'a region of uncontaminated beauty and pastoral dreams', the magical land she had sensed as she watched Dr Wyeth, the 'old plantation of days before the war'.

The idea of the 'old plantation' as a source of transcendent black singing had rarely, if ever, been voiced by antebellum planters them-selves. While some encouraged their fieldhands to sing in order to speed up the pace of their work, most seem to have heard in slave song simply savage wails, barbaric, uncivilised noise. White Southerners' rhapsodic accounts of black singing were an entirely retrospective affair, beginning only in the late nineteenth century. The end of Reconstruction saw the rise of a new Southern elite, an uneasy mix of planters and industrialists united by their determin-ation to reverse the fragile gains African Americans had won since the war. By the end of the century, the introduction of the sharecrop-ping system was supplemented by a campaign of disfranchisement, segregation and lynching, a full-blown racial caste system backed up, where necessary, by violence. Yet the new racial order was never as stable as most Southern whites would have liked. Despite all their efforts to keep African Americans tied to the soil, black men and women proved stubbornly mobile, leaving the farm, sometimes leaving the South, and in ways large and small, real and imagined, aban-doning old habits of deference.

Against that backdrop, Southern whites turned to visions of (in the phrase of the period) 'the old-time Negro'. By the late nineteenth century, that figure had the impress of science upon it. In 1888 the newly founded American Folklore Society declared its intention to collect and study 'the fast-vanishing remains of folklore in America', by which it meant 'relics of old English ballads', myths and tales of Native Americans, and 'lore of Negroes in the Southern States'. From the outset, the work of collecting the latter was dominated by white Southerners, who set up state and local folklore societies at the turn of the century that defined how the study of Negro folklore would be pursued for the next thirty years. Few of their members drew upon fieldwork. Instead, they excavated their memories, conjuring up the old-time Negro as a ghostly rebuke to the new, mourning the loss of a golden age of racial harmony, 'the happy days of the plantation' when blacks and whites had lived in friendship and peace. Women played a key role in this process as cultural caretakers, conduits of plantation lore, transforming their domestic seclusion into privileged access to a remembered world of tender emotion. As late as 1930, the folklorist Robert Winslow Gordon, who prided himself on his scientific rigour, spoke of their value as informants. 'Many a dear little Southern lady whose hair is now white [has told me] that she used as a girl to beg the Negro women to shout for her, and, if no men were present, had joined in with them – thus herself learning the art.'

Scarborough's hair may still have been brown, but she built a career as a Southern lady, even though by 1921 she had spent six years in the North. In that persona she found that her memories were transformed into knowledge, and she herself was accorded respect. She had grown up, she once remarked, as 'a queer combination of bookworm and tomboy', a studious girl who loved to climb trees and constantly butted up against social constraints. Once, when she was eight or nine, she attended a religious revival, watching in awe as men and boys stumbled forward to confess their sins and profess their faith, yet when she rose and attempted to do the same, she heard the room erupt in laughter and found herself shunted back to her seat. If to grow up female in the South was, by and large, to confront that kind of belittlement, here she could voice her ideas and emotions and no one would question her right to speak.

In Negro folk song, she believed she had found the subject she was born to explore. Her first forays into the topic came in 1915, when as head of the Texas Folklore Society she gave a talk on 'plantation melodies' for her presidential address. Later, when she began writing fiction (her first novel, *In the Land of Cotton*, a tale of white farmers in Texas, was published in 1921), she threaded black folk lyrics through the story and discovered that 'readers found them more interesting than anything I had written myself'. From the beginning, she took issue with mainstream folk-music studies. A voracious reader, she had ploughed through the books that defined the scholarly orthodoxy, the works of Northerners like Francis Child and George Lyman Kittredge, and while much of their argument struck her as insightful, their style and methods left her cold. She accepted the basics: a genuine folk song was of rural, communal origins, it had no single, definitive form, it was common property in the hands of non-professional singers who altered it freely according to their mood. Yet Child and Kittredge approached song-collecting as an act of taxonomy, endlessly classifying and cataloguing multiple variants. For Scarborough its lure was far more emotional, far more intuitive, an invitation to travel through time. 'How many memories of my childhood and youth are associated with loved black faces!' she rhapsodised.

> How I enjoyed the songs the Negroes sang, even though I was ignorant of their value! . . . I see a procession of black and yellow and cream-colored faces that have passed through our kitchen and house and garden – some very impermanent and some remaining for years, but all singing. Now, when I sit on a porch at night, I am in fancy back at our

old home, listening to the mellow, plaintive singing of a Negro congregation at a church a half-mile away – a congregation which 'ne'er broke up' at least before I went to sleep, and which gathered every night in a summer-long revival. I can project myself into the past and hear the wailful songs at Negro funerals, the shouting songs at baptizings and the creek or river, old break-downs at parties, lullabies crooned as mammies rocked black and white babies to sleep, worksongs in cotton field or on the railroad or street-grading jobs. All sounds of human activity among the Negroes in the South used to be accompanied with song. It is so now to a certain extent, but less than before.

In the modern world, she was convinced, genuine black melodies were fast disappearing, as those 'loved black faces' gave way to anonymous new ones who were no longer disposed to break into song, who had fully succumbed to the lure of what she could only regard as 'canned music'. The more she read, the more convinced she became. African Americans' too-enthusiastic embrace of modernity, in the form of education, factory labour and migration to cities, were eradicating what one commentator described as the Negro's 'highest gift, his spontaneity. Songs start from nothing, from the loading of a truck, the possession of a banjo, the half-remembered line of a hymn, and grow in an hour, never to be exactly repeated . . . The songs may live, but the best thing of all, the free impulse, the pattern of careless voices happily inventing as they go, if it dies it cannot be resurrected.' That 'free impulse', that 'golden source', still existed in the souls of some black Southerners, but its days were clearly numbered. 'The plantation Master and the plantation Negro stand today definitely at the parting of the ways,' lamented her friend and South Carolina novelist, Dubose Heyward. 'The call of the city has already been heeded. The migration has commenced. They will be taken from our fields, fired with ambition, and fed to the machines of our glittering new civilisation.'

In the face of that disheartening prospect, capturing authentic black songs became an imperative. Her sources she saw as impeccable: elderly white Southerners who had absorbed the melodies they had heard from black caretakers with the wholehearted devotion only children could show. Though she had her own vivid memories of such figures, by and large she let her informants speak for her. They told of stealing away to the servants' quarters, treasured illicit moments in childhoods otherwise ruled by decorum. 'I sat in the kitchen and learned songs, stories and the buck and wing dances, when I was first able to carry a tune until I went away to school at thirteen,' recalled Udly Jones Wheeler. 'I didn't know what I was singing, I just sang as he sang.' And they mourned the steady deterioration in the years that had followed. 'Once the trusted servant and almost constant companion of the white man, the Negro, since he became free, has become shiftless, uncertain in his responsibility, and morally outcast,' argued her informant J. E. Morrow. 'The happy days of the plantation have passed; with them have gone "Swanee Ribber", "My Ole Kentucky Home", "Uncle Ned", "Nellie Gray" and "Old Black Joe" . . . No longer does the Negro sit about his little cabin and sing his rich old melodies to the plinky-plinky-plank-plank-plank of his banjo. No more the pathos of a heart longing to hunt for the possum an' de coon on de ole Kaintucky shore; no more the pining for the home far away; no longer the passion of a bereaved heart in a plaintive "I shall nebber see my darlin' eny mo." The art of banjo playing has almost been lost and where it survives, the instrument has been prostituted to thumming out vulgar dances for dives or cheap ragtime songs for carnivals or medicine shows.'

Scarborough would not have phrased it so bluntly, but at heart she would have agreed. What she heard and saw in her informants' singing and dancing was an evocative contrast to the jangle of Victrolas that drifted through her windows in Manhattan. She had no doubts about the accuracy of such performances, their value as historical artefacts. Black people themselves were no longer singing, at least not the kinds of songs she was after. Dr Wyeth, in contrast, could evoke Uncle Billy's dancing and singing with scientific precision, and not only because he had memories to draw on. As Scarborough repeatedly maintained, 'the Negro is by nature a mimetic creature, dramatising all he knows, his experiences and the life about him, expressing everything in form and motion.' Like most other white Southerners of her generation, she assumed that slave songs and dances had originated not from an African inheritance, but from imitation of the slaveholding class. That inborn disposition to mimicry explained both the high class of melodies developed under slavery, when blacks were in constant contact with aristocratic whites, and the danger of urban migrations, since black men and women would inevitably take on the character of their surroundings. What Dr Wyeth was enacting was not just a dance but an intimacy, a tender care and reciprocity that once existed between the races. Seen in that light, his performance became not a mere copy, but an imitation of an original that was itself an imitation, a hall of mirrors whose multiple refractions devolved from a source that once had been white.

Hence Scarborough's sense that obtaining genuine black song need not involve speaking to genuine black people, apart from those born into slavery or, in some indefinable but palpable way, touched with the spirit of the Old South. Occasionally in her travels she stumbled upon them, and then it was as if time had stopped. Their backs stooped, their faces lined, in voices beautiful with old age's 'quavering sweetness' they sang songs that no one else remembered, and when she pleaded for more they smiled indulgently, as though at the vagaries of a demanding child.

And sometimes she got more than songs: memories of loved ones who had been lost to her. Once in Natchitoches, Louisiana, when she was wandering through the ruins of her family's plantation, an elderly black man approached her deferentially and introduced himself as Sebron Mallard, one of her late grandfather's slaves. Though he could not sing and could not help her directly, he was able to verify the antiquity of some of the songs she was investigating, and he had vivid memories of her father, a high-spirited boy who had run away to join the Confederates at age seventeen. 'I was ploughing when I got the word that Mister Johnny's daughter was nigh here, and I drapped the plough and made tracks toward you,' he explained. 'Mister Johnny war de youngest of all de boys, but he knowed how to work harder and laugh more than any of 'em.' He looked at her fondly. 'He said, "Li'l mistis, is you well? Is you happy?"'

'Yes, Uncle Sebron, I'm always well, and I'm very happy,' I told him.

He looked at me with dimming eyes.

'My ole pappy tol' me befo' he died that good luck would be bound to go with ol' Marster's fambly becase they was allus so good to their pore slaves. They brought us up mannerble, and I brought my chillun up thataway, too. And ain't none of us never been arrested nor had no trouble. But some of the young folks these days isn't that way and it makes trouble. Us old folks sees when dey do wrong, and it hurts us, but we can't do nothing, cause we's feble and we's few. White folks and black folks look like they ain't live lovely together like they used to.'

Voices like Mallard's, speaking words she could have scripted, were for Scarborough the black voices that mattered; to others she was largely indifferent. After leaving Natchitoches, she travelled to Texas and spent a few days with a friend, the state's governor, Pat Neff, who urged her to follow up an encounter he had on a recent visit to Central State Prison Farm. 'A Negro man came up to him after supper,' Scarborough related, 'and said, "Will you listen while I sing you a song?" He rendered a ditty whose refrain ran as follows:

If I had the gov'ner
Where the gov'ner has me,
Before daylight
I'd set the gov'ner free.

I begs you, gov'ner,
Upon my soul:
If you won't gimme a pardon,
Won't you gimme a parole?

Ten years later, chasing his own dream of authentic black voices,
John Lomax would record another pardon song by that same convict
in Angola State Penitentiary in Louisiana, but the prospect of hearing
him did not entice Scarborough. She enjoyed Neff's anecdote and
wrote down the lyrics, but, for her, the governor's rendition was real
enough.

Opposite the main archivist's desk in the Special Collections Library
at Baylor University hangs a portrait of Dorothy Scarborough. Painted,
most likely, sometime around 1920, it shows a small-boned woman
with light brown hair and hazel eyes behind wire-rimmed glasses,
her expression composed and thoughtful, her glance bright and alert
as a bird's. The heart-shaped face has a wistful smile and an under-
stated, not wholly realised beauty – like a bookish spinster in a
Hollywood movie, just before the hero removes her glasses and lets
down her hair.

If anyone ever let Scarborough's hair down, she kept it quiet. To
read the collection of her papers at Baylor, thick with manuscripts
and letters from correspondents, is to be struck by her remoteness:
carefully culled by her sister to remove anything unduly personal,
the archive contains virtually no letters *from* her, barely a trace of
her private voice. Neither can that private voice be made out in the
pages she wrote for publication, where she dwells at most length on
the memories of others and says relatively little about her own. What
we are left with is that face in the portrait, the voice that Scarborough
carefully cultivated: that of the archetypal Southern lady – 'our demure,
delicate, poised, other-minded Dot', as one of her friends put it. That

Dorothy Scarborough

voice is persuasive even in *On the Trail*, where she moves with a freedom that few Southern white women could have imagined. 'I have wandered through the colored quarters of many towns and cities, hailing many an old mammy and uncle to beg for songs,' she wrote. 'I have made friends with countless children, loitering to watch their play and hear their singing, stopping them from their errands, rousing them from their naps in public places. I have loitered in market places to watch the women buying their supplies, and overhear their conversation and their chance humming, and have strolled along levees and quays in many a town to hear the Negro men sing at their work.' That she seems no less refined and genteel for so doing simply heightens our sense of the magical landscape to which song-collecting transports her: a world where racial boundaries do not impinge upon her, where danger never looms.

There is one time in the book, and only one, when her safety is threatened. While gathering songs near Natchez, Mississippi, Scarborough encounters a baptism being held in a pond in the grounds of a mansion that burned in the war. She had seen the ritual once or twice in her childhood, but framed by the ruins of an old plantation this one unfolded with the power of a dream. The candidates for baptism filed to the edge of the water, ghostly figures enveloped in white, their voices raised in a weird, eerie dirge. As the preacher cried out in exhortation, each candidate plunged into the water and resurfaced thrashing and wailing in ecstasy, while the hundreds of black worshippers gathered at the waterside responded with shouts and groans. For a time Scarborough watched the service from the top of the mansion's old marble stairway, but the drama grew too intriguing, and as 'with each immersion the excitement grew, the shouting became more wild and unrestrained, the struggles of the candidate grew more violent', she moved into the crowd and pulled out her camera to capture the proceedings on film.

> The shouter would fall on the ground, writhing about as if in anguish, tearing her hair, beating off those who sought to calm her. Sometimes one, reeling too near in the throes of thanks-giving, would fall into the water and have to be fished out, somewhat subdued but still shrieking, and led off to dry in the sun.
>
> I tried repeatedly to get a picture of the scene, but each time I adjusted the Kodak, some shouter would start up beside me and all but push me into the pond. That little black box seemed to have an unfortunate effect on the crowd. One time I thought I would persist, but in the melee I was all but crushed. I was between the pond on one side and a barbed-wire fence on the other, with no chance for escape but a tree which I might have climbed had it not been a *bois-d'arc*, full of hard thorns. The crowd surged against me, and I had to put up my Kodak hastily and become as inconspicuous as possible. I do not think they meant to harm me, but it was merely a matter of emotional excitement. Even my pencil taking down songs upset them.

Reading Scarborough's account of the baptism, it is tempting to take it as a kind of fable, a distillation of the corrupting power she saw at work in the Machine Age. In the crowd she discovers the unfortunate effect that a machine – 'That little black box' – had upon the people whose rituals she was trying to capture. No wonder Scarborough so feared the impact of the phonograph: mechanical instruments like Victrolas and cameras created a dangerous kind of self-consciousness, and a primitive folk that had been simple and nurturing suddenly became a mob.

So powerfully does Scarborough evoke this moment that it comes as a shock to discover that throughout her research for *On the Trail* she collected songs with mechanical devices: a bulky disc recorder that she used near her home in Manhattan and a portable recording phonograph that she took into the field. Scarborough began hunting for the machines early on in her research, writing to Thomas A. Edison, Inc requesting 'a cylinder phonograph which can be used for home recording' in April 1921. Just what she recorded and when is uncertain – the cylinders wore out after a few playings and she apparently discarded them after a musician friend transcribed their contents – but in her sessions with her white informants she appears to have used the machine routinely. It seems almost certain that she had it with her when she turned up at Dr Wyeth's apartment, that he 'turned himself loose' on the banjo while facing a mechanical recording horn.

From the moment Scarborough embarked on her quest, she had to grapple with a dilemma that had vexed song collectors for over three decades: how best to capture authentic voices in the age of mechanical reproduction. That the arduous work of transcribing songs could be immeasurably eased by the phonograph had been apparent to song collectors virtually from the moment of the machine's invention, yet the very precision that first entranced Howard Odum made the cylinder recorder anathema to others, particularly those who had experienced precisely how useful its assistance could be. 'I lack entire faith in the [making] of wax records,' noted the folklorist Natalie Curtis Burlin, shortly after recording black students at the Hampton Institute in 1919. Mechanical accuracy, as she saw it, got in the way of folkloric truth, which celebrated 'the instinctive song of un-self-conscious people – a type of music which is by its very nature furthermost removed from all idea of mechanism.' Far more important was the folklorist's intuitive grasp of the songs she was hearing, gained from living amongst the singers until their rhythms become part of her own being. Scarborough had those words with her as she embarked on her project, and her own practice endorsed them. As a grand-daughter of slaveowners, she believed she had inherited a body of knowledge that enabled her to distinguish the fake from the genuine, and like Burlin, she saw folk-song-gathering as an intuitive and quintessentially feminine practice. In her account of her meeting with Dr Wyeth, she posed herself as dutiful Southern daughter, coaxing him back to a childhood soundscape of tenderness and emotion. To have shown the machine in her account would have shattered the illusion, revealing the modern researcher behind the plantation-bred lady, the writer and teacher who through her connections at Columbia had access to technological aid.

That technological aid was crucial to her project. Scarborough used her cylinder recorder to capture music and lyrics, then threaded bits of musical transcription through her account of her subjects' reminiscences. When her subjects remembered the music but forgot the words, her transcriptions indicated that too. What she was after was not a songbook, a set of playable musical arrangements – rather, an impressionistic record of her own journey, in which memories slid into half-remembered musical fragments, shards of melodies that the reader could just about hum but not in any real sense recreate. To describe this as documentation does not really capture it – it was more of a summoning of musical ghosts. Using a cylinder recorder allowed Scarborough to immerse herself in the illusion. With her hands freed from the work of transcription, she could slip into reverie, reliving, through her informants' mimicry, the transracial intimacy she imagined she had known as a child.

Compelling her informants to sit at a machine and sing their songs into a horn made for a different sort of collecting encounter, far more formal, controlled and artificial than she would ever admit to. Yet in many ways Scarborough's hidden machine is of a piece with other tensions at work in her story. For what is most intriguing about *On the Trail* is its erratic but unmistakable note of detachment, its intermittent reluctance to commit to the plantation myths that the book otherwise seems to purvey. Take, for instance, her discussion of that central Southern archetype, the mammy. Though for much of the book Scarborough relies upon formula, a conventional elegy to the 'crooning sweetness' of her remembered singing, to the wonder of 'a racial mother-heart which can take in not only its own babies, but those of another, dominant, race as well', at moments she abruptly steps back. 'What other nation of mothers has ever patiently and with a beautiful sacrifice put alien children ahead of its own?' she asks, adding 'in outward devotion if not in actual fact?' That the 'actual fact' might have been different, that the mammy might have been playing a role, that she might have felt hostility toward her 'alien' charges, was a possibility that few white Southerners ever broached.

'We wear the mask,' wrote the African American poet Paul Laurence Dunbar in a verse of which Scarborough was likely aware. Once Scarborough had completed her travels, she began writing the book in her New York apartment, and the longer she worked on it, the more her persona as a plantation-bred lady took on elements of a masquerade. To look at the life she developed in the 1920s is to be struck by its contradictions. On the face of it a professional Southerner, she claimed to find the North cold, arid and soulless, yet she never attempted to move away. Scarborough lived in New York till the end of her life, and her roots there became stronger as time went on. By the mid-1920s she was spending her summers not in lazy reverie at her sister's house in Virginia, but at her own cottage in Connecticut, where she cultivated a garden, wrote several novels, and enjoyed the relative quiet. Her New York apartment became a salon for minor literati, like her fellow book reviewers on the *New York Tribune,* friends like Fannie Hurst and Zona Gale, writing students like Carson McCullers, and displaced song gatherers like Emmet Kennedy. In time, those friendships became the most Southern thing about her. Her 1925 novel *The Wind* can only be described as an anti-pastoral: based on a tale Scarborough originally heard from her mother, it follows a young bride who moves to West Texas only to be driven mad by the bleakness of the landscape – above all by the 'wild shouting voice' of a howling wind that never lets her 'know the peace of silence'. Though for most of the decade Scarborough continued to write regional fiction (tales of white Texas farmers interspersed with scraps of black folk song, which 'seemed to me necessary to make the life of the section adequately real'), the setting became increasingly unspecific, and her final novel, 1932's *The Stretch-Berry Smile*, takes place largely in New York.

Far more than the Southern arcadia she sometimes evoked in her writing, New York City had been Scarborough's salvation. In Texas, and even in Oxford, her femininity constantly constrained her; in New York she could support herself as a writer, teacher and journalist, and she seems to have prized the crisp professionalism of that identity. She never married; she lived alone. And as much as at times she aimed to hide it, she relished the mobility and anonymity the city allowed, the possibilities for loitering, wandering, eavesdropping, the same pleasures, indeed, of collecting black song. 'She told him how on Saturday afternoons she would explore the town as if it were a jungle no one had seen before, would loaf for hours watching the life slip by on the East River, would visit the piers to see the ocean liners, would mingle with the foreigners in the tenement section,' she wrote in her final novel. 'On subways at rush hours, on elevated trains past the exposed domesticity of second-story windows, on buses up Fifth Avenue, up Riverside where grey battleships lay in the river, on ferry boats to Governor's Island with its army headquarters, to Staten Island and back to watch the miracle of the New York skyline at sunset, or as dusk brought out its million lights.'

It is impossible to know for sure where she wandered, what parts of the 'jungle' she ventured into, but they almost certainly included Harlem. She lived on the fringes of what she described as the 'greatest Negro city in the world', and in time she got to know people there. At Columbia she taught and befriended the West Indian journalist Eric Walrond, whose collection of short stories *Tropic of Death* she helped nurse into print, and through him she met Charles S. Johnson, Walrond's editor at *Opportunity* magazine, the journal of black arts and politics produced by the Urban League. Though he may not have known of her interest in black folklore, Johnson admired her fiction, its attention to regional particularity, a skill he believed black writers should cultivate. In September 1924, he invited Scarborough to serve as a judge for *Opportunity*'s upcoming literary contest, which would award $500 in prize money to the most promising African American writers. Over the next nine months, as she wrote the final drafts of *On the Trail*, Scarborough read hundreds of pages of African American fiction, debating their merits with her fellow judges on the short story panel, including the black critic Alain Locke. On 1 May, 1925, she joined Locke, Paul Robeson, James Weldon Johnson, Jean Toomer, Carl Van Doren, Carl Van Vechten and 300 other writers, artists and critics for a banquet ceremony at the Fifth Avenue Restaurant, awarding prizes to Langston Hughes and Countee Cullen for poetry, Sterling Brown and E. Franklin Frazier for essays, and Eric Walrond and Zora Neale Hurston for short stories. 'White critics, whom "everybody" knows, Negro writers, whom "nobody" knows, meeting on common ground,' marvelled the *New York Herald Tribune*. 'The movement behind it means something to the race problem in general; certainly it means something to American literature. We are on the edge, if not already in the midst, of what might not improperly be called a Negro renaissance.'

Scarborough stumbled upon that renaissance in the final stages of drafting *On the Trail*, and she could not have failed to miss its challenge to white Southerners enthralled by black singing, who claimed the authority to delineate authentic black voices, those that evoked 'our southern life'. 'The day of "aunties", "uncles" and "mammy" is gone,' retorted Alain Locke bluntly on the eve of the *Opportunity* dinner. Those words would recur in his much-heralded anthology *The New Negro*, published in December of that year. The old-time Negro, he continued, had always been 'more of a myth than a man . . . a stock figure perpetuated as an historical fiction partly in innocent sentimentalism, partly in deliberate reactionism.' Putting an end to that historical fiction demanded a reinterpretation of black folk song and tale, and of paramount importance in that process was 'the energy and awakening of the Negro scholar and folklorist', wrote Scarborough's student Eric Walrond. 'For it is more or less common property in these United States today that if you really want to get to the heart and spirit of the black people you must do it through the medium of one of their own.'

What Scarborough was hearing, all around her, was the sound of her own obsolescence, assertions that reminiscences of black song penned by Southern whites were, at best, inconsequential, revealing little more than sentimental platitudes about African American music's 'heart and spirit'. ('I am now struggling with Kennedy's *Mellows*,' wrote Locke to Scarborough, 'so charming in some respects, but so annoying in others.') Just what she made of these claims is unclear, since Scarborough never addressed them directly, but the tone of her comments suggests unease. 'I am considered something of an authority on Negro life and literature, and the Negroes of New York think of me as a friend who is willing to help in constructive ways,' she wrote to a journalist in the final months of completing her book. 'I am often asked by editors to review books on the subject and I frequently act as judge in contests . . . I am glad to do anything I can to help the Negroes develop their talents and find their audience, and I am gratified at the progress I see them making in education and citizenship and art.' If Scarborough's talk of her 'gratification' sounds an unmistakable note of condescension, it was surely fed by trepidation: fear that her authority as a writer was being undermined, that her subject matter was being stolen away.

In the end, that fear proved impossible to ignore. Before she could finish her book, she had to embark on one last journey, which for one brief, startling moment would open her tale to the modern world.

'For the last several years,' Scarborough observes in her final chapter, 'the most popular type of Negro song has been that peculiar, barbaric sort of melody called "blues".' It was, to her ears, at once disagree-able and compelling in its sheer oddity. Blues compositions had a jerky rhythm, 'like a cripple dancing because of some irresistible impulse', and the abrupt stanzas, three lines instead of the customary four, gave them the shock of the unexpected, 'like the whip-crack surprise at the end of an O. Henry story'. Broadly available on record-ings and sheet music, blues seemed on the face of it 'to have little relation to authentic folk-music of the Negroes'. But the music's singularity made Scarborough curious, and she set out 'to trace it back to its origin', through referrals and tips making her way to West 46th Street and the music-publishing office of W. C. Handy.

Scarborough had never heard of Handy before one of her corre-spondents, the Mississippi planter William Percy, passed on his name. Born to former slaves in Alabama in 1873, Handy had worked as a bandleader in the Midwest and the Mississippi Delta before settling in Memphis and, in 1912, publishing 'Memphis Blues', among the first pieces of sheet music with the word blues in the title. Its success led to others: 'Beale Street Blues', 'Joe Turner Blues' and 'St Louis Blues', which in the hands of the race-record industry became perhaps the best-known blues of all time. By the time Scarborough tracked him down, Handy had moved his thriving business from Memphis to Times Square and established himself as among the city's pre-eminent songwriters, though his international renown as self-proclaimed 'father of the blues' was still over a decade away.

Scarborough peppered the composer with questions. Did the blues meet the criteria to be considered a folk music, based in rural trad-itions, remote from the world of cities, commerce and machines? Had the form emerged anonymously? Did blues compositions spring up spontaneously? Were the songs, to any extent, sung communally – 'taken up by many singers, who change and adapt and add to [them] in accordance with their own mood'? Yes, Handy replied, all that was true enough, but it did not get to the heart of the matter. What gave the blues its real standing as folk music was that it was 'essentially of our race', rooted in a collective black past. 'Each one of my blues is based on some old Negro song of the South, some folk-song that I heard from my mammy when I was a child,' he explained. 'Something that sticks in my mind, that I hum to myself when I'm not thinking about it. Some old song that is a part of the memories of my child-hood and of my race.'

Scarborough presented Handy's words without comment, unable, it seems, to digest them, and her silence leaves questions hanging in the reader's mind and, perhaps, in her own. Had Handy really had a mammy, that archetypal badge of genteel Southern whiteness? Did he compose his songs out of a kind of nostalgia, of, necessarily, a different character from that infusing the plantation myth? Above all, by Handy's criteria, what did the term 'folk music' mean? Though Scarborough treasured authentic black song as the voice of an idyllic community, evoking the transracial intimacy she imagined she had known as a child, Handy, in words echoed by New Negro critics, asserted that the music's folkness lay in the fact that it was 'essentially of our race', born of a history from which she was excluded, a black experience that she could not share.

Perhaps in Scarborough's encounter with Handy, and in those unasked questions, lay the seeds of what would become a retreat. Though she planned for *On the Trail* to be the first of a series of books about black folk song, she never returned to the topic. As her novels of the late 1920s moved ever further from a Southern setting, those black voices that once seemed so necessary 'to make the life of the section adequately real' gradually lapsed into silence. The mounds of material on African American music she claimed to have accumulated appear nowhere in her private papers. When she died abruptly of influenza in 1935, she was at work on a book about song-collecting, but the manuscript described her experience in the Appalachians, in remote communities where she was a stranger, gath-ering traditional melodies from mountain whites.

In all kinds of ways this account of song-hunting differed from anything she had written before. Rather than relying on second-hand reminiscence, she describes collecting from the music's primary carriers, a remote, aloof people with whom she makes no claims of having a shared past. She depicts their 'incredibly arid and difficult' lives with the dispassionate concern of a social worker, pointedly acknowledging their jarring discrepancy from the South of plantation myth. '[O]ne sees log cabins or shacks, fields black and poor, people whose faces show the lines wrought by struggle, care, and despondency,' she observes. 'No beauty of Greek columns here – no dreaming lawns, no happy ease – but instead a terrible, proud poverty that cheats body, mind, and soul.' Collecting songs in this region means doing battle with isolation, reserve and suspicion. That she succeeds at all owes in part to the intervention of teachers and missionaries, but more importantly to her appeal to wonder: in a region still 'remote from the centers of commerce, inaccessible for lack of good roads', she offers her subjects the chance to hear their voices played back on a recording machine.

Ten years on from *On the Trail*, Scarborough again hunted for songs with mechanical assistance, but this time her narrative makes no attempt to hide the machine. Her introduction devotes three pages to her efforts to find the appropriate mechanism, in the process lifting the veil on her use of a phonograph a decade before. 'On my trips to collect material for *On the Trail of Negro Folk Songs* I had used an old-fashioned recording phonograph of a type not now manufactured, but that had been broken and so was not available,' she explains in her introduction. Though she still owned a Speak-O-Phone disc recorder, it was too bulky to take into the field; in the end, she consulted technicians at the Dictaphone Corporation, who built a cylinder machine to her specifications. 'The Dictaphone records, being of wax, are not permanent, and can be run off only a dozen to twenty, and they are less agreeable to listen to than the Speak-O-Phone records, which are practically as good reproductions of sound as the radio or the phonograph,' she observes. 'But the Dictaphone served my main purpose, which was to capture the tunes so that they could later be transcribed.' In the pages that follow, her Dictaphone becomes a central player in the drama, a bulky contraption arduously transported from the world beyond the mountains, a tool that her subjects regard with astonishment, an emblem of modernity.

It is hard to know what to make of this decision to push the Dictaphone to the front of the story. When she drafted the manuscript in 1932, no one was describing recording machines in this fashion – not ethnographers, whose scientific ethos demanded that they spotlight their findings and excise the tools by which they obtained them, and not even, at that stage, John Lomax, whose accounts of his field-recording experiments would not see print for well over a year. But perhaps it amounts to a hesitant new start, an attempt to find a new voice. In *On the Trail*, Scarborough had written as a fond Southern daughter, her expertise in black song based on the fact that 'I was a Southerner born and bred, and that I had been loving the Southern Negroes ever since I could remember anything'. Yet in the wake of the New Negro movement, she could no longer voice the old plantation platitudes, nor could she assume that her readers would accept her judgements simply because she was born in the South. In chronicling song in the Appalachians, she sought a visible, palpable badge of authority. Her recording machine transformed her into what we might term a documentarian, a fact gatherer driven by disinterested compassion. The Appalachians, she discovered, housed a genuine folk culture, a people immune to mechanically reproduced music. 'There isn't a radio in the district,' one of her informants noted. 'We have to make our own music and provide our own amusement.' Hence the care she takes to assure her readers that she employs the machine purely as a tool of transcription. To do otherwise, to produce recordings that were 'agreeable to listen to', would run the risk of corrupting the culture whose music she sought to preserve.

Scarborough's death cut short this tentative transformation, and we cannot be sure where it would have taken her. Perhaps it would have provided a new beginning, a new voice of authority, that would have allowed her to return to collecting black songs. Yet that seems unlikely. Even at the peak of her involvement, the songs had always mattered less to her than the affectionate exchanges she had in collecting them. Mostly, and of necessity, she had those exchanges with white informants, but every so often she had stumbled upon elderly black men and women born in the era of slavery, and then all the pleasures of the past rushed in upon her. Once, at a garden party near the Alabama-Mississippi border, she heard a haunting melody 'floating on the breezes'; parting a curtain of ivy, she found an aged black laundress 'engaged in the mysteries of the washboard', singing a song that Scarborough remembered from childhood, when she drifted to sleep in her mammy's arms. That was the way of Negro folk songs: their notes cracked open worlds otherwise inaccessible, 'songs I knew but did not know that I knew', memories she did not recall that she had.

Just how irrevocably that world was now lost to her had become clear in Handy's office. Though she presented him in *On the Trail* as benign and affable, yet another in her gallery of kindly old aunties and uncles, the reality of her encounter was far more unsettling than she ever let on. Soon after her visit, she wrote a draft account and sent it to her friend Ola Lee Gulledge, a musician and fellow Southerner who had transcribed her disc recordings and had accompanied her to Handy's office. Gulledge sent the manuscript back with puzzled comments scrawled across the margins. Why, she wondered, had Scarborough left out so much of what their visit had really been like?

> Why not say that it was typical of all publication offices –
> filled with vaudeville stars (both genders – black and white)
> and cigarette smoke. Do you think it out of place to stress
> how business-like it was – when the man said, 'Mr Handy is
> in his office, is very busy, and will not be able to see you' –
> and so forth.

Though Scarborough could present, if not assimilate, Handy's New Negro vision of folk song, what she could not abide, could not even acknowledge, was the brusque indifference she met with in his office. No greater contrast could be imagined with the world to which song-hunting had once transported her. Here the tenderness of her remembered South had been crowded out by a hard-nosed commercialism, faceless and altogether lacking in deference, as Scarborough found herself rebuffed in a smoke-filled office where white women and men jostled with black ones for the attention of a black entrepreneur. In the end, Handy's office is the silence at the heart of her tale, the unspeakable emblem of an unwelcome new world in which African Americans looked less like a 'folk' than ever before.

Chapter Four

Sound Photographs of Negro Songs

L ouisiana Highway 66 is one of those meandering Southern roads that seem to offer the traveller a straight shot into the past. In places little more than a dirt track, it winds past antebellum mansions shadowed by magnolias and crumbling churches overgrown by kudzo, and the humid air echoes with the plash of river-water from tributaries of the Mississippi that straddle the road. The great river itself surges against a levee a few hundred yards to the west, and to the east rise the Tunica hills, their bluffs and ravines thick with copperheads, bears and bobcats.

At a hairpin bend of the Mississippi, about fifty miles outside of Baton Rouge, Highway 66 terminates in front of a high wall topped with barbed wire, the entrance to Angola State Penitentiary. Founded in the wake of the Civil War by an ex-Confederate major, Samuel James, it was set up on the grounds of Angola Plantation, once a thriving agricultural centre whose owner had named it after the region that had been home to most of his slaves. James was an entrepreneur who designed his prison to turn a profit, and convicts figured into his scheme as cheap and eminently disposable labour. Housed in flimsy, ill-ventilated dormitories built over malarial swamps, convicts spent their days shackled at neck and ankle, tilling cotton and sugar cane and building levees, driven with a degree of brutality that eventually became a national scandal. In the early twentieth century, new prison administrators fired the worst of the guards, built new dormitories and abolished the much-despised convict stripes. But in the economic chaos of the Great Depression, Louisiana's governor left Angola to fall into decay, its guards took it over as a private fiefdom and convict stripes were brought back.

On a hot July day in 1933, a dusty black Ford drove up to Angola's gates bearing a portly white man in a Stetson hat who addressed the guard with the blustery charm of a Texan accustomed to getting his own way. His name was John Lomax, he was writing a book about folk music and he hoped to spend two or three days at Angola, hunting for songs among the black prisoners. He wanted to talk to the inmates in their free time – whatever time they had free from their prison labours – and then (with the help of his eighteen-year-old son Alan) listen to anyone who had songs to offer. The best of their findings they would record on disc, via a bulky mass of phonographic equipment that he had been loaned by the Library of Congress. It went without saying that he would do nothing to stir up trouble among the inmates; he was, after all, born and bred in the South. Lomax produced a sheaf of letters from powerful acquaintances, including an old friend of the prison governor. With visible reluctance, the guard opened the gates and waved his car through.

John Lomax arrived at Angola in a state of near euphoria. Aged sixty-five, he was a vagabond, quite a feat after a lifetime that sometimes had seemed to consist only of missed opportunities and failed hopes. He was born in 1867 in Goodman, Mississippi, his father a farmer and tannery operator, the family situated (as Lomax liked to put it) 'on the upper crust of the po' white trash'. Two years later, they boarded two covered wagons and moved to the Bosque Valley in Texas, looking for a place to establish a homestead. Lomax grew up immersed in farm labour, scratching corn and cotton out of the arid soil, attending school for short bursts between crops. Though he loved to read, cowboy stories especially, not until he was nearly thirty did he enrol at the University of Texas. He had hoped to become a teacher, but instead he spent most of the years that followed trapped behind a desk as a college administrator and later as a bonds trader in a Dallas bank.

Then came 1931, which brought catastrophe: the loss of his job, when the bank he worked for failed, and the death of his much-loved wife of thirty years. Lomax found himself an unemployed single father with two of his four children still living at home, and he might have succumbed to despair had his eldest son John Jr not persuaded him to return to his first love, song-hunting. Back in 1907 he had enrolled for a term of graduate study at Harvard and had been inspired by a course on folk expression and regional literature. On his return to Texas he took a cylinder recorder into the Brazos River Bottoms near Dallas, capturing enough cowboy songs to publish an anthology of them in 1910. His song-gathering had been hampered thereafter by the pressure of a growing family, but the book had remained in print, with a new edition published in 1929. In 1932 Lomax, Alan and John Jr drove across the US promoting it in public lectures. But the book sold poorly; the three men bickered frequently; they had several flat tyres. The trio returned to Texas uncertain about what to try next.

But John Lomax was nothing if not an optimist and an incorrigible entrepreneur. Midway through the dispiriting book tour, he had managed to secure a contract with Macmillan for a new volume of folk songs, a much bigger book than his cowboy anthology, drawing on fieldwork to be undertaken during the next summer among men and women from all walks of life. If his first book had focused on one picturesque group, this one would offer a portrait of a nation – a nation, he believed, that had a tradition of indigenous song as rich, robust and vital as anything to be found in Europe.

That conviction placed Lomax at odds with a generation of scholars, his teachers at Harvard among them, who believed that America had no indigenous music, no body of song developed on its own soil. Folk music was composed anonymously, transmitted orally, and suffused with the spirit of the peasantry, and since America was singularly lacking in peasants, no such tradition could have taken shape. Lomax rejected that argument flat out. Any ballad scholars who claimed there were no American folk songs had clearly not looked in the right place. The US proved to be rich in folk music once you ventured outside the confines of polite society, once you scouted among 'the down-and-out classes – the outcast girl, the dope fiend, the convict, the jail-bird, and the tramp'.

Chief among those 'down-and-out classes' were African Americans. Lomax's fascination with black singing stretched back to his childhood, and he would have pursued it in his studies at Harvard had his supervisor George Kittredge been remotely receptive. The unfettered emotion you heard in the spirituals, the vigorous exertion that echoed in the work songs: all of this spoke of a folk tradition as vital and spontaneous as the open air. In the 1910s Lomax began putting his thoughts about Negro music on paper, often attending services in black churches and taking down the words to the spirituals, occasionally employing a cylinder recorder to capture the elusive melodies. Those trips gave him material for a few published articles and a series of after-dinner speeches, but he knew that he had done little more than scratch the surface. The collections of black song published in the 1920s by people like his friend and fellow Texan Dorothy Scarborough only reminded him how much remained to be done.

Once Lomax had sold Macmillan his proposal, he began researching in earnest, travelling to Washington, DC, and the newly established Archive of Folk Song at the Library of Congress. Set up in 1928 as an adjunct to the library's Music Division, the archive was the brainchild of Robert Winslow Gordon, a forty-four-year-old Harvard graduate and folk-song aficionado. A man of obsessive enthusiasms, tall, thin and permanently dishevelled, Gordon had scraped together a living in the early 1920s as a folk-song columnist for a pulp adventure magazine, soliciting contributions from readers and building up a vast collection of work songs, ballads and chanteys. On the basis of that material and his encyclopaedic knowledge of folk-song history and style, Gordon persuaded the Library of Congress to set up a national folk-song repository. He would serve as the collection's 'Specialist and Consultant in the Field of Folk-Song and Literature', making and transcribing field recordings and classifying and studying the results.

Yet however pioneering Gordon's vision, the man himself proved supremely ill-suited to giving it form. No sooner had he established himself as the archive's 'Specialist and Consultant' than he retreated to Darien, Georgia, where he hid himself away in a one-room cabin and immersed himself in the minutiae of his subject (at one point he drove 2,500 miles to interview an informant about the real-life crime behind the ballad 'Cooney Shot Delia'). His priorities, it seemed, lay less with filling the archive than with 'solving the basic problems of folk song' in a mammoth text on the subject, very little of which ever got written. Absorbed in the excitement of his quest, he was incommunicado for months at a time, leaving letters from the library unanswered, occasionally issuing grandiose manifestos for the future of the archive when pressures from Washington got too intense to ignore. Meanwhile the four rooms in the Music Division set aside for the archive remained more or less empty, and the Music Division was fast losing patience. They were already planning to cut Gordon's funding when John Lomax stepped onto the scene.

The archive, it seemed, needed John Lomax. For his part, Lomax needed the archive – its stamp of approval, for a start, letters of introduction on library stationery that could get him past Southern prison officials. Above all, he needed recording equipment. Back in 1907 he had used a portable graphophone with a horn and a spring-driven motor that recorded on wax cylinders, the same kind of machine employed by Howard Odum and virtually every other folklorist in the field. It had advantages – it was lightweight enough to be easily carried, and the wind-up motor allowed it to run in remote areas – but the cylinders were fragile and the sound quality of the recordings was poor. By the early 1920s, recording companies like Okeh and Victor had devised a portable machine capable of recording wax master discs in the field, but the discs required factory processing to be transformed into permanent, playable records. Lomax wanted a device that was simple to use and easy to carry and that made durable, high-quality disc recordings that could be played back on the spot. No such machine had yet been devised, but late in the

spring of 1933 the library rustled up the necessary funds to pay a
recording engineer to devise an experimental model. Two weeks into
his journey Lomax collected the machine in Baton Rouge. Consisting
of two large batteries, a rotary converter, amplifiers, a button carbon
microphone, a speaker, cables and piles of blank aluminium discs,
it weighed over 300 pounds. In the end Lomax managed to transport
it only by tearing the back seat out of his Ford.

John Lomax's recording machine

Equipped with their machine, Lomax and his son Alan set out on
the road, by day speeding down rutted highways, by night camping on
beaches, washed over by birdsong and the cool Gulf breeze. Within
days, they found rich material. In a logging camp near the Louisiana
state line, they 'heard for the first time the wail of the Negro woodsman',
who echoed the shuddering crash of the pines in a cry full of 'music
. . . and mystery and wistful sadness'. At the Central State Prison Farm
near Sugarland, Texas, they met two 'lifers', Iron Head and Clear Rock,
who knew 'the words of enough folk songs to fill a volume of five hundred
pages'. Just as rewarding was the sweltering evening they spent near

Wingate, Texas, with Henry Trevillier, leader of a railroad track crew, who knew an endless stream of work songs and chants but insisted that they record him with his cabin door shut and his windows bolted, 'for his wife objected to his singing other than "sanctified" tunes'.

They were three weeks into their trip when they arrived at Angola, and at first the inmates proved a disappointment. Apart from a group of female prisoners who sang a haunting ballad of Christ's crucifixion – 'how Christ took his persecution, the crown of thorns, the cruel nails through his feet and hands . . . "and he never said a mumblin' word"' – the bulk of the convicts had nothing to give them. Undoubtedly, the prison itself was partly to blame since, unusually, at Angola Negro inmates were not allowed to sing as they worked. The Lomaxes spent three gruelling days attempting to coax songs from indifferent convicts before concluding that the effort was fruitless.

But just as they prepared to pack up their equipment, Captain Andrew Reaux of Camp A brought one last inmate forward. He was a 'trusty' – a convict of noteworthy skill and reliability – who had been at Angola for over three years. In that time he had won the confidence of prison officials, who had moved him out of the sugar-cane fields and allowed him to serve as Camp A's laundryman and, from time to time, awarded him the privilege of entertaining the inmates on their days off. The number on his convict stripes read LSP 19469. Reaux introduced him as Huddie Ledbetter, but everyone called him Leadbelly.

He was short and stocky, with coal-black skin and a chiselled, sombre, unwrinkled face; only his hair, grey at the temples, indicated his forty-eight years. Across his throat a long, deep horizontal scar could be glimpsed under the collar of his striped convict's overalls. In his arms he carried a battered twelve-string guitar,

John Lomax (right) and
Leadbelly (standing)

painted green and held together with twine, and his eyes bore the wary, deliberately blank expression born of ten years' confinement in three Southern penitentiaries for violent offences about which he remained stubbornly vague.

He began to sing, and John Lomax was transfixed. This was a find like no other. Spirituals, lullabies, cowboy tunes, shouts from the fields and the levee camp: Leadbelly appeared to remember every song that he had ever heard. He had a deep, booming voice that echoed down the prison corridors, and the propulsive twang of his twelve-string Stella set his vocals off to rich effect. Even when Alan set the recording machine whirling, the flood of songs never slowed. Leadbelly moved effortlessly from a novelty song, 'The Western Cowboy', to the old whorehouse ballad 'Frankie And Albert', to a prison lament called 'Angola Blues', much of which he seemed to have composed himself. He sang a Dallas saloon number, 'Ella Speed'; a song about cocaine, 'Honey Take A Whiff On Me'; and 'You Can't Lose Me Cholly', a dance tune that had been around for years. In amidst those raucous numbers was a gentle waltz called 'Goodnight Irene' that he sang in a lilting tenor. In the end they obtained seven discs, each so different from the other that it was hard to believe that they were sung by the same man.

These songs were nothing like the homogenised stuff that clogged up the radio airwaves. To Lomax's ears they sounded archaic, wholly unsullied by contact with whites. Even the more upbeat tunes, with their undercurrent of melancholy, spoke of a profound isolation. In Leadbelly, Lomax found what he was after: a living, breathing musical artefact, a black voice that was uncorrupted and pure.

'Everybody knows the story of how Leadbelly sang his way to freedom,' writes critic and historian Francis Davis, and it is true that the tale of the convict-turned-folk-singer commands attention in virtually every blues chronicle. Born in 1885 in Mooringsport, Louisiana, Huddie

Ledbetter won a pardon from his ten-year sentence in July 1934 after John Lomax returned, one year on, to Angola and recorded 'Governor O. K. Allen', a plea for clemency that Leadbelly composed and Lomax delivered to the state governor. That collaboration launched a stormy partnership. Initially employed as Lomax's chauffeur and manservant, Leadbelly travelled with him across the South, performing for black inmates in penitentiaries from Arkansas to South Carolina to give them an idea of the songs Lomax was after. Late in 1934 the pair arrived in New York, where Lomax regaled journalists with the pardon story, re-enacted it in a *March of Time* newsreel, and booked Leadbelly into high profile singing engagements up and down the East Coast. Though their relationship disintegrated quickly thereafter, Leadbelly's fortunes eventually revived, earning him recording contracts, concert bookings from Los Angeles to Paris and an enduring reputation as a folk musician *par excellence*.

What we know less well is the figure in the margins of that story, the man who took the recorded disc to the governor and thus, as legend has it, engineered Leadbelly's release. John Lomax spent little more than a decade documenting African American music, and his career has long been overshadowed by the achievements of his son Alan. Yet in those few years he transformed the search for authentic black song by spinning around it a new kind of romance. The black renegade, the outlaw, the convict in chains: they were carriers of the folk spirit, and they would give up their treasures to the brave and intrepid who dared to venture off the beaten path. Not for nothing did Lomax title his 1946 autobiography *Adventures of a Ballad Hunter*: for him song-collecting was a kind of safari, rough-hewn, vigorous and consummately masculine, full of the excitement of sleeping in the rough, eating round a campfire and driving down rutted, dusty back roads at midnight.

Inextricable from that sense of virile adventure was an evangelical enthusiasm for recording technology. Unlike virtually every collector who preceded him, in writing up his accounts of his findings Lomax made no effort to hide the machine. He felt, it seems, none of his predecessors' fear that the phonograph could distort the reality that it was meant to be capturing, or that admitting to using it compromised his authority. As he saw it, the phonographic apparatus that he brought with him to Angola made a truly objective study of black music possible for the first time.

> Through the Music Division in the Library of Congress, we were provided with the latest improved-model portable-machine for electrical sound-recording, with all the necessary accessories, including a fine microphone. Edison batteries, operating a direct current, enabled us to record singing wherever we found a good voice, in camp, cabin, or field. Likewise, a music-reproducing apparatus made it possible to play back at once any song recorded, to the very great astonishment and enjoyment of our black convict friends, nearly all of whom manifested an eager and enthusiastic interest in the project . . . Before starting on the trip, I was impressed with a cautioning word from Mr Engel, chief of the Music Division: 'Don't take any musician along with you,' said he, 'what the Library wants is the machine's record of Negro singing and not some musician's interpretation of it; nor do we wish any musician about to tell the Negroes how they ought to sing.' The hundred and fifty new tunes that we brought to the Library at the end of the summer are, there-fore, in a very true sense, sound-photographs of Negro songs, rendered in their own native element, unrestrained, uninflu-enced, and undirected by anyone who had his own notions of how the songs should be rendered.

'Sound photographs' were what Lomax was after: the black voice reproduced with machine-like precision. Lomax was convinced that metropolitan audiences would be transfixed by these rough, primal voices, and that it was those voices that needed preserving, not just the folklorist's transcription of them. The discs, in other words, were what mattered. 'The songs would make a sensation in cultured centers,' he noted after a visit to Parchman Prison Farm in Mississippi, 'if it were only possible to present them in their native, primitive style.' His purpose-built recording machine made that dream a reality. Caught on wax, those evanescent voices could be stored for posterity in a federal repository – as one of Lomax's informants would put it, in a building that would never burn down.

Yet if Lomax's enthusiasm for recording technology was, among song collectors, unprecedented, it was also fraught with contradictions. However much he waxed rhapsodic about his state-of-the-art recording devices, his aim in employing them was to escape from the phonograph, to step outside modernity, to find archaic Negroes who inhabited a world where time had stopped. 'Folk songs flourish, grow – are created, propagated, transformed – in the eddies of human society, particularly where there is isolation and homogeneity of thought and experience,' he explained. Hence his enthusiasm for recording in prisons, which supplied isolation and homogeneity in abundance. Faced with a recording machine, Lomax maintained, convicts revealed their essential simplicity, with hardened criminals transformed into giddy boys, 'contented and carefree as a group of children'.

> Their excitement over the strange machine merged into laughing delight as the singers listened to their voices coming back to them from the newly made records. One man, not knowing what was going on and brought in suddenly from the barn to sing before the microphone, crumpled and fell flat on his back in amazed terror on hearing his own voice from the machine.

Contrast this account to Howard Odum's encounter with the blasé, savvy Will Smith three decades earlier. What made the convict, for Lomax, an ideal subject was what he saw as the singular lack of (in his terms) 'contamination' insured by the conditions of prison life.

'Negro songs in their primitive purity can be obtained probably as nowhere else from Negro prisoners in state or Federal penitentiaries,' Lomax argued. 'Here the Negroes are completely segregated and have no familiar contact with whites. Thrown on their own resources for entertainment, they still sing [the 'distinctive old-time Negro melodies'], especially the long-term prisoners who have been confined for years and who have not yet been influenced by jazz and the radio.' He never doubted that such isolation was possible, even by the mid-1930s, when race records had been circulating for fifteen years. In stressing the shock of his 'convict friends' when they heard their own voices replayed on the phonograph, he echoed comic writers like Joel Chandler Harris, who back in 1880 had lampooned Uncle Remus's befuddlement at the workings of 'dish 'ere w'at dey calls de fony-graf', his naive astonishment at the disembodied voice booming out of the horn.

Yet time and again, Lomax would be bewildered by the worldli-ness of the men whose 'primitive purity' he was meant to be docu-menting. At no point did that bewilderment loom larger, or have more painful consequences, than in his encounter with Leadbelly, when he transported him from Angola to New York and put him on stage as an embodiment of the uncorrupted folk voice.

One key shaper of the Leadbelly legend was the *March of Time* newsreel, filmed in February 1935 a few weeks after Leadbelly and Lomax arrived in New York. By that time the spectacle of the singing ex-convict had already provoked a media frenzy, to such an extent that Lomax had removed Leadbelly from the city, brought his lover, Martha Promise, up from Shreveport, and secreted them in a friend's house in Wilton, Connecticut. There the film-makers arrived with barbed wire and guard dogs in an attempt to trans-form the rolling New England hills into a passable facsimile of the Angola swamps. The film that resulted was transcribed decades later by a German fan, Herman Gebhard. Reprinted in Charles Wolfe's and Kip Lornell's book *The Life and Legend of Leadbelly*, it is worth reproducing in full.

[Title: 'Angola, Louisiana'. At night. Leadbelly and other black convicts, dressed in stripes, are shown huddled round a fire. Leadbelly plays his guitar, the sound covered by orchestral music.]

ANNOUNCER: To the Louisiana State Penitentiary goes John A. Lomax, Library of Congress curator, collector of American folksongs.

[End of background music. Leadbelly sings and plays 'Goodnight Irene' as Lomax records him. Shot of the recording equipment in action. After a verse, Lomax interrupts.]

LOMAX: Just one more, Leadbelly! [Leadbelly starts again with 'Goodnight Irene'. He sings another verse.]

LOMAX: That's fine, Leadbelly. You're a fine songster. I've never heard so many good Negro songs.

LEADBELLY: Thank you, sir, boss. I sure hope you send Governor O. K. Allen a record of that song I made up about him, 'cause I believe he'll turn me loose.

LOMAX: Leadbelly, I don't know this governor. You mustn't expect too much of me.

LEADBELLY: But Governor Pat Neff of Texas, he turned me loose, when he heard this song that I made up about him.

LOMAX: So you were in the Texas penitentiary, too, Leadbelly?

LEADBELLY: Yeah, I was serving 35 years for murder, but it wasn't my fault. A man was tryin' to cut my head off.

LOMAX: Mighty bad, Leadbelly.

LEADBELLY: I believe Governor O. K. Allen, if you'll just send him a record of that song, I believe he'll turn me loose.

LOMAX: Leadbelly, I'll try it.

LEADBELLY: Thank you, sir, boss, thank you, sir, thank you!

[He begins to play again. Scene fades. Next scene begins with a hotel

entrance. Leadbelly, in jeans and with his guitar in hand, talks to the hotel clerk.]

CLERK: Yes, Mr John Lomax is staying here. He's in room 109. *[A typewriter is heard in the background.]*

LEADBELLY: Is that on the first floor?

CLERK: Yep.

[Leadbelly runs up the stairs.]

CLERK: Hey, hold on a minute!

[Inside Lomax's room. Lomax is sitting at a table, typing. A knock at the door.]

LOMAX: Come in!

[Leadbelly comes in.]

LEADBELLY: Boss, here I is!

LOMAX: Leadbelly! What are you doing here?

LEADBELLY: No use to try and run me away, boss. I came here to be your man. I got to work for you the rest of my life. You got me out of that Louisiana pen.

LOMAX: I – you can't work for me. You're a mean boy. You killed two men.

LEADBELLY: Please to don't talk thataway, boss.

LOMAX: Have you got a pistol?

LEADBELLY: No sir, I got a knife.

LOMAX: Lemme see it.

[Leadbelly produces a short knife. Lomax examines it and hands it back.]

LOMAX: What do you do with that thing?

LEADBELLY: I'll use it on somebody if they bother you, boss. Please, boss, take me with you. You'll never have to tie your stri –, shoe strings any more, if you'll let me, long as you keep me with you.

LOMAX: All right, Leadbelly, I'll try you.

LEADBELLY: Thank you, sir, boss, thank you. *[Claps his hands.]* I'll drive you all over the United States and I'll sing all songs for you. You be my big boss and I'll be your man. Thank you sir, thank you, sir.

[End of scene. In the next scene, Leadbelly wears a suit and plays his guitar, humming and singing 'Goodnight Irene'. Next to him sits Martha, elegantly dressed, smiling at him.]

ANNOUNCER: John Lomax does take the Louisiana Negro convict to be his man. Takes him north to his home in Wilton, Connecticut, where Leadbelly's long-time sweetheart, Martha Promise, is brought up from the South for a jubilant wedding. Then hailed by the Library of Congress' Music Division as its greatest folk song find in 25 years, Leadbelly's songs go into the archives of the great national institution.

[The interior of the archives is shown, with songbooks, etc., and finally, the original copy of the Declaration of Independence. Leadbelly sings 'Goodnight Irene'. Close-up of the Declaration. Scene and music fade out, orchestral music, titles and signature tune. End of newsreel.]

The first thing to say about the newsreel is that it is more or less correct on the facts. An itinerant guitarist and sometime farm labourer, Leadbelly had been in the midst of a thirty-year murder sentence at Central State Prison Farm in Sugarland, Texas, when he won a parole in 1924 by composing a song begging for a pardon and serenading the state governor. Ten years on he turned to John Lomax's recording machine to deliver his plea to Governor Allen, and though prison records would later reveal that he was released routinely (under a state law allowing double time off for good behaviour) it is clear that Leadbelly believed, or claimed to believe, that John Lomax's assistance had set him free. After his release on 1 August he bombarded his benefactor with offers to drive his car, wash his clothes and cook his meals. 'Dear Sir Just a few lines to let you no iom out and Here in Shreveport La, Looking for you,' he wrote. 'iom looking for you iom going to work for you Your servan Huddie Ledbetter.' On 22 September they met in Lomax's hotel room in Marshall, Texas, where, if we can believe the letter Lomax wrote the next day to his family, Leadbelly showed him his knife and swore his undying loyalty, even

insisting that Lomax would never again need to tie his own shoes.
Yet for anyone reading that script today, questions of accuracy can
only seem academic, overwhelmed as they are by its excruciating
depiction of Leadbelly as a hapless, hopeless, mindlessly criminal
darkie, a part that Lomax seems to have set out for him and with
which the singer seems to collude.

Yet it is important to recognise that there were other ways of
reading the story. 'Dear Mr Lomax,' wrote Zora Neale Hurston in early
January 1935, nine months before publishing her landmark folk-tale
collection, *Mules and Men*, and a few days after the news about
Leadbelly broke in New York. 'I am writing now because I admire
your work, and knowing what I am talking about, feel that it is something fine and necessary to American culture and art. May I have
the pleasure of talking with both of the Lomaxes as well as listening
to Leadbelly? This is the sort of thing I have been advocating all
along.' Hurston saw Lomax as a kindred spirit because he shared her
passion for the innate, untutored creativity of 'the Negro furthest down',
the man or woman in the gutter, the singer of rough, unadulterated
song. Like Hurston (but unlike many other black intellectuals, W. E. B.
DuBois and Alain Locke among them), Lomax firmly believed that
vernacular singers like Leadbelly needed no refinement, no polishing
– to do so, indeed, would devitalise what was already consummate
art. Whether Lomax responded to Hurston is unknown, but he was
clearly pleased by her praise. 'A Negro author', he scribbled at the
bottom of her letter when preparing his autobiography some years
later. 'See her excellent book.'

As Hurston's admiration makes clear, nothing in the tale of
Lomax and Leadbelly admits of easy characterisation. Most puzzling
of all are Lomax's motives in putting the singer in the public eye.
Even before he took Leadbelly north, Lomax was convinced that
genuine folk singers could not be transplanted. It is 'impossible to
transport Negro folk-singers from the South and keep them untainted
by white musical conventions,' he maintained in 1933. 'Contact with
whites soon brings about cheap imitations of ordinary music and

conversations, and the real charm disappears.' Indeed, that very vulnerability was why the recording machine was essential to start with. Captured on record in their native surroundings, the voices could travel thousands of miles and remain uncorrupted. By his own assumptions, to take Leadbelly with him was to court disaster.

That Lomax disregarded such apprehensions owed in part to the rigours of field-recording, for taking a 'sound photograph' in Southern prisons turned out to involve far more than simply turning on the machine. Power supplies could fail, machinery could break down, wax discs could warp in the heat. Prison authorities could be unco-operative; sometimes they refused him outright. 'I do not think there is a boy in the institution who would remotely dream of using a 'crude' or 'vulgar' song on the grounds,' wrote one prison superintendent in response to Lomax's appeal for 'the words and tunes of songs and ballads current and popular among prisoners . . . no matter how crude and vulgar they may be.' Attempts to help could be even more troublesome, since prison officials rarely understood what he was after. 'After a thorough investigation I find that there is at the present time a professional song-writer-journalist imprisoned here, whose term will expire on May 3rd 1935,' wrote the head of one penitentiary. 'This "lad" under the name of J. Solomon King, Jordan S. Murphy, and numerous other pseudonyms . . . is the writer of many songs including "If It Makes Any Difference To You", "The Kiss I Can't Forget", "Oh! What A Nice Place", "Someday Your Heart Will Be Broken Like Mine", "My Grand-Daddy's Sweetheart", "Smiling Through the Rain", "I'm Dizzy Over Lizzy", "If There's A Radio Station In Heaven (Mother Send A Message To Me)" . . . Trusting that the above information will be of some use to you in your compilation of All American songs.'

And then there were the prisoners themselves, who could be sullen, suspicious, lethargic or simply deaf to his needs. A few refused to sing anything but religious music; others were too exhausted from their labours to sing at all. Most vexing were the educated Negroes he met up with from time to time on his journey, the teachers and ministers who attempted to stage-manage his visits to remote black communities to ensure that nothing unseemly made its way onto Lomax's wax discs. Such individuals were 'blinding themselves to the power and beauty of the Negro's most significant artistic contribution,' Lomax complained. 'A bit of shallow instruction has had its inevitable result in a crop of false ideals. These Negroes are ashamed of their heritage and make themselves ridiculous (in most cases) when they attempt to ape the whites in the field of music.' Manoeuvring his way through the black South meant negotiating subtle gradations of class and respectability, an enterprise for which he was ill prepared. He and Alan may have been born in the region, but they were, nonetheless, outsiders 'amid a people we really know little about'.

What Lomax needed was an insider, and that was what Leadbelly provided. Through the autumn of 1934, Leadbelly and Lomax journeyed from Texas to Georgia, through six states and a dozen penitentiaries, and by the end of the first week Lomax saw just how useful his companion could be. Not only was Leadbelly an efficient driver and, much of the time, an exemplary manservant; guitar in hand in the cell block, he was unrivalled as a demonstration model. No longer need Lomax waste valuable time establishing confidence among the inmates. 'Other singers hearing him became ambitious to show me what they could do,' Lomax noted. 'I discovered that musicians among the Negro convicts in this prison camp, through Leadbelly's singing, quickly understood what I was looking for.'

What Lomax was looking for were 'the reels or so-called "jump-up", "made-up", or "sinful songs" of the blacks' – secular tunes that, he felt, were richer and more original than even the spirituals. 'Negro spirituals abound in idioms and phrases drawn directly from the Bible and from the older white spirituals,' he argued. 'The secular songs treat of subjects vital to the Negro's life, every day of the week – his hates, his loves, his earthly trials and privations.' Because some prisoners deemed such songs 'worl'ly' and 'sinful', the pair devised a collecting practice designed to allay inmates' suspicions, assure them of the songs' importance and entice them to contribute as best they could. At the heart of the practice was a kind of illustrated lecture. They would gather the inmates together, Lomax would speak about the kinds of songs he was after and then, as the folklorist introduced each number, Leadbelly would perform a few samples. The results, Lomax maintained, were electric. 'We sat at a point in the run-around while the men were crowded inside as close as possible to us, peering out between the iron bars,' he recalled of their first attempt, at a state penitentiary outside Little Rock. 'So eager were they to hear and see Leadbelly that at times some stood on the shoulders of others. When the twanging of his guitar strings rang out, supporting his rich booming voice, silence fell in the rows of cells suddenly and completely. The crap games ceased, the coon-can players dropped their cards, while from dim corners, where groups were mumbling prayers and songs and religious preachments, poured all the worshippers, including the black ministers. For the moment Leadbelly's "sinful songs" became more powerful than the "spirituals".'

That Lomax ended his journey with well over 200 disc recordings owed a tremendous debt to Leadbelly's mediation. In effect, the singer had become his collaborator, a fellow song gatherer, though Lomax never admitted as much: to do so would have confused their roles, and from his perspective it was essential that Leadbelly stay on the correct side of the line. Hefting the machinery, singing into it, was one thing; attempting to operate it was something else. At Cummins Prison Farm in Arkansas, after a particularly raucous illustrated lecture, Lomax found Leadbelly surrounded by inmates, flushed with pride and excitement, jiggling the controls on the sound equipment, eager as Lomax saw it 'to "show off" among his own color'. Lomax made clear his irritation and insisted that this should not happen again, but he recounts the incident as an amusing spectacle: the aborigine fingers the machine.

It is worth asking, as Lomax never did, just what Leadbelly would have recorded — and, for that matter, what he would have described had he ever recounted those prison sessions himself. He was a nominally free man spending his days on penitentiary corridors and his nights bunked in with the inmates in the segregated cell blocks. The surroundings were grim, sometimes gruesome. At one penitentiary, seeking a soundproof room for recording, they were directed to the execution chamber, where they elicited songs from the inmates a few feet from the electric chair. Leadbelly himself was an object of extreme curiosity. Far from encountering a fresh start, he found that his history always preceded him. 'Before we reached the farm I told Leadbelly that I would not mention, either to the guard or to the prisoners, his penitentiary record,' noted Lomax, 'but we had not been there an hour before all the Negro convicts knew his story . . . The same thing happened at every penitentiary we visited together.' What Leadbelly did not say directly, his growing unhappiness made unmistakable, and ultimately he did speak up. 'I'm tired of lookin' at niggers in the penitentshuh,' he told Lomax abruptly at the end of October. 'I wish we could go somewheres else.'

That was the reason, Lomax maintained, that they headed north. Leadbelly was bored and restless and desperate to see the Big City, and Alan (who had spent much of the autumn ill with malaria but who had joined them on the road in late November) was eager to show him the sights. Plus, word of Leadbelly had begun to spread. Lomax's *American Ballads and Folk Songs* had been published in late October, and it included many of the songs gathered from convicts and credited Leadbelly as an important source. The glowing reviews the book received provoked the head of the Modern Language Association to invite Lomax to unveil his discovery at their annual convention in Philadelphia in late December. Though Lomax claimed to be apprehensive – the idea, he said later, 'smacked of sensationalism' – he, Alan and Leadbelly duly took the stage with lecture notes and guitar at the evening smoker in the Crystal Ballroom in the Benjamin Franklin Hotel, billed as 'Negro Folksongs and Ballads, presented by John Lomax and Alan Lomax, with the assistance of a Negro minstrel from Louisiana' and sandwiched between a performance of Elizabethan madrigals and a sing-along of sea shanties.

What followed can only be described as a media circus. In the first week of January 1935, Lomax unveiled Leadbelly again and again, to gatherings of publishers, critics, musicians, radio broadcasters, folk-song enthusiasts, socialites and reporters from the *Nation*, the *New Yorker*, *Time* and what seemed like every newspaper on the East Coast. The pair fielded offers of radio broadcasts, concert bookings, a record deal and a contract for a book of transcriptions of Leadbelly's songs. Though some of this may have owed to Leadbelly's singing (which was, wrote the *Brooklyn Daily Eagle*, 'infinitely more genuine than the effete spirituals of Harlem'), to judge by the press coverage interest in the music was far outweighed by the lurid appeal of the singer himself. 'Murderous Minstrel', the *Time* headline, was typical. 'Lomax Arrives with Leadbelly, Negro Minstrel', trumpeted the *New York Herald Tribune*. 'Sweet Singer of the Swamplands Here to do a Few Tunes Between Homicides'. Clearly, what had taken shape on the penitentiary circuit as a sober and educative illustrated lecture was transformed in the hands of the press into a vaudevillian freak act.

John Lomax always claimed to have abhorred this, insisting that it was not his doing, and it is true that he might not have needed to do much: the simple outlines of Leadbelly's history, his double convictions for violent offences, conformed to the most hidebound racial typecasting. Yet it is impossible to absolve him of all of the blame. Lomax's posture to journalists – who were not allowed to address Leadbelly directly, lest they interfere with his purity – smacked of the antics of P. T. Barnum and set up Leadbelly as a savage curiosity, a home-grown Wild Man of Borneo. Even as he praised the 'absolute sincerity' of his protégé's singing, he let no one forget his criminal background. Indeed, despite Lomax's claims to the contrary, it is clear that in spotlighting Leadbelly as (in *Time*'s phrase) 'a black buck', journalists were not simply distorting his words. Back in the autumn, while recording at Atmore Prison in Alabama, Lomax wrote about Leadbelly to a friend in New York who then passed the letter along to the press:

My chauffeur, while Alan is sick . . . is a Negro who sang so
beautifully at Angola, a Louisiana prison farm, that I took one
of his records back to Baton Rouge, one hundred miles away.
When I played it for the Governor he issued a pardon.

Leadbelly is a nigger to the core of his being. In addition
he is a killer. He tells the truth only accidentally. He keeps
his promise rarely – when it suits his convenience. He has
no sense of loyalty or gratitude . . . I am thinking of bringing
him to New York in January. Then you would have a guest
[who] could entertain your crowd.

In bringing Leadbelly north, Lomax set out to create a new kind of
celebrity: a flesh-and-blood embodiment of life on the margins, a
living, breathing Left Wing Gordon. Yet, almost instantly, he became
obsessed with the danger that the experiment raised. Keeping
Leadbelly marketable meant keeping him 'pure', protecting him from
the malign influences which abounded in the city. In New York, this
proved almost impossible, since in Lomax's eyes those influences
loomed at every step. Since no hotel south of 125th Street would take
him, Lomax was forced to house Leadbelly in Harlem, where (though
he told Lomax he had sworn off whiskey) he spent his nights touring
the bars, eventually making his way to the Cotton Club and befriending
its headliner, bandleader and scat singer Cab Calloway. The sight of
Leadbelly returning the next morning, drunk, dishevelled and euphoric
(he told Lomax that Calloway had offered him $1,000 to sit in with
the band) convinced Lomax that extreme measures were necessary.
Though the press was still clamouring for a glimpse of the singer,
Lomax whisked him off to Wilton, Connecticut. In all, the pair's stay
in New York lasted less than two weeks.

Even so, Lomax judged, the damage had been done, and the
problem ran deeper than simple dissipation. That Leadbelly lied,
caroused and drank to excess was nothing new, and indeed nothing
more than Lomax expected. It was part of the role he was enacting as
Lomax's 'boy', his flunky, its script drawn straight from the paternalist

traditions of the Deep South. ('Boss, I'se nothin' but a nigger,' Lomax
reported Leadbelly saying back in November after one of his peri-
odic disappearances. 'There never wus a nigger whut would keep
his word – leastwise I never knowed none. I thought you knowed
dat.') What distressed Lomax far more was what he perceived as the
change in Leadbelly's stage performances, a change that acceler-
ated the longer they remained in the North. As their bookings multi-
plied around the East Coast, Leadbelly turned to new material,
introducing songs that he had learned from recordings by the yodelling hillbilly Jimmy Rodgers and Tin Pan Alley standards like 'That
Silver-Haired Daddy Of Mine'. With that came what Lomax saw as
a new kind of self-consciousness, a studied artifice that the press was
quick to decry. 'Already the pure nigger in him shows signs of becoming
corrupted,' carped a reporter for the *Brooklyn Daily Eagle*. 'A certain
striving for effect is noticeable in his performances, a trick, evidently,
that he picked up at Cab Calloway's.' What was being played out, as
though Lomax had scripted it, was his deep-rooted belief in the
vulnerability of the primitive artist, his conviction that mere exposure
to commercial music would inevitably result in adulteration. 'We
(Alan and I) are disturbed and distressed at his beginning tendency
to show off in his songs and talk when his money value is to be
natural and sincere as he was while in prison,' he wrote to his family
in mid-January. 'Of course, as this tendency grows he will lose his
charm and become only an ordinary, low ordinary, Harlem nigger.'

Had Leadbelly been corrupted, as Lomax always maintained?
Decades on, it is hard to disentangle the facts of these performances
from their resonance in Lomax's imagination, but there is reason to
believe that the man Lomax met in Angola Penitentiary was never
as unsullied as the folklorist made out. From the outset Lomax had
heralded Leadbelly for his purity of voice and repertoire. 'We saw no
printed page of music either in his prison cell or in his home,' he
maintained. 'His eleven years of confinement had cut him off both
from the phonograph and from the radio.' Yet in truth Leadbelly
enjoyed listening to the radio – he would later record a song titled

'Turn Your Radio On' – and his exposure to commercial recordings began well before he arrived in New York. 'I learned by listening to other singers once in a while off phonograph records,' he later recalled. 'I used to look at the sheet music and learn the words of a few popular songs.' That openness to all kinds of music would have served him well as an itinerant songster at juke joints and house parties, where he needed a wide-ranging repertoire to play whatever the crowd might demand.

Yet if much of what Lomax labelled Leadbelly's 'corruption' was a worldliness that was there from the outset, it is also clear that, to some extent, in the course of their journey, Leadbelly had changed. Back in September they had set out on the road as players in a joint drama, and at the outset they more or less agreed on the script, but exposure to the confident, bustling black world of Harlem made Leadbelly's part increasingly hard to sustain. In Wilton 'the most famous nigger in the world', as Lomax described him, returned to his role as valet and house servant (though the arrival of Martha Promise relieved him of cooking the meals and making the beds). In live performance and in recordings, he struggled to negotiate Lomax's confusing demands: that he clean up his diction and slow down his guitar work so that Northerners could make out his lyrics, and that he simultaneously appear wholly unadulterated, as 'natural and sincere as he was while in prison'. Meanwhile the folklorist cemented their informal relationship, signing Leadbelly up to a contract that gave the Lomaxes the bulk of his earnings. Since he did not trust him with even small sums, Lomax also insisted on pocketing the coins that Leadbelly earned each night passing his hat.

That Leadbelly grew increasingly truculent could have surprised no one but Lomax himself. As the weeks passed in Wilton, as the pressures in the household mounted, the singer disappeared for hours, sometimes days at a time, stumbling home morose and sullen, trailing bottles of gin in his wake. That, at least, was how Lomax described it, a chronicle of mounting dissipation; a more even-handed interpretation would have it that Leadbelly had simply had enough. In early

March he and Lomax set off across upstate New York and New England for a series of concerts on college campuses, and from the outset Leadbelly flatly refused to be chaperoned. In Rochester he headed for the city's black district and disappeared for twenty-four hours; in Buffalo he turned down a room at the 'colored' YMCA in favour of what an appalled Lomax described as 'a low, dirty back room . . . down an alley on Williams Street'. Though he passed the hat as usual during his shows, he refused to hand over the proceeds. 'I ain't goin' to sing no more for you unless I wants to, and I ain't goin' nowhere unless you bring Marthy along too,' he told Lomax.

The climax, as Lomax described it, came on 8 March 1935, the same day that the *March of Time* newsreel was released to theatres across the country. As Lomax read in the Grosvenor Library at the University of Buffalo, he was confronted by Leadbelly, who had traded his brown overcoat for a loud green and yellow checked suit and abandoned all traces of the old deference. 'I wants my money,' he announced. When Lomax refused, he reached for his pocket, where he carried a knife. At that moment an acquaintance walked up and Leadbelly retreated, but Lomax was deeply shaken. 'The experience has shattered my nerves temporarily as you can see from this writing,' he explained to his family. 'I think the main reason I feel about Huddie as I do is that he frightened me. The humiliation of that will be lasting.' The man who had approached him in the library was every jumped-up, citified Negro who had ever strutted his way into Lomax's nightmares, and that encounter brought their relationship to an end. 'The little drama was played out,' Lomax would write one year later in *Negro Folk Songs as Sung by Leadbelly*. 'He had been changed by a little prosperity, and possibly through our own mistakes in dealing with him, into an arrogant person, dressed in flashy clothes, a self-confident boaster.' Two weeks after the library incident, Lomax put Leadbelly and Martha on a bus back to Shreveport.

A year later, in April, 1936, one day after he sent his editors at Macmillan the corrected proofs for the Leadbelly book, Lomax drove from Austin to Central State Farm in Sugarland, Texas, to collect another black convict and set out on the road. James Baker, who went by the nickname of Iron Head, had impressed him on his first recording expedition in 1933 with his wide repertoire of 'jumped-up' songs and his rich and resonant voice. Though Lomax originally thought him a 'triple murderer', he was, rather less dramatically, an habitual burglar whose repeat offences had put him in Sugarland under a sentence of ninety-nine years. In preparation for another trek through Southern prisons, Lomax contacted Texas governor James Allred, whom he knew slightly, to arrange to parole Iron Head into his care. He would take charge of the convict for the next four months while they drove across the South making recordings, at the end of which time, if all went well, Lomax would set up Iron Head in his own business weaving rugs from corn shucks (the craft he had learned in prison) and Iron Head would be a free man.

The journey that ensued makes a bizarre coda to the Leadbelly saga, with Lomax apparently acting on a compulsion to repeat the experience in every detail. 'Among his own kind,' he wrote a few days after their departure, 'Iron Head . . . is developing some Leadbelly ego and is beginning to cause me some worry.' Taking Leadbelly's place as servant and assistant (though he never learned to drive, so it was Lomax who acted as chauffeur), Iron Head, like his pre-decessor, grew ever more sullen as he performed for the assembled inmates in prisons from Mississippi to North Carolina, only to have Lomax confiscate the coins he was given each time he passed his hat. When the pair arrived in New York at the end of May, Lomax predicted disaster. 'Tell Alan that I drove [Iron Head] to the YMCA at 135th Street yesterday and did everything but tuck him into his bed,' he reported. 'If I stay up here very long . . . I have decided to send him back home on a bus. In a city he is only in the way. There is nothing for him to do except get into trouble, and he is certain to do that.' The journey ended like the one before it: the same one-way bus ticket, the same anger and bitterness, the same perplexity at the convict's ingratitude. Only this time no one except Lomax's family was listening. The press showed no interest in Iron Head; nor did the New York folk-song enthusiasts who had been mesmerised by Leadbelly one year before. When Lomax contacted Mary Elizabeth Barnicle, the professor of folklore at New York University who had lent him and Leadbelly her house in Connecticut, she at first claimed to be too busy to see him, then turned up for a brief visit, during which she seemed remote and indifferent. 'She expressed no interest in Iron Head,' he noted with some bewilderment. He did not know, nor did she tell him, that she now had her own folk-music project: helping Leadbelly launch a second career.

In a climate-controlled room at the Barker Center for American History at the University of Texas at Austin are housed the hundreds of boxes and files that comprise the Lomax Family Papers. Here in amongst photographs, clippings and family correspondence (much of which, at the time of writing, is closed to researchers) are the material remains of Lomax's encounter with Leadbelly. I have come to explore the encounter's beginnings, the letters Lomax wrote on the road in 1933, the earliest account of his first prison trek. Though I have come across them already in bits and pieces, quoted in Nolan Porterfield's biography of John Lomax, I am after a first-hand glimpse, in hopes of finding something that might reveal his motives, that might make the man himself come through.

What takes me by surprise is the fact that these are love letters. Sometime in the spring of 1933, one year after the death of his wife, Lomax began courting Ruby Terrill, a forty-eight-year-old Latin instructor and dean of women at the University of Texas. Little more than a few dinner dates had passed between them by the time he set out for the South's penitentiaries, but while on the road between June and August he wrote to her regularly, describing the sights and sounds in detail and slipping in his feelings along the way. 'Because Alan will drive recklessly and because you are a lovely person, I say now

that I love you.' Though he claimed to have little hope that she might
return his passion, he pleaded for her forbearance. 'I have no means
of knowing whether my outpourings about this somewhat unusual
journey have for you any particular interest, but . . . should it turn
out that for any reason you do not care for my letters, will it be quite
fair to ask that you do not tell me just now. I am lonely beyond words.'

Grieving, lonely and vulnerable, Lomax wrote in the hopes of
showing his beloved that he was capable of heightened emotion, and
what provoked that emotion, along with Miss Terrill herself, was the
sound of the black convict's voice. The work cries of the prisoners,
he told her, were full of 'music and mystery and wistful sadness', and
the more intense the suffering, the greater the power of the voices
that conveyed it. What thrilled him above all was 'the simple direct-
ness and power of this primitive music, coupled with descriptions of
a life where force and other elemental influences are dominating.'
The sights and sounds of that primal world, he was sure, would haunt
him for years to come. 'As I think back, and in my dreams, lines of
stripe-clad convicts file before me. Down in Tennessee they wore
chains and in their singing you can hear the swish of the pick and
the clank of the chain.'

That John Lomax filled his love letters with the sound of 'the
swish of the pick and the clank of the chain' may seem incongruous
or even perverse, but to Lomax, and apparently to Miss Terrill (who
would marry him twelve months later), there was nothing untoward
about it. What he was responding to in those penitentiaries, what
would take him back again and again, was the resonance he heard
in those voices. Its visual counterpart can be seen in the photograph
he chose in 1934 to illustrate the first published account of his trek,
which showed a white prison guard armed with a shotgun overseeing
a line of black convicts digging a trench, their backs bent, their heads
bowed, without a trace of self-assertion. This was the sound that
Lomax was after: a voice of unutterable melancholy, 'of hopeless
longing, of remoteness, of quiet resignation to the inevitable'.

'The truest, the most intimate folk music,' Lomax wrote, quoting the music critic Henry Krehbiel, 'is that produced by suffering.' In an American context, no suffering produced richer, more resonant music than that of African Americans. Such had been an article of faith as far back as the abolitionist movement, but in the hands of Frederick Douglass it had been tied to a political critique of cruelty and injustice. That the slaves could sing as they did demonstrated that they could feel, proof in itself of the monstrousness of a system that made them out to be chattels. Yet even abolitionism contained a kernel of what Lomax was experiencing, this transcendent thrill at the sight of black suffering, at the sound of a black man's pain. Over time, that sensibility would attach itself to the post-emancipation South's convict lease system. The same haunting sound that transfixed John Lomax caught the imaginations of others, like the Southern novelist Samuel Derieux, one of Dorothy Scarborough's informants, who wrote of his delight in spending Sunday afternoons lazing in meadows, soaking up the voices of gangs of black convicts singing as they laid down the roads. Howard Odum, too, was mesmerised by the 'chain gang songs and jail house blues', with their echoes of 'stripes and chains, guards and guns, sometimes cruelty and hardships, sickness and death'. The sound that drew them, and that obsessed John Lomax, might be described as the convict pastorale, a song of melancholy yearning, with the black man in prison stripes, laying roads, splitting rails, moaning in anguish, serving as a minor gateway to the sublime.

That experience of the sublime lay at the core of Lomax's love letters. What Lomax sought to convey to Ruby Terrill was his encounter with what the Romantics had defined as an 'uncontrolled category of perception', 'distinctly pleasurable but definitely unbeautiful'. The convicts as Lomax described them were a kind of human landscape, fierce and insensible, no more aware of their own rugged beauty than was an Arctic glacier or a desert crevasse. One night, on the road outside Tuscaloosa, Lomax gazed for a time on Leadbelly's profile in the light of a blood-red moon as he 'drove steadily and silently, his black, black face shining like a bronzed statue'. No matter how glorious the settings they passed through, scenic grandeur seemed to leave him untouched. 'I can find no little feeling for beauty in him,' Lomax claimed, little sense of wonder, empathy or love. 'Penitentiary wardens all tell me that I set no value on my life in using him as a travelling companion,' he told a friend. 'He is as sensual as a goat, and when he sings to me my spine tingles and sometimes the tears come.' For Lomax, Leadbelly's sheer animalism made the delicate nuances of his voice all the more haunting, an emotional response so deeply engrained in him that he could not see the questions it was beginning to raise.

Those questions began heating up in March 1931, when nine black youths, one aged only thirteen, were arrested in Scottsboro, Alabama, on charges of raping two white women on a freight train. Despite flimsy evidence, they were quickly tried, convicted and sentenced to death, and their convictions withstood appeal after appeal, even after one of the women recanted her story. By the mid-1930s the case of the Scottsboro boys had become an international cause célèbre, and in its wake the American Left launched a wholesale critique of Southern criminal justice. The radical journalist John Spivak investigated prison conditions in Georgia and saw black convicts treated with a brutality that almost defied description. Spivak photographed prisoners shackled at the wrist and the ankle, left hanging from stocks in 102-degree heat, pulled and stretched along the ground until their arms were nearly wrenched from their sockets. His account, published in 1932 as *Georgia Nigger*, was an impassioned attack on the barbarism and cruelty that bolstered the power of the South's ruling class, and its impact was felt, indirectly, by John Lomax, who reached Georgia with Leadbelly in December 1934 only to find that Spivak's book had preceded him. 'The trouble we have had in Georgia has been due to the fact that the hospitality of the Prison Board has been shamefully abused by visitors from the North who have come here and invented, after having been the guests of these gentlemen, horrors and cruelties even worse than those practiced in the Dark Ages,' he wrote in disgust to Ruby Terrill. 'It took me nearly three days to break down the opposition.'

Clearly, for Lomax, Spivak's critique was wholly unfounded, and over the years he would take great care in his own writing to avoid the appearance of an exposé. At times, this meant rewriting his field notes. In one of his earliest letters to Ruby Terrill, he described a song relating the 'terrible story of the fear of a Negro as he sees the "Captain" riding up with the bullwhip in his hand to punish the black for an offence. Here the chorus was made up by the line "Great God Almighty!", uttered in a voice that mingled terror with . . . [a] horrible shrinking from physical pain.' As set out here, the song spoke of current prison practices, punishments carried out in the here and now. Six months later, however, when Lomax published an account of his trek in the *Musical Quarterly*, that song had become an historical artefact, describing the days long gone 'when convicts were leased by the State to owners of large cotton and cane plantations', a song of past sufferings to which the prisoners listened in 'awed and reminiscent silence'.

Had Lomax been asked, he would doubtless have replied that such alterations did not amount to whitewashing. Southern penitentiaries housed hardened lawbreakers who had been convicted fairly and were treated humanely; those few who were innocent and had been imprisoned unjustly were generally 'Negroes who have been convicted on Negro evidence only. Negroes do "gang up" on each other.' The melancholy voices of black prisoners resulted not from ill treatment, but from an essential restlessness – 'the Negro's desire, as one said, "to git away f'om here. I jis don' nachly like dis place."' While Lomax listed 'the injustice of the white man' as one of the subjects of black prisoners' songs, this was simply the misfortune borne of the heritage of slavery, not systematic oppression in the present day. Yet even as Lomax dismissed it, the Left critique of Southern criminal justice would have a profound impact on him, particularly at the end of the decade, when Leadbelly returned to the public eye.

The comeback began inauspiciously. At the end of 1935, Leadbelly had moved from Shreveport to Dallas, where he washed cars in a filling station and saw a few lawyers. From them he discovered that Lomax claimed to be entitled to two-thirds of the money earned by his performances; he also claimed to hold full copyright on his songs (which would prevent Leadbelly from performing them himself). In response, Leadbelly embarked on a legal battle that would last, in fits and starts, for two years, even as he hatched plans to return to New York, convinced that there was an audience for his music and determined to show Lomax that he could manage without his help. By a stroke of luck, the gas station manager nursed his own dreams of adventure. When he realised who Ledbetter was, he sold his business, rented his house and drove Leadbelly back to Manhattan, booking him for a week's engagement at the Apollo Theater in Harlem. The show they devised was a singing and dancing extravaganza with two lines of chorus girls, a jazz pianist and Leadbelly in convict stripes re-enacting the pardon story. But within a few days the show folded; black New Yorkers, as Leadbelly's biographers put it, 'stayed away in droves'. The African American press was no kinder. 'The advance publicity stated that this man had been in two jails under murder charges and that the wardens, on hearing him work out on the guitar and vocally, set him free,' wrote the music critic of the *New York Age*. 'Maybe they did, but after hearing the man myself, I'm not so sure that musical excellence prompted the two governors' actions. It may have been that both they and other inmates wanted some peace during their quiet hours.'

In despair, with no money coming his way, he turned to Mary Elizabeth Barnicle. A mainstay of New York's radical circles, Barnicle was a one-time suffragist born and bred in New England, who moved to New York after World War One and took part in labour and civil rights struggles. As a folklorist, she focused on political, occupational and sexual lore, encouraging her students to see folk music not as a quaint 'survival' but as a vital form of communication and protest. Though at first she had regarded John Lomax as a kindred spirit, she had grown to detest his treatment of his protégé and had said as much to the singer himself. Within weeks of Leadbelly's return to New York, she was paying him to perform for her classes and serving as his unofficial manager, guiding him into the radical folk-singing circles that she saw as his natural home.

Those circles were large and thriving in the mid-1930s, the heyday of the Popular Front, when all shades of Left opinion united to oppose fascism abroad and racial and class oppression at home. For many, folk songs became a key tool in the struggle, a voice of popular resistance, a music that spoke the people's language, fostering a feeling of shared identity and purpose. In the same year that Leadbelly returned to New York, the American Music League, a Communist Party affiliated collective of musicians and music lovers, announced its intention 'to collect, study, and popularise American folk music and its traditions'. With Barnicle's help, Leadbelly soon joined Woody Guthrie and Aunt Molly Jackson (a miner's wife from Kentucky whose career was also managed by Barnicle) in a new pantheon of Left icons, revered as living, breathing incarnations of the essential radicalism of American vernacular song.

Just how this would affect John Lomax became clear in August 1937, when Leadbelly was profiled in the *Daily Worker* by the African American novelist and Mississippi native Richard Wright. A member of the Communist Party since the early 1930s, Wright had befriended Leadbelly that summer after moving to New York from Chicago, while at work on what became *Uncle Tom's Children*, the short story collection that would make his name. His article in the *Daily Worker* amounted to a radical rewriting of the Leadbelly saga. Under the headline 'Huddie Ledbetter, Famous Negro Folk Artist, Sings the Songs of Scottsboro and His People', Wright described Leadbelly as an 'embodiment' of 'the entire folk culture of the American Negro', who composed songs born of his life experience 'of dodging white mobs, of wandering at night to save his life . . . and of seeing black men drop dead from the heat of Southern suns in the cotton fields.' John Lomax was the story's arch villain, a calculating bully who, contrary to legend, played no part in Leadbelly's release. 'When Ledbetter won himself a pardon for a second time out of a Southern prison by composing folk songs, the Southern landlords exploited him, robbed him of his self-made culture and then turned him loose on the streets of Northern cities to starve,' Wright argued. 'John A. Lomax, collector of American folk songs for the Library of Congress, heard of Ledbetter and went to see him in prison. And here begins one of the most amazing cultural swindles in American history.' 'Beguil[ing] the singer with sugary promises', persuading him he would make him rich, Lomax used Leadbelly's singing talent to manipulate prisoners into 'confid[ing] their folk culture in him'. In New York he 'gave out a vicious tirade of publicity to the nation's leading newspapers' depicting Leadbelly 'as a half sex-mad, knife-toting, black buck from Texas'. Swindled out of his songs, exploited and vilified, Leadbelly was then cast aside. Only his rediscovery by the Left kept him alive and believing in himself. 'The folks in the Workers' Alliance [a Popular Front organisation] are the finest I've ever known', Wright quoted Leadbelly as saying. 'I feel happy when I am with the boys in the Workers' Alliance. They are different from those Southern white men'.

Owing in large part to Wright's article, by the end of the decade Leadbelly had become a Left cause célèbre. Whether the singer himself would have told the same story is open to debate. Much evidence suggests that the welcome he found in radical circles was not as wholehearted as Wright made out, that he was occasionally met with incomprehension from comrades whose ideas of authentic black folk song were no more elastic than those of John Lomax. The composer Earl Robinson described inviting Leadbelly to sing at Camp Unity, a Communist Party summer retreat, where he performed 'Ella Speed' and 'Frankie And Albert', sensational ballads of murder and sex. 'The camp was in an uproar,' recalled Robinson. 'Arguments raged over whether to censure him, or me, or both of us.' Leadbelly placated the crowd the next night by performing 'Bourgeois Blues', an attack on segregation in Washington, but the matter was not always settled so easily. Even his most broad-minded comrades could be dismayed by his love for the song creations of Tin Pan Alley, his desire to spice up his sets and recording sessions with songs by movie cowboy Gene Autry, yodelling hillbilly Jimmie Rodgers and the latest Bing Crosby hit.

Nonetheless, what remains indisputable is that the Left brought Leadbelly an eager audience, more respect than John Lomax could ever have given him, and influential friends who were prepared to fight battles on his behalf. Wright was one; another was Lawrence Gellert, an activist and folk-song hunter who befriended the singer in the late 1930s, advising him on his legal wrangles, helping him to engage a lawyer and providing invaluable moral support. Gellert was a long-time critic of John Lomax's song-gathering practices. Late in 1934, after the publication of *American Ballads and Folk Songs* and as news circulated of his discovery of Leadbelly, Gellert unleashed a scathing attack on the folklorist in the letters column of the radical journal *New Masses*. In sharp contrast to the publicity to come sensationalising Leadbelly's criminal record, Gellert turned the spotlight on Lomax, in his eyes an archetypal racist driven by a reactionary nostalgia for the shuffling Sambo of Southern lore.

Gellert knew field-recording, and the South, at first hand. Born in Budapest in 1898, he emigrated to America at the age of nine and grew up on New York's Lower East Side, where he found his way into radical circles through his older brother Hugo, an artist and political cartoonist. Failing health in the early 1920s sent him south to Tryon, North Carolina, where he moved into the town's black section, got involved with a black woman and, inspired by the singing he heard in his neighbourhood, acquired a cylinder recorder and began documenting African American song. In contrast to Lomax, who sought in black music sounds of 'primitive purity' and 'wistful sadness', Gellert was after (as he put it) 'propaganda', music 'as a weapon' in political struggles. He shared the Communist Party's conviction that America's oppressed black masses formed a potential revolutionary vanguard, and he believed that those political sympathies allowed his black subjects to drop their guard and perform songs that few white people were ever in a position to hear. What he captured on disc, he believed, made a sharp contrast to Lomax's recordings: not 'the nonsensical jingles served up for the white man's amusement', but the songs of resistance and rage that black people sang amongst themselves.

To those who made claims for Lomax's humanitarianism in championing an obscure black convict, Gellert bluntly disagreed. 'Getting "our niggers" out of difficulties with the Law when we need them to work or to entertain our crowd is a time-honored custom with the Southern landlords,' he argued. 'Along with Jim Crowism, the whole vicious system of sharecropping, lynching, and the oppression of the millions in the Black Belt, the practice is rooted in the feudal traditions that still dominate the Gentlemen's South.' 'Our niggers' were those who broke the rules in acceptable ways, drinking or carousing or pulling a knife in a juke joint on a Saturday night. Those lawbreakers it was easy to tolerate: they confirmed the white Southern conviction that Negroes were amoral and animalistic. In essence, they legitimised segregation, demonstrating through their sheer dissolution that white Southerners needed it to protect themselves.

Yet the Lomaxes of the world were nowhere to be found when it came to those black convicts who raised awkward questions. They were silent on the case of Angelo Herndon, a nineteen-year-old Party activist from Georgia, sentenced to twenty years in prison for distributing Communist leaflets. And they had nothing to say about the Scottsboro boys, the case that in Gellert's eyes demonstrated the true face of the South. Seen against that backdrop, Lomax's sponsorship of Leadbelly revealed itself as nothing more than racist paternalism. 'Imagine Ben Davis Jr, editor of the *Negro Liberator*, going to Governor Talmadge of Georgia with [a record] sung by Angelo Herndon and getting a pardon for him! Or ditto Governor Miller of Alabama with a record sung by nine Scottsboro boys in chorus!'

It is a measure of the potency of Gellert's critique that, though he surely did not know it, the recording that he mockingly envisioned had actually been within Lomax's grasp. In late October 1934, at the peak of international outrage over the Scottsboro verdicts, Lomax arrived at Alabama's Kilby Prison to hunt for songs among the inmates. There he had his first significant dispute with Leadbelly, who fought with him over money and disappeared for two days, leaving Lomax the arduous task of recording at Kilby on his own. Two years later Lomax would describe this stop at length in the Leadbelly book, yet nowhere did he note the presence of Clarence Norris and Heywood Patterson, the leading Scottsboro defendants, who were interned at Kilby on death row that same week.[*]

Clearly, there were limits to what Lomax would capture in his 'sound photographs'. Voices that challenged, that expressed resistance, he could not acknowledge, could not even hear. As the decade wore on, as Scottsboro continued at stalemate, Popular Front folklorists took up Gellert's contention that what Lomax recorded was not true and unmediated, that, on the contrary, the machine could lie. The authentic black voice as they heard it was the voice of resistance, and no such voice would reveal itself to John Lomax, who 'embodies the master-slave relationship intact'. What he had captured on those prison recordings had been shaped by his plantation mentality and, most likely, by coercion and fear. Gellert, for one, had no doubts about the tactics that Lomax must have employed. 'On Southern chain gang and jail, where Mr Lomax got many of his songs, officials are perverts, sadists and murderers, with a hatred and ill will towards their charges unequalled anywhere outside of Fascist Germany,' he argued. 'I'll wager that many a work-tired Negro in dirty bedraggled stripes was yanked off a rock-pile by bribed plug ugly guards and ordered to "sing for the gentlemen".'

It is symptomatic of Lomax's obliviousness to the criticism his

---

[*] In a further twist to the tale, it seems that at least one of the Scottsboro Boys had heard of Lomax's prison recording project and would have been a willing participant. Sometime in 1936, the twenty-three-year-old defendant Olen Montgomery began writing blues songs from his prison cell. After the lyrics to his 'Lonesome Jailhouse Blues' were published in the *Labor Defender*, he attempted to get hold of an eight-string guitar. He had heard about inmates making records in jail, and he thought this could bring him a new career and a new reputation. 'If I live,' he wrote to his lawyer, 'I am going to be the Blues King.' (Goodman, *Stories of Scottsboro*, 270–1.)

work was arousing that he himself provided the evidence that would have allowed Gellert to claim on that bet. Late in the 1930s he wrote to a friend reminiscing about his first penitentiary recording tour, the same one on which he met Leadbelly, and fondly recalled an occasion when an inmate refused to cooperate:

Some time ago when I was recording Negro work songs in the Nashville Penitentiary I found an enormous Negro man, Black Sampson by name, who had been a section hand, a levy camp worker, a steamboat roustabout and a labourer in a Railroad construction gang. He could sing many of the songs used by the Negroes in all sorts of gang work. Moreover he had a wonderful, rhythmic, baritone voice. But he would not sing the Negro songs of labor because he had 'got religion' in the penitentiary and had been told by his pastor that these songs were 'sinful'. For two days he tantalised me by singing these songs, always where the microphone could not catch his voice.

The last afternoon of my stay the Warden of the penitentiary came by and asked if I had got everything I wanted. I told him of Black Sampson's refusal to sing for me. 'Go bring Black Sampson here,' he said to one of the guards. Soon the big black man, frightened but smiling ingratiatingly, came into the room. 'Black Sampson,' said the Warden, 'stand up before the microphone and sing whatever this white man tells you.' Black Sampson shambled up to the microphone. I started the machinery whirling for the recording, but Black Sampson did not sing. He prayed, 'Oh Lawd, you see what a fix yo po black man is in. Heah he is down in the de world where he has to do ev'ything this white man tells him to, but Oh Lawd, I hope you will understand and forgive me for de sin I is about to commit and not charge it up against a po Negro who caint hep hissef. For Jesus sake, Amen,' and then he sang some beautiful work songs.

Meanwhile our machine had recorded both the prayer and the songs. I call this my prize record.

For what may perhaps be obvious reasons, history has not been kind to John Lomax. He swaggers through the pages of recent accounts of the blues much as Wright and Gellert depicted him, all bluster and bombast and self-satisfaction, treating his black subjects with a high-handedness so monumental it is almost disarming. What emerges is a portrait of a ruthless, exploitative tyrant who paraded Leadbelly on stage in convict stripes and enriched himself on his humiliation. In the end the depiction resembles nothing so much as Dorothea Lange's famous 1936 photograph of a white plantation owner in the Mississippi Delta, a burly, suspender-clad patriarch with one foot on his car bumper, exuding unassailable confidence in his authority as three ragged black men sit hunched and cowed on the porch steps behind.

Yet that portrait, with all its harsh outlines, simplifies far more than it illuminates. Certainly, it cannot account for the memories of many of those who knew and worked with him, even some whose politics differed sharply from his own. 'Now Mr Lomax, my God he hated old Roosevelt, hated the whole damn New Deal, he was very very conservative in his politics,' recalled the song collector John Henry Faulk, a Left activist who would later fall victim to a McCarthy-era blacklist. 'But he was such a dear old soul. You would delight in his stories and accounts of people.' Asked why a man of such engrained limitations would devote himself to black musicians, Faulk pointed to a sheer breadth of vision that his backward racial opinions made all the more remarkable. 'Because Lomax was unquestionably a genius,' he explained. 'He was a man of a magnificent mind but he never put two and two together. He would just say, "These [crimes against blacks] are aberrations of lawless people."' Those who watched him in the field testified to his extraordinary ear for exceptional voices and his capacity to treat black informants with sensitivity and tact.

Harold Spivacke, head of the Library of Congress's Music Division, accompanied him to a segregated prison in Virginia and watched him sit for hours with a blind banjo player, singing songs and swapping life stories, leaving his recording machine untouched in the car. When Spivacke recorded the man the next day, so comfortable was he before the microphone that 'all I had to do was turn over the records'. As a song gatherer, he came to realise, Lomax was 'a consummate artist', a view with which John Henry Faulk concurred: at coaxing songs from shy and unforthcoming people, Lomax was 'the best I ever met'.

In his hidebound racial attitudes Lomax was a man of his time and place, worse than some and better than many. While he never stopped believing that the South treated African Americans justly and fairly, he could also speak up to demand that it accord with its professed ideals. Threaded through his correspondence are letters he wrote to Southern state governors, urging them to investigate prison conditions and free any convicts unjustly interned. In the summer of 1941 he wrote to the governor of South Carolina to protest what he had seen at a convict road camp, 'a hundred Negroes resting in their quarters, all fastened together on a single long chain'.

> In making my reports to the Library of Congress I have found so much unjust criticism and misinformation about the treatment of Negro convicts in the South that a year or so ago I wrote a news article explaining the widely misunderstood term 'chain gang'. In this story I stated that I had never seen two convicts chained together. (As a matter of fact no instance of physical brutality in all my experiences have come under my personal notice.) I can no longer make this claim . . . I do not know of the special reasons that make it necessary for these men to be chained together on their rest day. I only know that I have never before seen a practice which seemed to me so unnecessarily inhumane.

Unquestionably, as Faulk himself noted, Lomax 'never questioned the system', never believed that it should be changed. (Indeed, even in this letter he muted his criticism: his own correspondence reveals that he saw prisoners in chains on his penitentiary recording tour of 1933.) Yet by his standards he was acting magnanimously, championing the cause of Negro prisoners to whom no one else was attending, 'the forgotten ones who have no influential friends', no radical lawyers or New York folk musicians raising money on their behalf. That such actions should leave him branded a racist left him bewildered and angry, and the more it happened, the more infuriated he became.

What was most frustrating was being dismissed as some kind of throwback when, more than anyone, he could see just how innovative and influential his work had been. Even while Depression-era radical folklorists recoiled from his reactionary nostalgia, they were swept up by the romance that he wove around the recording machine. Lawrence Gellert, for example, began making disc recordings of black song in the mid-1920s, but in none of his early accounts did he reveal the means by which the songs were acquired. His articles in the *New Masses* in 1930 and 1931 posed his song-collecting as a process of eavesdropping and chance, and he presented his findings as overheard treasures carried along on the Southern breeze: 'I heard a washerwoman striding along the road with a bundle of laundry balanced on her head sing this'; 'A tray boy in an Asheville, NC, sanatorium sang this one'. Compare that to his introduction to *Negro Songs of Protest*, published in 1936:

> For more than a dozen years I lived alternately in Tryon, NC, and Greenville, SC. I enjoyed the friendship and protection of influential whites. And with impunity I haunted the Negro quarters. Long and painstakingly I cultivated and cemented confidences with individual Negroes without which any attempt to get to the core of the living folklore is foredoomed to failure.
>
> Repeatedly from these vantage points I invaded the Black Belt. Armed with a mechanical phonograph, a sawed-off megaphone and a bundle of blank aluminum records (my recording outfit) I trekked, railroaded and hitch-hiked the length and breadth of the deep South . . . I slept on dirty floor pallets in

miserable ghetto hovels or ramshackles half disappeared in
malarial swamps . . . Through GA, the Carolinas, way over the
Mississippi and Louisiana even, in city slums, on isolated farms
out in the sticks, on chain gangs, lumber and turpentine work
camps, I gathered more than 300 songs of the black folk – songs
that reveal for the first time the full heroic stature of the Negro
dwarfing for all time the traditional mean estimate of him.

Here the machine – 'my recording outfit' – gives the passage a gritty
power that it would not otherwise have. Gellert vests his authority in
the fact that he 'armed' himself with this equipment and carried it
'the length and breadth of the deep South'. Though he despised what
he saw as Lomax's colonialism, knowingly or not he paid homage to
his influence, echoing his sense of song-gathering as rugged adventure, charged with the excitement of a guerrilla ambush or a wilderness trek.

The historian William Stott has written suggestively of the 1930s
'documentary spirit', the heroic resonance that attached itself to the
mechanical reproduction of sound and image, most famously to
the photographs of Walker Evans and Dorothea Lange. Used prop-
erly, the camera could go beyond art and artifice to capture (in James
Agee's phrase) 'a portion of unimagined existence', hidden truths of
a hidden America that had gone unnoticed for too long. In Lomax's
hands, sound technology carried those same connotations, and over
the course of the decade, his ambition to capture forgotten voices
(combined with the macho thrill of hefting the equipment) caught the
imagination of the Left. By 1940 left-liberal folklorists like Herbert
Halpert and Benjamin Botkin had taken recording machines beyond
the Archive of Folk Song, into the Federal Theatre Project, the
Federal Music Project, and the Federal Writers Project, where they
documented everything from children's rhymes to occupational lore
to (in a project that Lomax himself helped initiate) the life histories
of African Americans who had been born as slaves. Underlying these
recording efforts was a commitment to a broadly inclusive American

culture, a celebration of those voices of resistance and struggle that the powerful would prefer to drown out. That celebration owed a great deal to John Lomax's innovations and influence, for embedded in his search for authentic folk voices on the American margins was an expansive energy whose radical potential Lomax himself could never really acknowledge, could not perhaps altogether perceive.

Of all the fallout from Lomax's collision with Leadbelly, all the invective and accusations, none of it was as painful to him as the drama that played out with his son Alan. From the beginning, and even as tensions had mounted, Alan had always been close to the singer, who seemed genuinely fond of the 'Little Boss', and Leadbelly's return to Shreveport left Alan (as Lomax put it) 'cut up'. In its aftermath Lomax wanted his son's life to get back to normal. Above all, he wanted him to return to his studies at the University of Texas. Alan had enrolled there in 1933 after a year spent at Harvard, but since then their song-gathering treks had left his studies disrupted. Lomax had great hopes for his son's academic achievements, believing him capable of taking folklore to a new pinnacle of scholarly renown. Alan, however, had plans of his own, and eventually Lomax assented: he would return to university in the autumn, but first he would head out on the road, collecting songs in Florida and Georgia with Mary Elizabeth Barnicle and Zora Neale Hurston.

The third of Lomax's four children, Alan was his father's favourite, like him bright and quick-witted, gregarious and charming, prickly and pugnacious. Nearly everyone who met him agreed that there was something special about him. Spotting him on the street in Austin, Lomax's friend Roy Bedichek discerned a figure straight out of Walt Whitman, 'bare-throated, bearded, rough, but clean inside and out', 'as picturesque and belligerent a vagabond as I ever saw'. To Carl Sandburg, he seemed 'intensely American and flagrantly and vagrantly modern, somewhat of my own trend except that I could never begin to catch him in certain areas of mental efficiency'. From early on, his sharp mind and winning manner made him the focus of his father's sense of thwarted ambition. On the road in 1933, as they battled heat, mosquitoes, recurrent malaria, and a disc recorder that continually broke down, Lomax watched with pride and satisfaction as Alan threw himself into the work. That trek convinced him that, if nothing else, his son was a natural folklorist. 'We did well for so short a stay,' he wrote to Ruby Terrill from Galveston, Texas, 'thanks to the fine impression Alan makes by his earnest sincerity.'

Alan Lomax

Yet for all the pleasures of that journey, one source of tension simmered between them. Back in 1932, while an undergraduate at Harvard, Alan had been arrested for taking part in a political demonstration demanding the release of Edith Berkman, a Communist Party

activist and union organiser who was facing deportation. That incident, which prompted him to withdraw from the university, left John
Lomax angry and distraught. 'It distressed my father very, very much,'
Alan would later recall. 'I had to defend my righteous position, and
he couldn't understand me and I couldn't understand him. It made
a lot of unhappiness for the two of us because he loved Harvard and
wanted me to be a great success there.' In the months that followed,
arguments raged between them about Alan's 'communistic activities'
and 'communist friends'. Indeed, in taking Alan out on the road,
Lomax may well have hoped to ease the tensions that had grown up
between them, as well as to get him away from unhealthy influences.
'He needs to build himself up physically,' he wrote to Ruby Terrill,
'and he will also benefit from the breaking of associations with
extreme radicals and rebels against society (the most of them Jews)
that he has consorted with at the University.'

Faced in 1935 with the prospect of Alan's trek south, at the outset
he did not put 'Miss Barnicle' (as he always called her) in that category. For all their political differences, he considered her a friend,
delighting in her flattery (she once introduced him to her class at
NYU as 'a ballad in himself'), her merry disposition, her silvery laugh
and her 'generosity to me and mine' which he deemed 'quite past
understanding'. Barnicle had lent him her house in Wilton, introduced him to New York literati, and lifted his spirits during the
darkest days with Leadbelly. 'I am quite satisfied to have Alan under
her influence,' he wrote to Ruby Terrill as the summer trek loomed.
'For many of her judgements I am in disagreement. She is, however,
wholesome and honest and seems fond of Alan and he of her. I know
she would save him from harm even as you and I. Then he must go
his own way some time.'

The journey began in June. While Lomax travelled back to Austin,
Alan, Barnicle and Hurston headed to St Simon's Island off the coast
of Georgia, equipped with a recording machine provided by the Library
of Congress. The result, Alan wrote in August, was 'the most exciting
field trip I have made', an adventure whose story 'really can only be

told in a long, rambling novel'. With Hurston's help they rented 'a little Negro shantey' in an isolated island community and found themselves 'on such friendly terms with the Negroes as I had never experienced before'. Issuing a call for folk singers, on the first night they found their front yard jammed with musicians, and in a week's time they had made forty recordings of spirituals, work songs, ring shouts and 'jook' music. Then they moved on to Hurston's home town of Eatonville, Florida and to Lake Okeechobee in the Everglades, where 'folk-songs are thick as marsh mosquitos'. After that, 'for various reasons', Hurston had gone back to New York, but he and Barnicle sailed on to the Bahamas. 'Here we came and here we have remained ever since, bewitched by these fairy islands and busy recording the live[lie]st and most varied folk-culture we had yet run into'. At the end of the summer, the pair travelled back to New York, having gathered some 200 discs for deposit at the Archive of Folk Song. Back in Texas, Lomax read his son's letters with pride and pleasure, then waited impatiently for his return.

The first inkling he had that anything was amiss came in mid-September, when he received an indignant letter from Hurston:

My dear Mr Lomax,

I thought once that this letter would not be necessary, but what I heard two nights ago make me feel that it is.

Miss Barnicle is not the generous disinterested friend of yours that you think. If she has her wish, Allan [sic] will not be back with you for years to come, if ever. She is trying to get him something to do so that he will not return to college this year, but will stay here in New York. For one thing she has a certain attachment for the boy and the next, she is trying to build herself a reputation as a folklorist thru the name of Lomax.

When she proposed that I go on this trip with them one of the things she earnestly urged upon me was that I must help her to get this lovely young man out of his stifling atmosphere. He had a backward father who was smothering Allan with fogy ideas both of mind and body. I heard how you took that gentle poet and artist Leadbelly and dogged him around and only her sympathetic attitude and talks with him (when you were not present, of course) kept the poor fellow alive and believing in himself. Leadbelly got no ideas of persecution from the Negroes in the [V]illage as you supposed. He got them right there in the house in Wilton. Why? She was attracted to him as a man by her own admission. And next, she like all other Communists are making a play of being the friend of the Negro at present and stopping at nothing, *absolutely nothing* to accomplish their ends . . .

One of the things that she is working hardest for is that Allan shall not return to Texas this fall. She says he does not need the schooling and he needs New York and freedom. I promised that I would help all I could to persuade him to that end. But Mr Lomax when I met Allan and he told me his plans and talked about you in the way he did, I just could not find it in my heart to destroy the boy. That is what it would amount to in the end . . . When I left Allan in early August he was in the notion of doing what you wished. Saturday night he came here and told me that [he] did not intend to return to Texas unless he couldn't find anything to do here. That you had written to him urging him to come home as soon as possible but that he wasn't going if he could help it. So you see, what she said was her objective on this trip south seems accomplished. I have not mentioned details and incidents because that would be too tiresome but I do know what I'm talking about. And none of it would add to your happiness. She knows that I see thru her and do not approve. She has used a great deal of sophistry on Allan to cover up and I have merely let him know that I do not

think that she is clean. He is so terribly young and men
are dumb for the most part before the tricks of women
anyway.

At the core of Hurston's long, furious letter was an accusation: that
Barnicle and the other 'Reds' with whom Alan was associating were
intent on turning him against his father, and that the crux of their
indictment was his treatment of Leadbelly. Just how Lomax responded
to this is hard to gauge. What evidence there is suggests that he
ignored it, at least at first. At this point Barnicle was still writing
him warm and effusive letters, and he continued to like and trust her.
(That, Hurston had written, was precisely the response the other
woman was counting on: 'She knows that I know, Oh God, just too
much, but I am certain that she feels sure of you to the extent that
you would never believe a word against her. Further you are a white
Southerner and I am a Negro and so I am certain that she feels that
. . . you would never believe me.') In any case, whatever fears he
had about Alan soon abated when his son returned to the University
of Texas, where he received a degree in philosophy in 1936.

Yet in the long run, Lomax may well have cast his mind back to
Hurston's warnings. Over the next few years, as Barnicle staked out
a career as Leadbelly's manager, she and Alan maintained a close
friendship, and as Alan became a fixture of New York's radical folk-
music circles, his ideas about folklore collecting aligned themselves
ever more pointedly with the Left. In 1937 he replaced his father as
Assistant Curator at the Archive of Folk Song, and in the ensuing
years he filled the archive's shelves with material that John Lomax
would never have countenanced, from proletarian folk songs by Woody
Guthrie to militant union tunes by Aunt Molly Jackson to an eight-
hour interview with Jelly Roll Morton, an attempt to document the
'folk roots' of jazz, a music that his father detested. He even pushed
for the accession of commercial recordings. In 1939 he spent several
weeks surveying the output of the race and hillbilly labels, ultimately
drawing up 'A List of American Folk Songs on Commercial Records',

which the archive made available to all who requested it. That process convinced him that folklorists' obsession with salvaging pristine rural purity had deafened them to what was most vibrant. What was most stunning was the sheer variety of those recorded voices: some rough and primitive, some urbane and sophisticated, but all revealing hidden currents of feeling, songs of love and lust and longing, of anger and fear and hard times. 'The commercial recording companies have done a broader and more interesting job of recording American folk music than the folklorists,' he told Harold Spivacke. 'Every single item of recorded American rural, race, and popular material that they have in their current lists and plan to release in the future should be in our files.'

Underlying all these initiatives was a new, politicised vision of what constituted folklore, a vision that was sweeping through the radical Left. Material that his father (and, indeed, Hurston) would have dismissed as purely a product of urban corruption seemed to Alan to be authentic and vital, part of what his friend Benjamin Botkin termed 'living lore'. Unlike the folk song John Lomax searched for, living lore was not confined to prisons or similarly isolated rural enclaves. As 'folklore in the making', it proliferated in the metropolis: in the songs and tales of seamstresses, construction workers, bus drivers, street peddlers, and the 'symphony' of urban night life – 'taxi dance halls, night clubs, honky tonks'. That such songs were sometimes recorded commercially did not place them outside the category. As Botkin explained, the authenticity of living lore lay in something recording did not eradicate: its audible, palpable social dynamics. Like 'the blues and reels and the work songs and "hollers" of the Black South', it was a direct 'expression of social change and culture conflict'.

It was that vision of living lore, that search for social change and culture conflict, that led Alan to what would become his best-remembered expedition. In 1941 he and the musicologist John Work and the sociologist Lewis Jones, both African American academics from Fisk University, launched a two-year survey of black music in

Coahoma County, Mississippi, based in the county seat of Clarksdale. Though the region was overwhelmingly rural, this was no search for pre-industrial musical relics: instead the aim, as Alan put it, was 'to explore objectively and exhaustively the musical habits of a single Negro community in the Delta, to find out and describe the function of music in the community, to ascertain the history of music in the community, and to document adequately the cultural and social backgrounds for music in the community'. Far from using the phonograph to escape from the phonograph, they were out to trace the phonograph's influence: the records to be found on local jukeboxes, the recordings to be found in people's homes, and the recording artists who influenced the repertoire of local musicians. Of particular interest were local guitarists like McKinley Morganfield (whom the locals called Muddy Waters), who described their collections of phonograph records, or like Son House and Willie Brown, who had made commercial recordings themselves. Those aims marked the study as a direct assault on folkloric nostalgia. 'It is a folklorist's illusion that folklore communities are pure, that the pure old tradition is the one most worth studying,' Alan observed in his field notebook. Above all, he sought testimony of the music's relation to broader patterns of social life, including the racial injustices that his father had downplayed or denied.

For John Lomax, watching from the sidelines, all this seemed horribly misguided, and by the early 1940s he was writing to Alan weekly, sometimes daily, to tell him so. The task of a folklorist, he reminded his son, was 'to record what you find, regardless of its import', not to seek support for a political dogma, which simply meant distorting the truth. The problem with 'advanced Negroes' like the scholars from Fisk was that they set out to rewrite history, to present their people as they wished they were, in defiance of the unvarnished facts. Privately he feared that Alan had become 'hopelessly involved in the slimy toils of Communism', and nothing he did seemed capable of having any impact upon him. While Alan wrote a few brief replies to his letters, more often than not he left them unanswered. In that silence Lomax felt himself repudiated as a reactionary embarrassment, 'a bourgeois Southerner (I am so branded in your mind by Miss Barnicle)'.

While none of this owed directly to the debacle with Leadbelly, it could not be readily disentangled from it, for as Alan became a folklorist in his own right, he brought Leadbelly along with him. Once the singer reconstituted himself as a proletarian folk artist and began performing in New York under Barnicle's management, Alan helped to support him, recording him again for the Library of Congress and lending him money when his fortunes flagged. In 1938 Leadbelly and Martha stayed with Alan in his apartment in Washington and were thrown out of the building by Alan's racist landlord, an incident that Leadbelly commemorated in his song 'Bourgeois Blues'. One year later, when Leadbelly was involved in a stabbing and arrested on murder charges, Alan put up the money for his bail, then dropped out of Columbia (where he had begun a doctorate in anthropology) to help raise funds for his defence. Once Leadbelly was released from Riker's Island, Alan became his most ardent promoter. In March 1940 they appeared together at a 'Grapes of Wrath' evening at New York's Town Hall, a benefit performance for migrant farm labourers, and throughout that spring and summer he featured the singer on a radio series on American folk song that he wrote and directed for CBS. Listening to the broadcasts from Austin, John Lomax declared Leadbelly bereft of any appeal (though more listenable than another regular artist, 'the Oklahoma Dust Bowl man', Woody Guthrie, whom he judged 'an absolute zero on any program at any time'). Meanwhile Lomax was acutely aware of how he himself was figuring in the evolving Leadbelly legend. That same summer he had a bruising encounter with Mary Elizabeth Barnicle, who no longer made any pretence of civility and brusquely told him that all of New York condemned him for his treatment of the singer.

In response Lomax's own estimation of Leadbelly turned increasingly caustic. 'Save for being a triple murderer, a drunkard, a congenital liar and a super double super hypocrite, Leadbelly is a most excellent guitar picker,' he told a journalist in 1944. 'He quickly spoiled his singing by adopting the patter of the city slicker.' By then it had become clear that his relationship with his son had irrevocably changed. While Alan never criticised him in public, never expressed anything other than pride in his father's achievements, in his actions he had quietly, remorselessly distanced himself. Once, it had seemed as though their shared love for folklore would act as a bond between them, as it had when Alan was a small, sickly child, when he carried him outdoors on hot Texas nights and sang him folk songs to lull him to sleep, and as it had on their penitentiary trek in the summer of 1933, when he watched Alan fiddle with the controls on the disc recorder to hide the tears welling up in his eyes. In his son, Lomax wrote in a moment of anguish in 1940, he had invested 'the core and center of my being'. Small wonder, then, that in Leadbelly's renown he saw the gulf that had grown up between them, all the ways in which his favourite child had gone astray.

In the final years of his life, the Left's focus on living lore steadily pushed John Lomax to the sidelines, and he watched with growing bitterness as his vision of field-recording was harnessed to a politics that he abhorred. Briefly employed as a kind of *éminence grise* as folklore editor on the Federal Writers Project, he was soon replaced by Benjamin Botkin, and when he returned to the field with a disc recorder, the Library of Congress showed polite but perfunctory interest. In response, Lomax devoted himself to battling what he saw as the Left's distortions. He was outraged late in 1938 when the poet Sterling Brown, who headed the collection of Negro folklore for the Federal Writers Project, alleged (inaccurately) that Bessie Smith had bled to death in a car crash in the Mississippi Delta because white ambulance staff had refused to respond to the call. The tale instantly entered Left mythology and Lomax threw himself into its refutation, amassing a pile of letters from Mississippi health-care officials to document their timely response. Brown's accusation, Lomax fumed to Alan, was 'an outrageous slander on the Southern white man'. What was at stake here was the region's essential decency and justice, a belief that not even Lomax's tour through Southern penitentiaries could shake.

In February 1947, eleven months before the heart attack that killed him, he published his autobiography, *Adventures of a Ballad Hunter*. The original manuscript contained a lengthy account of his travails with Leadbelly, clearly an attempt to get the last word, to set out the definitive story and free himself from lingering charges of exploitation and racism. His publisher, however, thought its inclusion 'unwise'. Lomax based his account on extracts from his letters to Ruby Terrill, which revealed more than he realised of his convoluted racial assumptions. Though Lomax could not see this – he felt sure that any sensible reader could see that he had behaved with complete justification – his editor insisted that the chapter's inclusion might provoke a lawsuit. In the end, Lomax deleted the chapter entirely and mentioned Leadbelly only in passing.

Instead, he told the story of his friendship, at the age of nine, with a neighbour's eighteen-year-old black servant, Nat Blythe. It was Nat, he explained, who inspired his interest in African American music. He had taught Nat to read and given him lessons in history, geography and maths, and in return Nat taught Lomax about black song and dance. 'From Nat I learned my sense of rhythm. He danced rather than walked,' moving with 'such enthusiastic abandon that all of us would join in the patting and dancing.' Three years after they met, Nat received $1,000 from his master and set out for the city to seek his fortune. 'I have never since seen or heard of him,' he concluded. 'His Negro friends think he was murdered for his money, and his body, bound with baling wire and weighted down with scrap iron, thrown into the Bosque River. As I have traveled up and down the South these recent years, I find myself always looking for Nat, the dear friend and companion of long ago. I loved him as I have loved few people.'

Lomax asks us to see his journeys across the South as searches for an intimacy that he had lost. Perhaps this story reveals more than he intended: not just about his attempts to befriend Leadbelly and Iron Head, but about how at some level he needed them to go wrong. Nat Blythe, he suggests, was killed not by whites but by fellow Negroes en route to the city, like him seduced by the false promises of the modern age. Lomax's spectacular ruptures with his black protégés allowed him to relive the pain of that loss, to reassure himself that the intimacy he had cherished could not be recaptured, to persuade himself that it was modernity, not Southern injustice, that had destroyed that beautiful dream.

Chapter Five

Been Here and Gone

When they looked back to the beginning, Frederic Ramsey, Charles Edward Smith and William Russell remembered the run-down building on the corner of U Street in Washington, with a hamburger joint on the ground floor and no indication of anything else. It was the late 1930s, they were white and this was a segregated black neighbourhood, but they opened the door alongside the burger shop and climbed the rickety stairs. On the top floor was a large, dingy room, the dank, chill air barely affected by the coal-black iron stove. Only the bar, the jukebox and the battered piano indicated that this was a nightclub, which for a time had been called the Music Box but now had been rechristened the Jungle Inn. Behind the bar, mixing a drink for a customer, was a light-skinned black man of uncertain age, thin, slow-moving (in retrospect they realised he was sick), and the look he gave them was sombre and grave. At first he did not seem to believe that they were interested in hearing his music, the hits he had generated on the Victor label before his fortunes turned sour in the Depression. But eventually he unplugged the jukebox and sat down at the piano, and before he played, when he flashed them a brief, wary smile, the light glinted on a diamond in his front tooth.

So incandescent was that introduction to Jelly Roll Morton that the three men tended to downplay what led up to it: the years spent listening to race records and foraging for those they could not easily find. Ramsey's passion for Morton's recordings had hit him in the early 1930s when he was a student at Princeton, around the same time that it overtook Charles Edward Smith, but it was William

Russell who had heard him first. Back in 1929, when he was teaching music composition at a high school in Staten Island, he asked his students to bring in some of their parents' records from home. As a classically trained violinist, he expected the exercise would demonstrate the supremacy of the European tradition, but among the discs was 'Shoeshiners' Drag' by Jelly Roll Morton and His Hot Jazz Peppers, and from the first bars Russell was hooked. The sheer complexity of it was what was most striking: the dazzling, rich, polyphonic rhythms, as intricate as anything Schoenberg had devised but so much more vital and free. Since childhood he had nurtured ambitions to be a composer, but this was so much more imaginative, so much more sophisticated, than anything he wrote could possibly be.

In the years that followed, Russell made it a mission to acquire all of Morton's recordings. Expense was not an issue: no one else seemed to want them, and you could buy them in bulk for as little as twenty-five cents a box. The problem was finding them. Morton had recorded his sides for Victor and Gennett in the early 1920s, and since then black consumers had consigned him to the margins. Finding his recordings meant devising strategies to unearth what African American listeners regarded as outdated, obsolete rubbish. Very occasionally he got lucky and found a cache of old Mortons in music stores in midtown Manhattan. More often, he took the subway up to Harlem and combed dime stores and junk shops and the Salvation Army. In 1934 he took a job as an accompanist for a theatre troupe and began criss-crossing the country, and on his travels he rummaged for old records in St Louis and Detroit and the South Side of Chicago. Eventually, in 1936 he helped to set up a trading post for old records in Manhattan, the Hot Record Exchange, and there he crossed paths with Ramsey and Smith. They made an odd trio – Russell an eccentric, close-mouthed, balding curmudgeon, Ramsey a suave, garrulous six-foot-five bohemian, Smith a boyish, earnest, resolute Marxist who wrote jazz criticism for the *Daily Worker* – but they learned to share the labour between them, trading tips and comparing finds and canvassing for each other's wants.

Still, for all that the quest for old Mortons consumed them, the man himself seemed fated to exist only as an evocative name on a faded label, a genius whom the undiscerning had forgotten and whom no one knew how to track down. Then in 1937 Charles Edward Smith moved to Washington to work for the Federal Writers Project, and that spring he read a single, astonishing sentence in the jazz magazine *Down Beat*: 'To many who have wondered what has become of "Jelly Roll" Morton, this may be good news – Morton is featured at the Jungle Inn, local sepia spot, where he is billed as "The Originator of Jazz and Swing".' Within weeks Smith had become a club regular, as were Ramsey and Russell when they were in town, and soon Morton's presence was well enough known that a coterie gathered around him. Apart from the poet Sterling Brown (who sometimes joined Morton at the keyboard), most of the enthusiasts were white, record collectors who steered Morton away from composing new material (he occasionally dreamed of writing pop songs for jukeboxes). Sitting round, asking him questions, they found that it was easy to get him to talk, and so they urged him to tell stories and spin out the numbers he remembered from old New Orleans.

In a short time, Smith discovered just how keen Morton was to claim a formative place in jazz history. Late in March 1938, Morton tuned in to one of his favourite radio programmes, *Ripley's Believe It or Not*, and heard an interview with the composer W. C. Handy, who was introduced as the father of blues and jazz. Neglected by record buyers, forgotten by jazz fans, his songs reworked and his royalties stolen by younger composers, Morton felt insulted beyond endurance, and in response he unleashed a 4,000-word letter to the jazz and African American press:

Dear Mr Ripley:

For many years I have been a constant reader of your cartoon. I have listened to your broadcast with keen interest. I frankly believe your broadcast is a great contribution to natural science.

In your broadcast of March 26, 1938, you introduced W. C. Handy as the originator of jazz, stomps, and blues.

By this announcement you have done me a great injustice
and you have almost misled many of your fans . . .

It is evidently known, beyond contradiction, that New
Orleans is the cradle of jazz, and I, myself, happened to
be the creator in the year 1902 . . . In the year 1908 . . .
I met Handy in Memphis. He was introduced to me as
Prof Handy. Who ever heard of anyone wearing the name
of a professor advocate Ragtime, Jazz, Stomps, Blues,
etc? . . . Of course, Handy could not play any of these
types and I can assure you has not learned them yet . . .

Mr Handy cannot prove anything in music that he has
created. He has possibly taken advantage of some unprotected
material that floats around . . . This very minute, you have
confronting the world all kinds of Kings, Czars, Dukes,
Princes and Originators of Swing (*swing* is just another name
for *jazz*) and they know that the titles are deceiving . . . I
would like to put a lie tester on many of these make-believe
stalwarts of originality. Mr Ripley, these untruthful statements
Mr Handy has made, or caused you to make, will maybe
cause him to be branded the most dastardly impostor in the
history of music . . . Music is such a tremendous proposition
that it probably needs government supervision . . . There are
many who enjoy glory plus financial gains and abundance,
even in the millions, who should be digging ditches or
sweeping the streets. Lack of proper protection causes this . . .
I only give you facts that you may force your pal to his
rightful position in fair life. Lord protect us from more Hitlers
and Mussolinis.

Very truly yours,

Jelly Roll Morton

Originator of Jazz and Stomps

Victor Artist

World's Greatest Hot Tune Writer

Temperamental, monomaniacal, Morton saw himself on a mythic scale, and for that reason Smith recommended him to Alan Lomax. Though Lomax was not a jazz fan, he and Smith both frequented the watering holes of Washington's radical Left, and Smith knew of Lomax's desire to create a new, progressive canon of American folk song, a more expansive sense of who 'the people' could be. Perhaps Lomax even told him of a book he had been reading, Howard Odum's *Rainbow Round My Shoulder*, which had got him thinking about new uses for recording equipment, how it could capture not only songs but the sound and flavour of vernacular speech. What had enchanted him about Odum's book was the sheer musicality of Left-Wing Gordon's seemingly verbatim reminiscences, the way he moved back and forth between speaking and singing and seemed to make no real distinction between them. That Morton could prove just as eloquent an informant Smith could not have doubted. Morton was an unparalleled raconteur, and since he had begun his career in New Orleans at the turn of the century, he could provide a kind of folk history that folklorists had roundly neglected, of African American secular song in its earliest, seediest, most disreputable days. Lomax was intrigued enough to book the Coolidge Auditorium at the Library of Congress for several recording sessions, to be held at intervals from late May until the middle of June 1938. '[Morton] will trace by piano and narrative the trend of popular American music from the standard sentimental songs, through ragtime and up to jazz,' explained the *Washington Daily News*. 'The Man Jelly Roll, also a singer of real caliber, will tell stories into his records, old song legends of the South, particularly New Orleans. The piano as a secondary medium will illustrate the stories. In short, history illustrated with music.'

Yet even though Ramsey, Smith and Russell expected great things from the sessions, once they heard the copies of the recordings that Lomax dubbed for them, they were astonished at how extraordinary an informant the man had turned out to be. All Lomax had needed to do was sit Morton at the piano, turn on the machine, ask a few questions and keep the glass of whiskey replenished, and Morton unleashed a flood of melody and anecdote. Lomax asked him about the men and women he had known in his early days in New Orleans, and Morton told him about the great musicians like Tony Jackson, a sissy-man and a fabulous composer and one of the greatest pianists who ever lived, and Buddy Bolden, the blowingest man since Gabriel, who blew his brains out through his trumpet and ended up in the crazy house. He remembered the Broadway Swells, the gang of toughs he used to run with and sing with and march with in the Mardi Gras parades. They were musicians and sweetback men who lived off the earnings of fifth-rate whores, and he had been bewitched by their sense of style, their red flannel undershirts and jackets with turned-up collars and cork-soled shoes with gambler designs on the toes, and the moseying walk they called 'shooting the agate', their hands at their sides, their index fingers extended, moving in a slow, deliberate strut. He told Lomax about the rough camaraderie of the honky-tonks, where St Charles millionaires rubbed shoulders with longshoremen and guys from the levee who didn't bathe more than once in six months. Some of them were gamblers with names like Chicken Dick and Boar Hog and Sheep Eye, men so mean and heartless they could chew up pig iron and spit out razor blades. He demonstrated how they played cards, what they called a Georgia Skin Game, slapping his hand on the piano bench to mimic the sound of the card hitting the table. Listening to the discs, Smith, Ramsey and Russell recalled him at the Jungle Inn reminiscing over the battered spinet piano, the way that his speaking voice itself became music, soft and guttural and melodic by turns, and as he played, his heel thumping out the beat, he tilted his head back and closed his eyes.

There could be no question that the recordings were poetry, the full nine hours of them, but one moment stood out above all. It came in the last session, on 12 June, when Morton was remembering Storyville, the city's red-light district, where music poured out of all the houses and everyone was wild about the blues. All you had to do was walk down Basin Street and you would hear it through the open windows, from the small-time cribs where they charged fifty cents to the mansions like Lulu White's where the mirror alone cost $30,000. Women sang blues in the doorways to tout for business and to convey every imaginable shade of feeling, and when he started playing piano in the district, he learned to sing them too. By then he had picked up the name of Sweet Pappa Jelly Roll, and he wore a Stetson hat and a peacock-blue coat and eighteen-dollar striped trousers that fit as tight as a sausage, and all the women who saw him were just dying to turn his damper down.

Then Morton paused and in a soft voice recalled the first blues he had ever heard. One day as a young boy, visiting his godmother in the Garden District, he heard music drifting from the house next door, home to a singer and prostitute named Mamie Desdoumes. 'On her right hand she had her two middle fingers between her forefingers cut off,' he remembered, 'and she played with the three, cause she played a blues like this, all day long when she first would get up in the morning.' And as his fingers teased out a few halting, stumbling notes, he sang:

> I stood on the corner, my feet was dripping wet
> I stood on the corner, my feet was dripping wet
> I asked every man I met.
>
> Can't give me a dollar, give me a lousy dime
> Can't give me a dollar, give me a lousy dime
> Just to feed that hungry man of mine.
>
> I got a husband and I got a kid man too
> I got a husband and I got a kid man too
> My husband can't do what my kid man can do.
>
> I like the way he cooks my cabbage for me
> I like the way he cooks my cabbage for me
> Looks like he sets my natural soul free.

The song ended there, Morton's lilting, feminine vocal submerged beneath the hiss of the needle on vinyl, but that melody, those lyrics, in their sheer mournful magic lingered on. It would be another twelve months before they heard the song again, during a recording session of New Orleans greats that Smith and Russell assembled in New York City, Morton playing that hesitant three-fingered piano as Sidney Bechet and Frederic Ramsey listened in, and more years still before Ramsey went to New Orleans and tracked down Mamie's house on Toledano Street. But from that moment they were caught in its echoes, intent on recapturing the world it evoked: the vanished enclave of Storyville, where the air smelled of sex and blood and longing, and where pimps and whores sang the blues.

Today, some seventy years after he sat down at the piano in the Coolidge Auditorium, Jelly Roll Morton's Library of Congress interview has become the stuff of legend: a set of recordings of unparalleled frankness and vigour, so obscene in places that some of the sessions remained buried in the library vaults for a full fifty years. Yet what has been forgotten is the singular context out of which they emerged, the community that pushed Morton forward and that, in the wake of the interviews, determined to build on Lomax's initiative. In the autumn of 1938, weeks after the Library of Congress sessions had been completed, a group of Morton aficionados secured a book contract for what they envisioned as a new kind of jazz history, for which they would track down every New Orleans musician who might have memories of the music's beginnings. The result, published in October 1939, was *Jazzmen*, the first history of jazz by American writers and the first anywhere to be based on research. Its rhapsodic portrait of the music of Storyville created an international sensation and helped to generate what became a New Orleans revival, an attempt to recapture what was imagined as black music at its most authentic and vital, the sound of the turn of the century red-light district, of New Orleans in its glory days.

Charles Edward Smith, William Russell and Frederic Ramsey,
July 1941, the day after Jelly Roll died

Since then, if Smith, Ramsey and Russell are remembered at all,
it is as reactionary antiquarians, 'moldy figs' opposed to musical innovation in any form. The New Orleans revival, one historian has argued,
was 'the longest lasting movement in jazz but . . . the only one to
have produced no music of value'. Certainly it produced neither
music nor scholarship bearing any relevance to the blues. No books
chronicling blues history give *Jazzmen* so much as a mention: it is a
minor footnote to a different story, a brief flurry in the development
of a different musical form. That blues and jazz are separate, distinct
musics has been an axiom of blues history since the 1960s. Yet to
go back to the interwar years is to find that the matter is not so
simple. Throughout his interview with Alan Lomax, Morton used the
words 'jazz' and 'blues' more or less interchangeably, as did race-
record advertisements in the African American press, where the term
'blues' simply signified 'black popular music', whether or not it had
the so-called blues chord progression or an AAB rhyming scheme.

No less so than Dorothy Scarborough or John Lomax, the *Jazzmen* cohort were visionaries and dreamers obsessed with uncovering uncorrupted black music, yet they envisioned that purity in the red-light district, in the terrain of urban dissipation that the likes of Scarborough most feared. That they found authenticity in the metropolis to some extent comes down to politics. The 1930s saw the emergence of a transatlantic circle of jazz aficionados who understood jazz as an urban music and whose romance with its collective improvisations was infused with the politics of the Popular Front. Yet, though the *Jazzmen* writers were on the Left (Ramsey a pacifist, Russell a New Deal liberal, Smith, some claim, a Party member), politics alone does not explain the lure that Storyville held for them. While conventional folklorists had been driven by nostalgia for music heard in live performance, the *Jazzmen* set were impelled by commercial recordings – records by Jelly Roll Morton and Joseph 'King' Oliver that were manufactured in the 1920s and that sometime in the early 1930s Smith, Russell and Ramsey began to collect.

'There is a world of difference between the blues as collectors know them and the folk stuff [that the Lomaxes] waxed for the archive,' Smith explained in 1939. The latter was simply anachronistic, the product of folklorists' imaginations, while the real blues, the blues that mattered, was the product of the modern world. 'Most of us' (he was writing to his fellow collectors) 'think that folk music went into a decline in the last century to make way for a few bright blasts on a golden horn.' That horn first sounded in Storyville. It signalled the rise of a blues that was urban, sexual and proletarian, first voiced by prostitutes touting for business and echoed by the rough, dirty melodies blown out of Buddy Bolden's cornet, Kid Ory's trombone and Sidney Bechet's saxophone.

Behind the publication of *Jazzmen* lay a circumstance that the recording industry had not anticipated: the mass production of popular music generated a vast amount of waste matter, some of which could have a second life. That resurrection began in the early 1930s, and it proved no less startling to the musicians whose recordings aficionados were after. One young enthusiast, Kenneth Hulsizer, found as much when he tracked down Jelly Roll Morton at the Jungle Inn and began bombarding him with questions about the supporting players – in collectors' argot the 'personnels' – on his 1920s recordings. Though to Hulsizer's delight he 'looked much like his pictures in the old Victor Race Catalogues', Morton was by then poor, embittered and bewildered by Hulsizer's interest. It took some time for Hulsizer to convince him that he was not a talent scout or an FBI agent but simply in search of information about wax platters that Morton had forgotten about long ago.

> He had never heard of a record collector. I was the first one he had ever met. When I asked him if he had any of his old records, he laughed and said, 'No, what would anyone want of those old things.' Records were merely something made to get a little money and to spread his name. A profitable sort of publicity device. The only music that counted was the music that you played directly to people who applauded and paid to hear you.

Though Morton's dismissal of phonograph records stemmed in part from his roots in New Orleans jazz, whose trademark improvisations the recording process curtailed, his bewilderment when confronted by a record collector appears to have been broadly shared. What seemed inexplicable was the urge to hoard something intended as so ephemeral. Pressed by the thousands in factories, sold for small change over the counter, recordings by the 1930s had a briefer shelf life than ever before. With the coming of the Great Depression, race labels of the 1920s like Okeh and Gennett had been forced out of business. In time, they were replaced by new, larger enterprises – 'empires of sound', one historian has called them – that supplied recorded music for jukeboxes and the radio, generating a steady stream of popular hits. Radio and jukeboxes institutionalised the value of novelty, playing recordings for a few weeks or months before replacing them with others more freshly pressed. Such built-in obsolescence seemed distinctly at odds with the collector's quest. Historically, collectors had amassed paintings, ceramics, exotic plant specimens, unique items of enduring cultural value, not mass-produced commodities designed to be discarded fast.

Yet it was precisely in the 1930s, as their shelf life contracted, that race records became collectable objects. That was when the passion first hit Frederic Ramsey. Born in 1915 in Pennsylvania, Ramsey had grown up in a swirl of art and ideas. His father, Charles Frederic Ramsey, himself the son of an artist, was an abstract painter who had served as the director of the Minneapolis School of Art until being dismissed as a socialist. The family resettled in New Hope, Pennsylvania, where they found a community of dissident intellectuals (including a pair of Quaker social scientists, Edward and Emily Mead, whose daughter Margaret was Fred's babysitter). From early on, the younger Ramsey displayed a flair for the written word. Valedictorian of his class at Solebury School, he enrolled at Princeton to study modern languages and represented the university on a goodwill trip to France, where he researched an essay by interviewing James Joyce, a feat considered so audacious it was reported by the *New York Times*. His senior thesis on the fictional techniques of Rabelais won him the Prix France-Amerique for sensitivity to European culture. When he moved to New York to take a job in publishing, his teachers and acquaintances expected great things.

All of which made what happened next seem inconceivable. While he was at Princeton, Ramsey had begun amassing disused recordings by Joe Oliver, Kid Ory and Jelly Roll Morton, black musicians whose names did not figure on the hit parade. Occasionally he could find the discs at the record store across from the university library, but mostly it meant making trips to New York, scavenging through junk shops in midtown or going up to Harlem and making the rounds of the general stores. On the eve of his move to New York, in the summer of 1936, he had a letter read out on the WABC radio broadcast *World of Swing* identifying himself as a record collector, and among those who responded was the show's scriptwriter, Charles Edward Smith. 'I liked your letter for its emphasis upon the good jazz of other years,' Smith wrote. 'It's worthwhile skimping on current stuff to get together a worthwhile collection of the best men of the past.'

That shared quest to find discs by 'the best men of the past' cemented Ramsey's friendships in New York with a group of like-minded enthusiasts: Smith, John Hammond, Marshall Stearns, Stephen Smith, Charles Payne Rogers and William Russell (with whom Ramsey found an apartment). By the time Ramsey moved to New York, those scattered aficionados were already coalescing into a subculture. In 1934, Smith had published an article called 'Collecting Hot' in the men's magazine *Esquire*, and what had been a pastime or an interest abruptly had an identity attached to it. As Smith explained it, collectors were defined by their passionate commitment, driven at once by the sound of the music and, not inconsiderably, by the thrill of the chase. Race-record sales in the 1920s had depended on mail order and on stores in black neighbourhoods (and the most unlikely outlets would stock them, from pharmacies to funeral parlours). Finding those discs several years on meant canvassing the black sections of cities for commodities long ago discarded or forgotten. William Russell, a classically trained composer and violinist whose passion for the recordings of Jelly Roll Morton led him to abandon composing entirely, learned to go door to door in Harlem and on the South Side of Chicago, where the Depression had transformed streets like Cottage Grove Avenue into 'one solid row of junk shops . . . [with] Victrola records stowed away in every corner'. 'Make out a want list of all the things you would take in any kind of "beat up" condition,' he wrote to Frederic Ramsey on the eve of one such expedition. 'Just list the things you don't have, which you can hardly expect to find new, and would be willing

Fred and Amelia Ramsey, 1950

to take even badly worn, or else mark "good condition only" after title.' While finding mint-condition recordings was best, scratches could be welcomed as badges of honour, physical evidence of the collector's discernment, his capacity to reclaim material that undiscriminating consumers had consigned to the rubbish heap.

Behind that capacity for discrimination lay a kind of ad hoc training. Most of the early collectors, like Ramsey, were products of the Ivy League, where they nurtured their passion for music in campus clubs devoted to the appreciation of 'hot jazz'. In 1935 Stearns and Hammond, both Yale graduates, founded the United Hot Clubs of America, a campus network committed to advancing the jazz recording as 'a worthy cultural object of study'. Hot Clubs functioned as an informal tutorial in taste and aesthetics, dedicated to the practice of studious listening, of applying intellectual effort to mass-produced objects and learning to distinguish the fake stuff from the real. And though they thrived on an atmosphere of tribal commitment, they did not generate a party line. Indeed, to read the bits of journalism and criticism produced by the likes of Smith, Stearns and Hammond is to enter a world of intense antagonisms, of passionately sectarian schisms over which performers and which recordings most fully embodied the true spirit of jazz.

For Smith, Russell and Ramsey the answer was clear: the true spirit of jazz could best be discerned on a set of recordings made in the 1920s for the Gennett and Victor labels by Jelly Roll Morton, Joe 'King' Oliver, Kid Ory and Louis Armstrong, all of them black and all of them natives of New Orleans. The intensity with which they held to that view was only in part a response to the music. Just as centrally, they were disputing an assumption that they discerned both within collectors' circles and in the pages of the popular press: that while jazz was undeniably black in its origins, only white musicians, with their greater capacity for creative thinking, had transformed it into art. 'There will always be wayward, instinctive and primitive geniuses who will affect us directly, without interposition of the intellect,' wrote Gilbert Seldes in 1923. '[Yet] the greatest art is likely to be that in which an uncorrupted sensibility is *worked* by a creative intelligence. So far in their music the Negroes have given their response to the world with an exceptional naivete, a directness of expression which has interested our minds as well as touched our emotions; they have shown comparatively little evidence of the functioning of their intelligence.' Fifteen years on that attitude persisted. Ramsey and their cohort discerned it above all in the popular fascination with Bix Beiderbecke, the white Chicago cornetist who played beautifully, lived dangerously and died young of alcoholism in 1931. That fascination – which reached a peak in 1938 with the publication of the novel *Young Man with a Horn* – valorised Beiderbecke as jazz incarnate, a self-willed outsider in thrall to primitive sounds that by sheer creative brilliance he raised to the status of art.

By the late 1930s, Ramsey lamented, even in collectors' circles 'everyone was talking Bix and Chicago'. To do so, as he saw it, was to buy into a story that pushed black creativity to the margins. Even while Bix fans lauded jazz as a kind of outsider art, they replicated the racism of the hit parade, in which white musicians like Paul Whiteman and Benny Goodman were propelled to the foreground while brilliant black innovators like Johnny Dodds and Tommy Ladnier were left to die in obscurity and want. The more they argued with their fellow collectors, the more Smith and Ramsey longed for some new kind of jazz chronicle – not yet another piece of jazz criticism, but a different sort of story that would put the focus on black creativity where it rightfully belonged.

Then in the autumn of 1938, a few months after Jelly Roll Morton completed his interviews at the Library of Congress, Frederic Ramsey was approached by an editor at Harcourt Brace, where he worked as a clerk in the sales department, and asked to comment on a manuscript on jazz. He returned it the next morning with the margins full of invective. It was a miserable book, as miserable as virtually everything written on jazz, all uninformed claims and superficial opinion, with no sense of where the music had come from or why. Smith had told him about Morton and his sessions with Lomax, so he knew that a deeper and more vibrant story was out there, and reading this manuscript convinced him that it had to be told. He knew about the writers and photographers Smith was meeting in Washington, Alan Lomax and Benjamin Botkin among them, who were forging new, progressive forms of documentation that pushed the experience of marginal peoples to the foreground and gave them space to speak for themselves. Jazz needed that kind of story: a definitive account of its origins, which could only come from the mouths of the musicians who had created it. Most importantly, he knew the men who could uncover the tale. He and his friends, he told the editor, 'could do a better book'.

Open the cover of *Jazzmen* and turn to the frontispiece, and you see what was designed to distinguish this book from everything ever published on jazz:

> Now here is the list about that Jazz Playing. King Bolden and myself were the first men that began playing jazz in the city of dear old New Orleans and his band had the whole of New Orleans real crazy and running wild behind it. Now that was all you could hear in New Orleans, that King Bolden's band, and I was with him and that was between 1895 and 1896 and they did not have any dixie land Jazz Band in those days . . . So you tell them that Bunk and King Bolden's Band was the first ones that started Jazz in the City or any place else. And now you are able to go now ahead with your Book.

The quote came from a letter to Ramsey and William Russell from William Geary 'Bunk' Johnson, an elderly trumpet player whom they found picking sugar cane in New Iberia, Louisiana. Ramsey and Russell had been steered to Johnson by Louis Armstrong and a few other New Orleans musicians, who thought they remembered 'someone called Bunk' playing in the city in the early days. Johnson's claims to have been there at the beginning, which he would ultimately parlay into recording sessions and concert appearances, were central to the sensation that *Jazzmen* created, and to the ridicule that has enveloped the book ever since. While Bunk was a consummate talker, he was quickly revealed to be unreliable: ten years younger than he claimed and never a member of Bolden's ensemble. That Ramsey and Russell swallowed his tales has led many historians to bemoan them as credulous dupes and to dismiss the value of the book outright. 'So eager were they for the "truth" about the origins of jazz that the authors of *Jazzmen* took Johnson largely at his word,' laments Peter Goldsmith. As a consequence, he concludes, 'musicologists have since been left to sort fact from fiction in his account of the turn-of-the-century bands'.

Yet to lambast *Jazzmen* for its failure 'to sort fact from fiction' is to misconstrue what the book was about. Steeped in the methods and ethos of the Federal Writers Project, the book's writers set out to compile (in the phrase of the period) a 'folk history', whose value lay in the sheer vigour of the testimony of the people themselves. Their introduction emphasised the importance of first-hand accounts of jazz's beginnings, of gathering memories of participants and witnesses and getting them down in their subjects' exact words. 'One or another of the authors has interviewed every living jazz musician who could contribute factual material,' they noted. 'In some cases, their remarks were directly transcribed in shorthand; in others, careful notes were taken. The sum total of information obtained in this manner was then typed and made available to all the contributors.' They presented the book, in other words, as a collaboration between the (mostly) white interviewers and their (mostly) black subjects. The truth they aspired to was poetic, not literal, conveyed not by solid nuggets of information independently verified by outside authorities, but by colour, by atmosphere, by the quality of feeling that the tales evoked.

Nowhere were those tales more vivid, more atmospheric, than in the accounts of Storyville, in William Russell's phrase 'the most glamorous, as well as the most notorious center of legalised vice in history'. Established in 1898 (and taking its name from the alderman whose city ordinance created it), it flourished until 1917 when it was shut down by the federal government, a region of thirty-eight blocks bounded by Canal, Basin, North Robertson and St Louis Streets, which were turned over entirely to brothels, cabarets and saloons. By the late 1930s, it had already been the subject of mythologisation, most notably as the culminating chapter in the 1936 book *The French Quarter*, Herbert Asbury's 'informal history of the New Orleans underworld'. Like his best-selling 1928 *The Gangs of New York*, *The French Quarter* was a rambling compendium of scabrous rumour and salacious anecdote drawn from police blotters, old newspapers and interviews with elderly crooks. Asbury emphasised the vice and dissipation that had shaped the city from its beginnings, the voodoo rites and gambling dens and weird African dancing in Congo Square. While he notes the city's racial dynamics, he does not object to them – they feature in the story largely as atmosphere. The rise of the racially mixed district of Storyville figures as both climax and turning point: the moment when prostitution gained unprecedented visibility, but also when it began to decline, for as Asbury concludes with blasé, man-of-the-world irony, middle-class girls are now as loose as prostitutes, and Americans as a whole have embraced the wickedness they once felt compelled to segregate.

There is one mention of jazz in *The French Quarter*, though it does not figure in the index and is so fleeting that it is easy to miss. Midway through a discussion of the decor of the brothels on North Basin Street, Asbury turns to the entertainment that the brothels relied upon, the 'groups of itinerant musicians' they sometimes employed:

One of the most popular of these combinations . . . was a company of boys, from twelve to fifteen years old, who called themselves the Spasm Band. They were the real creators of jazz, and the Spasm Band was the original jazz band. There were seven members besides the manager and principal organiser, Harry Gregson, who was the singer of the outfit – he crooned the popular songs of the day through a piece of gas-pipe, since he couldn't afford a proper megaphone. The musicians were Emile Lacomb, otherwise Stalebread Charley, who played a fiddle made out of a cigar-box; Willie Bussey, better known as Cajun, who performed entrancingly upon the harmonica; Charley Stein, who manipulated an old kettle, a cow-bell, a gourd filled with pebbles, and other traps and in later life became a famous drummer; Chinee, who smote the bull fiddle, at first half a barrel and later a coffin-shaped contraption built by the boys; Warm Gravy; Emile Benrod, called Whisky, and Frank Bussey, known as Monk . . . Cajun Bussey and Stalebread Charley could play tunes upon the

harmonica and the fiddle, and the others contributed whatever sounds chanced to come from their instruments. These
they played with the horns in hats, standing upon their heads,
and interrupting themselves occasionally with lugubrious
howls. In short, they apparently originated practically all of
the antics with which the virtuosi of modern jazz provoke the
hotcha spirit, and sometimes downright nausea.

If nothing else, Asbury's account is intriguing in its sheer brevity –
clearly, in 1936 to speak of the 'New Orleans underworld' did not
necessitate speaking of jazz. (Compare this to Al Rose's 1974 book
Storyville, New Orleans; even while denying that jazz began in
Storyville, Rose still felt obliged to devote a full chapter to the
subject.) Just as clearly, to speak of jazz's origins did not necessitate
speaking of black musicians. While Asbury's account does not mention
race, the fact that (as he explains in a footnote) Harry Gregson was
now 'a Captain of Detectives in the Police Department' makes it
almost certain that the Spasm Band's members were white.

For Asbury, clearly, such an ensemble seemed an apt point of
origins for the hit-parade swing of the 1930s, which he disdained as
a music of 'antics', a cheap, mass-market amusement not particularly
marked by race. As connoisseurs of race records, the *Jazzmen* writers
had a different story to tell. They were out to authenticate those
Mortons and Olivers, to flesh out the purity that they heard in the
music, and that meant establishing a place of germination and a line
of transmission. While Asbury's Storyville is simply a vice district,
Jazzmen's Storyville is a community, a black proletarian haven where
outcasts and disreputables expressed resistance, found training and
fellowship, and created a new art form.

From the outset, Smith and Ramsey were aware of a potential
danger in their project: they could be seen to be catering to the
voyeuristic taste for 'slumming' most famously associated with Carl
Van Vechten, the Jazz Age music critic and Harlem habitué whose
fascination with African American arts was permeated with an intense

investment in exoticism (he famously celebrated Bessie Smith as an 'elemental conjure woman' with a 'plangent African voice'). Van Vechten's passion for Negro arts (as well as his willingness to wield money and influence on artists' behalf) had helped many black artists but repelled others, and both Ramsey and Smith (they were less sure about Russell) were determined to avoid any parallels. In they end, Smith sought help from the poet Sterling Brown, who he had got to know at the Federal Writers Project and at the Jungle Inn. 'I said we were trying to avoid the Van Vechtian line, etc,' Smith reported to Ramsey. 'I was glad I did, for Sterling told me his feeling about how the Negro should be discussed racially, and it's the same as ours. That is, where heritage is legitimate, such as pentatonic scale, ok, but don't try to explain his hot virtues by his savage breast – in other words, environment shapes us. I agree with him, and I'm sure you do, and I learned from him that this is a very very important issue with Negroes, that they do not care to be set apart anthropologically even when this is supposed to be a compliment.' In the end, Brown was sufficiently impressed with their project to offer them his poem 'Ma Rainey', and Smith urged Ramsey to go through the manuscript with its inclusion in mind. 'I hope, in view of this, you'll go through the stuff once again (especially Russell's) and cut out – just DELETE – all adjectives or phrases or comparisons that are AFRICAN – "like an African dancer" – "His African voodoo ancestors", etc. Sterling, I know, would not have any part of a book that had any trace of that in it and, believe me, he is representative of the most progressive Negro thought.'

Aligning their book with 'the most progressive Negro thought' meant framing their black protagonists as creative geniuses. At the centre of their story, the starting point in their line of transmission, was Buddy Bolden. Though Ramsey, Russell and Smith seem to have assumed that they were the first to write about him, Bolden had in fact been discussed in the New Orleans black press back in 1933, in an article entitled 'Excavating Local Jazz' by an African American journalist named E. Belfield Spriggins. Spriggins had interviewed

Bolden's trombonist Willie Cornish, and he described the 'sensation' King Bolden created 'many years ago . . . [in] popular dance halls around the city' with a number since labelled 'Buddy Bolden's Blues' (or 'Funky Butt'). For Spriggins, Bolden was one name among many, and he mattered simply as the creator of the first local jazz hit. But listening to the stories they were told by Bunk Johnson, Willie Cornish and Jelly Roll Morton, the *Jazzmen* authors seized upon Bolden as the music incarnate: battered by poverty, disdain and racism, but able to fight back through 'an innate power of invention', an intuitive, untutored brilliance that had all New Orleans running wild before it finally drove him mad.

Though Bolden was, in their eyes, a genius, his talent flourished because of his surroundings, the low-life barrelhouses and honky-tonks of Storyville. This, to Ramsey, Smith and Russell, was the side of the red-light district that mattered: not the lavish pleasure houses Asbury dwelled upon, where blacks entertained but were kept out as customers, but the gutbucket dives like Pete Lala's Café or the Big 25, where black musicians played after hours. It was a common mistake, Charles Edward Smith once remarked, to assume 'that the musicians found no appreciative audience in dives and didn't play their best there'. On the contrary: 'jammed every night with river rowdies, card sharks, roughnecks, pimps, and all varieties of male parasites', clubs like Lala's brought performers and spectators together in a kind of ecstatic fusion, the musicians 'dragging out the blues with a slow beat and fierce intensity' as the rough-edged habitués egged them on. Hustlers and roustabouts were there to relax, whores were there to drum up business, and together they set the tone. 'Inside the low, smoky room, the musicians sweated for their bread, delivering "gully-low" stomps and blues, the kind that the respectable "dicty" people pretended to hate, but yelled for as soon as they had a few drinks under their belts,' wrote Ramsey. And if a few, like Johnny Dodds, 'hated the long hours, the low pay, the sweat, the obese, waving back-sides', others, like Bolden, found it exhilarating, playing louder and louder to send the dancing crowd into a frenzy, then dropping the volume to take inspiration from the sound of their shuffling feet.

For the *Jazzmen* writers, black popular music was born in that atmosphere of underworld communion, and with Bolden as its guiding spirit, what followed took the shape of a tragedy. Storyville figures in the book as a ribald, plebeian Garden of Eden, and its closure in 1917 amounts to an expulsion from paradise. Travelling to New York and Chicago, the musicians were hit by the virulent racism from which the Storyville community had partially sheltered them, and on top of that, exploitation by the commercial record companies. Over the course of the 1920s, great artists like Oliver and Morton were recorded by the Victor and Gennett labels, run by men with little knowledge of music and even less concern for art, who used them for a time and then let them go. So Jelly Roll Morton ended up mixing drinks at the Jungle Inn; Kid Ory worked on a chicken ranch; Joe Oliver sold apples on street corners and pushed a broom in a pool hall before dying of a broken heart. Most telling of all, Bunk Johnson, 'the ideal successor to the throne of King Bolden . . . [with] an unprecedented sense of swing and feeling for the low-down blues and gutbucket style', had never been deemed worth recording. The conclusion seemed clear: the history of jazz on record was one of cheapening and adulteration, with brilliant black innovators either ignored entirely or cavalierly discarded, the credit for their innovations assigned to white imitators, themselves descending into poverty.

That invective against commercial recording might seem an odd conclusion for record collectors to draw, yet the *Jazzmen* writers' attitude toward their collections had always been ambivalent. On the one hand, and in marked contrast to traditional folklorists, they welcomed the recording process, regarding commercial discs as (in Smith's phrase) 'a transcribed history', artefacts that contained forgotten echoes of a marginalised, rejuvenating national heritage. As the writing of *Jazzmen* itself proved, commercial recordings could prompt curiosity, debate and historical research and investigation, and they kept echoes of New Orleans alive. Yet that process was blighted by acquisitive, racist recording executives and (they implied) by the record-buying masses, who were fickle and undiscerning at best. It was due to that sheer lack of discernment that hot jazz was not and would never be popular. The nature of the popular market meant record companies would always be loath to record it, preferring a music of 'shallow emotionalism', music that, as Smith put it, 'plucked at the surface emotions with a monotonous persistence'.

There was, however, one recording that they hoped would tell a different story. Throughout their research for *Jazzmen*, Ramsey and Smith kept hearing rumours of a wax cylinder made sometime in the mid-1890s by Buddy Bolden. The story seemed just about plausible: the 1890s had been the decade when phonograph companies first got off the ground, and some had made recordings of local musicians for their salesmen to use when demonstrating the technology. Bolden's trombone player, Willie Cornish, told Smith that he thought he remembered the band being employed by some 'white company' to perform in front of a bank of recording phonographs, and while he did not have any of the resulting cylinders, he knew a woman who might have hung onto some. Smith tracked her down and she apologised. She had indeed owned a box of old cylinders that might well have included something by Bolden, but she hadn't listened to them for decades. For the past forty years they had been stored in her living room just a few feet from where they were standing – 'just sitting there', she said, gathering dust – but finally she had tired of looking at them. About one year earlier she had thrown them out.

In a sense, that tale of the Bolden cylinder loomed over the New Orleans revival. It accounts at once for the frenzied hopes that animated their searches for old recordings – who knew what one might unearth at the local Salvation Army? – and for their wistful near disappointment with those recordings that they actually found. Much as they loved those Mortons and Olivers, they inevitably ran a poor second to the sound that collectors imagined: African American music at its purest, in the rough democracy of Storyville, where they

liked their blues 'mean and dirty' and where Bolden would call out
to his band:

> Way down, way down low
> So I can hear those whores
> Drag their feet across the floor.

Today little remains of what was once Storyville. Long before the
environs of Iberville and Basin Streets had been engulfed by the
waters unleashed by Hurricane Katrina, the buildings that housed
the 101 Ranch and Pete Lala's Cafe had fallen victim to urban renewal.
Even as Smith, Ramsey and Russell were writing, New Orleans was
calling on the newly created United States Housing Authority to pull
down the old buildings and construct public housing for low-income
families, and in the process erase the physical remnants of a place
and a period the city now deemed an embarrassment. Some of the
most famous street names were changed: Franklin Street, where Pete
Lala's had stood, became Crozat; Basin Street became, for a time,
North Saratoga. In 1942, William Russell wandered round with a
camera and captured the transformations in progress, the broken
glass, the 'No Trespassing' notices, the boarded-up facades of the
cribs and dance halls.

Perhaps the steady, relentless disappearance of those final bits
of material evidence helps explain the lush romance of the revivalist
portrait, an aura that rapidly intensified. In the years that followed
the publication of *Jazzmen,* as the city fathers belatedly realised that
the jazz heritage constituted a potential tourist attraction, enthusiasts
who came to the city in search of the remains of the old dives and
barrelhouses found that they had to rely entirely on their imaginations. The saloons on Bourbon Street seemed a poor substitute, with
their crowds of drunken college students and sailors on shore leave,
and the most avid collectors lamented the passing of a place that had

created great art, forged a community and invested pleasure with raucous protest. 'The barrelhouse was the refuge of the tragically destitute, the blindly rebellious, the abjectly sodden,' explained the critic Rudi Blesh in 'Jazz Begins', part of a 1946 collection of essays that he helped to edit with Frederic Ramsey. 'For this was the haunt of the blues, music of tragedy, dull despair, flaming revolt. Through the foul, smoky air loud with the clatter of cups, the shrill-edged laughter, rowdy shouting, and drunken snores and weeping, rang incessantly, day and night, the stark, simple blues.' And as important as the music, in this portrait, was the man who created it.

> In a dark corner, hunched over the battered upright piano, the aged, rosewood 'box', sat the 'beater', a lonely figure, 'stacking the blues', tapping his foot, humming in a rough voice the bare and melancholy phrases, the dark words:

> > Got to keep movin'
> > Blues fallin' down like hail
> > I got to keep movin'
> > Blues fallin' down like hail
> > I can't keep no money
> > For a hellhound on my trail
> > Hellhound on my trail

The first time I read this passage, over half a century after Blesh wrote it, I had to stop and read it again. Abruptly, bizarrely, the role of the forlorn brothel pianist was being performed by the wrong actor, and that foul, rowdy ghetto barrelhouse had acquired a soundtrack that seemed entirely out of sync with the script. But that reaction to Robert Johnson's 'Hellhound On My Trail' was my moment of dissonance, not Blesh's, for as it happens, the jazz collectors who celebrated Storyville lionised Robert Johnson too. As early as the late 1930s, Johnson's recordings were circulating among a small but ardent group of New Orleans enthusiasts, Frederic Ramsey, Charles Edward Smith and John Hammond among them. (In 1939, Hammond loaned his copies to Alan Lomax, who included eight Johnson titles on his 'List of American Folk Songs on Commercial Records'.) What captured their imaginations in Johnson's music was the same kind of magic they heard in Morton: a music as 'dry on the ear as some wine may be on the tongue', infused with 'an unquenchable power . . . a power direct and unornamented, completely unmixed with cloying sweetness, languor, or sentimentality'.

In their attempts to account for that power, to find a story of origins with which to make sense of it, the record collectors who generated the New Orleans revival were the first blues historians. To dismiss them for finding the wrong story is to overlook the work such tales perform. In purporting to reveal 'the object of study in the moment of its emergence' as Eric Lott puts it, 'the pure thing (unadulterated by later, superfluous changes)', stories of musical origins are always social and political fables. For the aficionados of old New Orleans, purity took the form of a lonely man 'stacking the blues' at a battered brothel piano, a proletarian soothsayer, an underworld bard telling stories of longing and lust. Just what vision and values that figure connoted depended on who was conjuring him up. As the historian and jazz aficionado Eric Hobsbawm notes, for revivalists '"New Orleans" became a multiple myth and symbol: anti-commercial, anti-racist, proletarian populist, New Deal radical, or just anti-respectable and anti-parental, depending on taste.' Some clearly found the raunchy, disreputable setting enticing, and not all were as scrupulous as Smith and Ramsey about steering clear of 'the Van Vechtian line'. The best that can be said, and it is not inconsiderable, is that they felt no need to pathologise Storyville, that they were bewitched by not the threat but the promise of black urban life.

For a time, Storyville would cast that spell even upon Alan Lomax. While on the face of it Lomax played little part in the revival (apart from producing the recordings that, in a sense, started it all), in truth he had never stopped thinking about the tales that Morton had told him. They simmered in his imagination even in the Mississippi Delta, where in 1942 he spent a fruitless afternoon trying to coax stories of the red-light district and examples of 'that early blues' out of an elderly brothel pianist named Jaybird Jones, who unlike Morton proved singularly monosyllabic. In 1949, seven years after Morton's death and three years after Rudi Blesh worked out a deal with his estate to issue a selection of the Library of Congress recordings, Lomax went to New Orleans to look for the traces Morton left behind. He had been there with his father fifteen years earlier, trawling the dance halls (with a brace of detectives in tow) in a quest for uncorrupted singers, and then he couldn't get away quickly enough – the younger Negroes, he wrote, 'were on the whole ignorant of the songs we wanted and interested only in the blues and in jazz'. But this time the city seemed different, as he heard Jelly Roll's stories confirmed by other musicians like Johnny St Cyr and Omer Simeon, and as he wandered around the Iberville Housing Project and imagined the streets as they once had been, the cribs and the dives and the sweet hot music pouring out of every window. The result of his visit, published in June 1950, was an elegiac celebration of New Orleans jazz titled *Mister Jelly Roll*.

In many ways *Mister Jelly Roll* marked the culmination of the New Orleans revival, as well as the gospel of living lore that had shaped Lomax's folkloric practice. In Morton's account of his Storyville past, Lomax found social change and culture conflict in abundance: a music 'of protest and of pride', created in a polyglot city by a fractious mix of Creoles and darker skinned, working-class blacks. With its 'streets thronging with pimps, chippies, rotten police, and Babbitts on a binge', Storyville had given birth to 'a truly fresh stream of culture', a 'lusty and life-giving proletarian art'. In its sexual robustness, Lomax heard a full-blooded contrast to the sentimental tones of the 'sweet' music generated by 'the marketplace of Tin Pan Alley'. While jazz was 'a marvel that has spawned a monster – a monster entertainment industry . . . whose million orifices pour out each week the stuff of our bartered dreams', Morton showed its utopian beginnings, commercial black music as it might have been. In his Storyville blues Lomax heard what Ramsey, Smith and Russell had heard: 'a rich evocation of underground America', a rough-edged, egalitarian world where pimps and whores could double as artists, exulting in the 'ecstasy' of cultural creativity, in the germination of a new art form.

Ironically, however, even as *Mister Jelly Roll* hit the bookstores, the New Orleans revival was beginning to flag, and with it the rhapsodic tale of the red-light district as the birthplace of black proletarian art. The reasons for this are complex, but in part they come down to politics. From the outset, the revival's vision of New Orleans jazz as 'a music of protest and of pride' had been steeped in the politics of the Popular Front, that coalition of liberal, Left and radical opinion that fused solidarity with the labouring masses with an impassioned commitment to racial justice. As Lomax and Ramsey and Smith envisioned it, New Orleans jazz was a music that 'did not draw a color line', whose defiantly black and working-class roots affirmed the creative vitality of black urban life. Yet those allegiances, and even that language, came under fire in the Red Scare that followed World War Two. Among the casualties was Lomax himself. In September 1950, a group calling itself Counter-attack, made up of one-time FBI agents, published a pamphlet entitled *Red Channels: the Report of Communist Influence in Radio and Television*. It urged the blacklisting of 151 allegedly subversive writers and artists, including Langston Hughes, Lena Horne, Pete Seeger, Orson Welles, Dorothy Parker and 'Alan Lomax. Author, *Mister Jelly Roll*'. In response, Lomax sailed to London, where he remained for the next ten years.

The collapse of the *Jazzmen* collective was less dramatic. None of its three main contributors fled the country, none were jailed or blacklisted, but the energy and collectivism had gone out of the enterprise, and all of them fell on hard times. Only William Russell continued to devote himself to the gospel of Dixieland. In 1944 he had founded a record label, American Music, to record Bunk Johnson and other New Orleans jazz artists, but audiences dwindled and the enterprise never really made money, and eventually he had to give it up. Charles Edward Smith retreated from jazz research altogether, though in his case that retreat was forced upon him. In 1950 he stepped off a curb in Manhattan and into the path of a speeding car. The accident, which nearly killed him, left him sick, depressed and penniless. Eventually, he moved to a one-room New York apartment and put all of his papers and records in storage, but he could not keep up the payments on the storage space. Ultimately it all disappeared, all his records, all his photographs, all his research for his planned books on Storyville, jazz and Jelly Roll Morton.

In a sense, those individual stories were symptomatic, for by the early 1950s it was unmistakable that the romance of Storyville had decidedly palled. Those years saw a growing enchantment with the power and purity of rural American cultures. In coffee houses, on university campuses and at music festivals across the US, that enchantment gave birth to a folk revival. Yet in a climate of Cold War reaction, this folk-song movement had a different tone from its predecessor in the late 1930s, when such songs were taken up as living lore, for their illumination of class and ethnic struggle. 'For those of us whose revival began around 1958,' writes Robert Cantwell, such political associations 'would have been, in our naive and compliant youth, a barrier to any enthusiasm for folk songs.' Nor did it have room for the sounds of the metropolis, what Benjamin Botkin had called the symphony of urban nightlife. The aftermath of World War Two had seen a massive increase in black migration to cities, and with it rising rates of male unemployment and of families headed by women. That in turn encouraged the growth of a virulent critique of black social 'pathology', as liberal social scientists argued that the city's vicious leisure pastimes and 'matriarchal' families were creating a society of damaged black men.

Even as early as the late 1940s, an awareness of that argument was trickling into the work of jazz critics, beginning to qualify their celebration of the vitality of the black urban experience. Even Rudi Blesh expressed something of it in his 1946 book *Shining Trumpets*, denouncing the pernicious influence on race recordings of unscrupulous black entertainers who had been 'corrupted by city ways'. Such musicians, he suggested, were effectively perverting black musical traditions, hearing in the blues simply a 'lascivious song', echoing with 'drunken snores in the barrelhouse, the snarl of the hop-head, prostitutes' shrill laughter'. While the music, he maintained, did 'have all these things in it', such listeners missed the underlying tone of lament: the fact that, 'in all of this, a lost race is searching for home'. The core of the blues, Blesh suggested, was a spirit of alienation. In the years that followed, as more white writers latched onto the music, that claim would become an article of faith. But few of them would make room for the barrelhouse, for the laughter of prostitutes or the snarl of hop-heads. The world they depicted would be pastoral and, with barely a woman in sight, singularly free from the disorganisation so evident in the black urban world.

There is no more dramatic example of this critical about-face than in the work of Frederic Ramsey. In the years that followed World War Two, his interest in New Orleans jazz slowly diminished. He got married, had a child and moved to a remote, hilly corner of New Jersey, where he built a rambling wooden house with big windows and unfinished walls, grew his own vegetables, and brewed his own beer. Though still a passionate fan of black music, he was nonetheless ready to leave New York. As early as the mid-1940s, he had stopped going to Harlem to collect race records – there were, he told a friend, too many muggings, and the whole experience of being there now felt exhausting.

Besides, he had a new obsession. One night after the war and before his marriage when he was strolling through Greenwich Village, he wandered into the Village Vanguard and found Charles Edward Smith deep in conversation with the nightclub's featured entertainer, Leadbelly. Up to then, Ramsey had never been particularly drawn to Leadbelly's music, but hearing him sing that night he was transfixed. Leadbelly's voice 'was rough and grainy, and some of its raw tones came up as if scraped out of his throat' he recalled eight years later. 'It rang out with intensity because he often shouted with violence . . . The hollers he yelled out were almost impossible of notation in our occidental music scale.' Above all, what made him exceptional was 'his extraordinary ability to tell a story'. Leadbelly spoke and reminisced as he sang, and his songs themselves formed a narrative, as he moved from blues to work songs to cowboy tunes to reels, like a 'record collector who, with a large library to choose from, spends an evening pulling out his favorite discs in a sequence both varied and suggestive'. What that sequence suggested was a tale that none of his recordings had captured. In 1948, with the help of a wartime innovation, the tape recorder, he spent three days in Leadbelly's apartment, as the singer recreated the stories and songs of his youthful wanderings through the cotton fields and timberlands of Texas and Louisiana. Though Leadbelly was weak and sometimes faltering, Ramsey was transfixed by what resulted, a tale of picaresque adventure. 'Rambling,' Ramsey concluded, 'was strong in Leadbelly's blood.'

Eventually, Ramsey took to rambling too. In 1951 he and a friend, the photographer John Vachon, drove from New Jersey to North Carolina and across the South to Louisiana, drinking in the sight of crumbling levees, tumbledown cabins and black women picking cotton in headscarves. Two years later, with a letter of support from Sterling Brown, he received a Guggenheim Fellowship for a project on 'jazz backgrounds', aiming to dig further into the Southern landscape, taking photographs and making recordings. In February 1954 he, his wife Amelia and his three-year-old son Loch left home in their battered 1941 Chevrolet coupe for a six-month trek across the rural South. The trunk of the car held two cameras, a Rolleiflex and a small, unobtrusive Leica, and two tape recorders that Moses Asch of Folkways Records had loaned him, a state-of-the-art, two speed, high-fidelity model and a Magnemite Portable, hand cranked and battery operated, for sites with no ready source of electricity. Late in March they drove into the Talladega National Forest in the northeast corner of

Alabama. The land there was thin and worn and had long ago been given over to sharecroppers, and with the roads and hills so often impassable, little seemed to have changed for the last eighty years. 'Life in the country extremely old – mud chimneys, small old cabins, a hog on every farm, jugs on poles for martin nests', he reported to Asch. 'The mule and the wagon are the principal modes of transportation.' They settled into a tourist cabin, the only white faces within miles, and while Amelia befriended the landlady and Loch rode his tricycle in the dirt tracks, he made the rounds of the front porches, asking for people who sang 'old-timey' songs. Everything about it enchanted him: the decrepit cabins, the lined faces, the quavery voices. At first he kept his cameras and tape recorders in his bag, but soon he simply stopped putting them away. Everything seemed to demand to be photographed; everyone had a story to tell.

The result of Ramsey's quest was a ten-volume LP anthology, *Music of the South*, issued on Folkways Records, and a book-length photographic essay entitled *Been Here and Gone*. The book makes a startling contrast to *Jazzmen*, setting out a new kind of blues origins story, rooting the music not in the urban underworld, but in a region where time had stopped. Mechanisation, he explains, has not reached these lands: 'here, hands are still striving to accomplish tasks set almost a hundred years ago.' The landscape still bears the imprint of slavery: 'Nearly everything that is lived in, or that houses livestock or farm implements, was built long ago.'

At the centre of that primeval landscape, the emotional core of the book, is the figure that Leadbelly had got him imagining, that of the wandering blues singer. He is, Ramsey explains, a dying breed, for these 'men who carried the devil on their backs, the box pickers and songsters who were the vagrants, easy riders and drifters of a period just past, are hardly ever to be encountered along Southern highways today.' The book sets out to track down the last of them, these sharecroppers, ditch diggers, loggers and mule skinners who took to the highway in despair of their lot. The music they produce, as Ramsey presents it, bears little resemblance to the rough, dirty blues of Morton's New Orleans. The blues of the wanderers is a song of melancholy, growing organically out of the pain and privation of their experience. Their feelings of torment infuse the blues verses that thread through the text, placing the voice of the wandering bluesman in a melancholy counterpoint with Ramsey's own.

I got the blues so bad, it hurts my feet to walk,
It has settled on my brain, and it hurts my tongue to talk.

Been Here and Gone paints a stark portrait, a world of poverty, hopelessness and degradation. Yet the tones of that portrait render it more than just pitiable: there is something enticing about it. Time and again Ramsey suggests that this rural world is alive in ways ours is not, rich in a sense of community and in a music – the blues – that is intensely personal and infused with passion. The cabins in Ramsey's photographs here are held together with junk, with chicken wire and bits of scrap metal, and yet the lives led within them contain subtler, more substantive forms of abundance: music that, like all else, is made by hand and permeates daily work and pleasures. In the mouths of the men he encountered, music became 'a personal expression. The music that was everywhere had been welded to a way of life.'

Suffusing Ramsey's text is a sense of deep longing for that way of life. As he paints it, this is a world of direct connections, unlike our own, where the stuff of life is swamped by the glut of commodities, drowned out by the din of mass-market pop. Preserving that world, or at least commemorating it, was for him an urgent mission – far more urgent, it would seem, than making an open stand against racial injustice. Though he wrote in the midst of the Civil Rights movement, the words racism and segregation do not appear in his text. *Been Here and Gone* is permeated with a sense of loss, a sense of a way of life and a people about to vanish, a disappearance that Ramsey attributes to an inevitable process of modernisation: 'tractors will replace mules, automobiles and trucks will push aside wagons.

Machines to plow and cultivate and harvest will do the work of men and women in the fields.' There's no mention of the political turmoil that was pushing young people out of the rural South, no acknowledgement that, in truth, many of the people in his photographs might welcome seeing some of the old ways go.

In a Cold War culture in which radicalism had been pushed to the margins, Ramsey had come to recoil from the politicised vision that had guided the folklore narratives of the Popular Front. Looking back on his time with Leadbelly, he was filled with disgust at the way the Left had exploited the singer, taking a gentle, humanitarian soul and forcing him to parrot the party line. 'I had looked vainly [in previous studies]', he explained, 'for accurate and convincing accounts of the persons who were making [black] music.' In *Been Here and Gone* he sought a new kind of accuracy, one that distanced itself from what was fast being deemed, in disparaging tones, the 'sociological' thrust of interwar writing on black song. Stripping away that distorting framework, he sought to capture the truth of the music: not its politics or its social dynamics but its heartfelt poetry, its rich emotion, which could only by corrupted by the invasive forces of the urban world. As he explained to the *New Yorker*, the soullessness of modern mass culture was infecting even the most remote corners of Alabama and Mississippi: 'The kids down South, more's the pity, would rather listen to some jukebox cutting loose with rhythm and blues than learn the good old music.'

That sense of longing for the purity of a black rural idyll had never been present in *Jazzmen*, but Ramsey had come to feel that his earlier enthusiasm had been misplaced. 'It is beginning to be evident that perhaps as high as eighty per cent of all New Orleans jazz musicians either come from the country, or spring from families moved in from the country,' he wrote to Moses Asch. 'Again, don't let Charles worry that I'm trying to *take away* from New Orleans. I think I'm adding to it by digging origins, showing how the lusty, hard-working families came in and brought their strength with them – their marching strength, their blowing and dancing strength. The music took shape here, but it, like many cultures that have flowered in many cities, had deep country roots. Roots in the country ways, roots in country ruggedness. Roots in the singing in the churches, and roots in the plantation blues.'

For Ramsey, uncovering the truth of black secular music now meant uncovering those 'deep country roots'. As he wrote, he steadily chipped away at the portrait of black music he had helped draw in *Jazzmen*, disentangling the blues from jazz to imagine it as a discrete musical form, a hermetically sealed harmonic landscape cut off from the taint of modernity. This was, as he put it, the 'plantation blues', and his photographs enveloped it in the sepia-tinged aura that phrase suggests. Ramsey's archetypal bluesman could have stepped out of the mid-nineteenth century; indeed, he exists out of time altogether. His hands toughened by labour, his face free from artifice or contrivance, he stares unflinchingly into the camera, a man among men, a heroic wanderer, a hardbitten loner with a guitar.

Chapter Six

The Real Negro Blues

If you had been walking past the building on that night in January 1944, you might have heard a raspy voice, a guitar and the crackle of scratched vinyl, and perhaps you would have looked up. At first, your gaze might have dwelled on the crest over the doorway, the inverted triangle bearing the words 'Spirit Mind Body', but finding the sound would have meant looking still higher, at the row of small anonymous windows on the fourth, fifth or sixth floor. Perhaps curiosity would have impelled you to slip inside the building, past the distracted young man at the reception desk, past the sailors loitering in the lobby, up the staircase, down the dark hallway, until you could crouch outside the door. Then, if you peered through the keyhole, you would have seen the revolving disc, the cardboard boxes full of records, and the angular man kneeling by the turntable, his eyes closed, his face taut with the absorption of a monk in prayer.

Somehow you might have formed the impression that few other people entered that room. Maybe it was the spartan decor – the narrow iron bedstead, the desk with one chair, the bedside table holding a half-empty bottle of whiskey and a single clouded glass. Maybe it was the air of preoccupation conveyed by the sheer number of records and the tattered copies of *Record Changer* stacked at the foot of the bed. Most likely, though, it was the man's face, a certain fierce self-containment about it. But had you felt emboldened and knocked and told him you had been drawn by the music, he might have surprised you. For though he would not have said much about himself – he might not even have revealed his name – he would have rifled through the cardboard boxes and shown you the treasures of his collection, battered records by obscure musicians of whom you would certainly never have heard.

He estimated that these boxes housed about 300 records in total. Not nearly as many as other collectors, not nearly as many, indeed, as he wanted – he was currently drafting a want list that comprised, at last count, about 1,200 items – yet, modest as his collection might be, every item in it was choice. If a record did not thrill him, he would not buy it (or if he had, inadvertently, he would not keep it long), even if it came recommended by the few collectors whose taste he respected. Owning a complete set of an artist's recordings, collecting master numbers in sequence, acquiring unissued pressings simply for their obscurity: such motives might compel other collectors, but none appealed to him. What he was after were magical sounds, by their nature rare and elusive. He prided himself on tolerating no junk.

He had made that rule ever since the day late in the 1930s when he wandered into a Salvation Army warehouse in search of cheap books and noticed a battered disc with the word '*sardana*' printed on a green Columbia label. From his researches into old world folk dances (he'd been reading up on the subject for a couple of years), he knew the *sardana* was a circle dance native to Catalonia, revived in the nineteenth century and now a kind of national emblem. That it had made its way onto a phonograph record surprised and intrigued him, so he started looking for other examples, and soon what began as a casual hobby became something far more involving. There were simply *so many* records to trawl through. Ever since the radio had replaced the phonograph as the main source of music in most people's homes, junk shops, general stores and furniture retailers had been inundated with discs, some of them used, some still in their packing crates, for sale for as little as a dollar per box. By the early 1940s still more resources appeared: trading magazines like *Record Changer* and stores wholly devoted to second-hand records, like Fichtelberg's at Sixth Avenue and West 44th Street, or the shop a few blocks further north that all the collectors called Indian Joe's. Suddenly he was finding all kinds of extraordinary examples of Spanish and South American folk music recorded in the 1920s on Victor and Columbia's foreign-language labels, *gardanas* and *munieras*, melodies he had only imagined, and the more he unearthed, the more he coveted (he still hoped to find a *zamacueca*, a dance of the Indians of the Chilean uplands). But beyond that, he sometimes thought, he had been bewitched by the discs themselves, by the unforthcoming black surfaces, the gaudy green and purple labels, the spiral grooves that, when set in motion, released magical sounds from distant lands.

Somehow, at some indefinable point, he had crossed a threshold from buying to collecting. The odd thing was that, up until then, he had never been drawn to recorded music – certainly not the treacly big-band standards that dominated the jukeboxes by the early 1940s, and not the recordings he'd heard a decade earlier, when he spent several months immersed in the stuff. A year or two after he graduated from high school, he worked for a summer for a family friend in a shop that sold records in a black neighbourhood. Day after day he stood at the counter playing customer requests, blues by Bessie Smith, Ma Rainey, Victoria Spivey and Lonnie Johnson, all of which struck him as cheap and tawdry, and that gut-level aversion to race records stuck with him for the next ten years. He cringed now to recall that, only two years ago, the owner of one of his regular haunts, the Central General Store on Long Island, had sent him a list of mint condition Paramounts, two great unopened boxes that he had unearthed at the back of the store. None of the discs had ever sat on a turntable, and he could have had them for a dollar apiece, but at that point he still dismissed as worthless anything with the word blues in the title, so he forwarded the list to a friend, a Seattle-based collector named Harry Smith, who promptly bought up every last one.

It took him another few months to discover that there were blues and *blues*. Late in 1942, at Smith's suggestion, he sent away to the Library of Congress for the nineteen-page 'List of American Folk Songs on Commercial Records' compiled by Alan Lomax at the end of the 1930s. What he read there confounded everything he had ever assumed about race records. The dizzying variety of musical styles, the sheer oddity of the song titles, the abundance of fire and brimstone sermons ('Babylon is Falling Down' by the Reverend F. W. McGee, 'Black Diamond Express to Hell' by the Reverend A. Nix): it all hinted at sounds richer and stranger than anything he had encountered before. Most intriguing of all were Lomax's mentions of blues recordings, for if many sounded predictably urbane and sophisticated ('De7069, "Chain Gang Blues" by Kokomo Arnold, mod[ern] t[ext] m[elody] and s[tyle], sings in Chicago night clubs'), a few promised something undiluted and raw. 'Co11420-D, "Depot Blues", Charley Lincoln, completely authentic rural blues, primitive g[uitar] s[tyle]'; 'PA12752, "Good Times Blues", Ramblin' Thomas, authentic rural blues, simple, v[ery] f[ine]'; 'Pe7-05-81, "Cross Road Blues", Robert Johnson, individual composition v[ery] f[ine], traces of voodoo'. A few weeks of digging and writing to dealers brought him a copy of the Robert Johnson, and then his curiosity became an obsession. By January 1943, he had compiled a sixteen-page want list that he sent to record traders across the country, and soon he acquired enough blues recordings to file them in their own cardboard box.

What mesmerised him about these discs was something he found hard to describe, harder, at least, than with the Spanish folk music, where he had listened out for a certain simplicity in the accompaniment, a way of handling the guitar and Galician bagpipe that evoked the rural vigour of the Spanish landscape. With the blues he was after a quality of voice. He heard it in Six Cylinder Smith on Paramount 12698, 'Oh, Oh, Lonesome Blues', how he would lift his voice at the end of each line, then abruptly drop it again, and in Ed Bell on Paramount 12546, 'Frisco Whistle Blues', where he careened from a growling bass to a high-pitched wail, and in Ishman Bracey on Paramount 12970, 'Woman Woman Blues', with his choked, broken falsetto repeated every third line until the effect was hypnotic. A decade before, when he clerked in the record store, he had encountered nothing as compelling as this. Blind Lemon Jefferson had been perhaps the closest, 'a real old-fashioned singer' as the ads had billed him, whose recordings practically flew off the shelves, but by comparison he sounded tame and prosaic, with a taste for crude double entendres that probably accounted for his appeal to the citified set. The voices he was hearing now had nothing jocular or sophisticated about them. The greatest were swamp primitives, barely civilised, like Bullet Williams or Jelly Jaw Short, who had a voice he threw around like a voodoo doctor, shouting and mumbling and growling and wailing, or Tommy Johnson, whose eerie rolling guitar set off his singing's naked emotion, passionate and yet wholly artless, none of the ersatz folkishness of a Leadbelly, with all his straining for dramatic effects.

One year on and he could go by instinct, or such a finely tuned sense of labels and master numbers that it amounted to the same thing. He knew now that label colour distinguished the early from the late-issue Vocalions, that Okeh reached its peak with its 05000-06000 series, and that high-numbered Paramounts were almost always worth hearing, since the best singers seemed to have been recorded just before the company went out of business. And sometimes he searched for recordings whose existence he simply imagined. In the most recent *Record Changer*, he had placed the following ad:

BL. ON BL.-LABEL VOCALION
ANY WITH S. A. MASTER #'S

'Blues on black label Vocalion, any with San Antonio master numbers' – in other words, any Vocalion blues made in the same studio that had recorded Robert Johnson. One such extraordinary voice, he reasoned, might have been followed by others just as exceptional. Guesswork was the best he could do in the face of the mysteries these discs presented, these singers whom no one remembered, who seemed to have come out of nowhere and then vanished without leaving a trace.

On the face of it, it might seem odd that the recordings he sought proved so elusive. Since America entered the war, the supply of used records had never been greater, with government scrap drives encouraging people to hoard far more shellac than the war effort needed, and boxes upon boxes of discs turned up in junk shops, great groaning masses of them. Yet while you could find Blind Lemon Jefferson everywhere, the titles he sought had never sold very widely and probably had not been pressed in large numbers to start with. Few other collectors bothered to buy them, so advertising in *Record Changer* was pointless (although he doggedly continued to do so), and while he still made his weekly pilgrimages to Fichtelberg's, the Central General and Indian Joe's, often he came home with nothing. Lately, he had experimented with bypassing the regular sales channels entirely. He struck up a correspondence with Ellis Horne, the clarinet player in Lu Watters' band, who agreed to look out for the discs on his want list and send them to him in exchange for New Orleans jazz rarities. A month ago he travelled to Camden, New Jersey, where Victors and Bluebirds had been manufactured, in the hopes of finding former employees who had taken test pressings home. And just last week he journeyed south and knocked on doors in the black section of Charlotte, North Carolina, where cabins were lit by kerosene lamps and records played on hand-wound Victrolas, but at one house a dog attacked him and at another a man pulled a knife. After that he decided to stick to the shops.

Today, though, he had been lucky. At Indian Joe's north of Times Square, near the back of a bin marked 'miscellany', he found a record in a sleeve so tattered he almost flicked past it, until something about the name caught his eye. It was Paramount 13110, 'Some These Days I'll Be Gone', sung by an artist called Charley Patton. Alan Lomax, he recalled, had listed a couple of discs of religious music by a duo called Patton and Lee – 'street singers', Lomax had called them – but those had appeared on Vocalion, so it might not be the same man. The record itself had so many scratches it looked to be almost unplayable. Normally he'd have tried it out in the shop, but the phonograph was mobbed by Kenton and Miller fans engaged in their interminable three-minute playbacks, so he went to the counter where

Joe was dozing and paid a dollar for it and a Gennett by Sam Collins. He had just finished listening to the Collins when you knocked on the door.

And perhaps it would have been then that he picked up the Patton, slipped it out of its sleeve, and put it on the turntable. At first you would have heard nothing but hisses and crackles, but then you might have flinched at the intensity, a rumbling, growling voice, deep and sepulchral, welling up within the surface noise as though echoing from another world. So thick and slurred was the delivery that you would have strained to make out the lyrics. But if you tore your attention away from the sound, you would have seen the man nodding and smiling, his back straight and his brow furrowed, as though every pore in his body were listening, and even before he replaced the tone arm and turned up the volume and his neighbour began to pound on the walls, you would realise that he had found it, the voice he'd been searching for all along.

There is an historic landmark that has gone uncommemorated in the borough of Brooklyn, New York. In the early twentieth century, the neighbourhood known as Williamsburg was home to a polyglot population: Italian and Polish immigrant families pushed out of overcrowded Manhattan; Irish families who'd been there a bit longer; and single men of various ethnicities attached to the nearby Navy Yard. To cater to the latter, in 1904 the Young Men's Christian Association opened a lodging house at 179 Marcy Avenue, near a stop on the BMT subway line and a few blocks in from the Williamsburg Bridge. And it was there at the Williamsburg YMCA, in a single room sometime in the mid-1940s, that the Delta blues was born.

It was born, that is, in the imagination of one of the YMCA's long-term residents, an impassioned record collector named James McKune. Born sometime around 1910, McKune was the driving force behind the cohort of music enthusiasts who powered the blues

James McKune's high school graduation photo, c. 1928

revival of the 1960s, when white Americans found new meanings in old recordings that African Americans had long since cast aside. Based in and around New York and calling themselves the Blues Mafia, McKune's coterie set up record labels, issued LP anthologies and wrote liner notes, articles and books of blues history that framed the blues as we now know it, a music of pain and alienation, a cry of African American despair. Giving life to that tale were the rough, ragged voices of Delta loners like Charley Patton and Robert Johnson, the prized items in their collections of 78s, which they invested with the mystical passion that John Lomax had invested in Leadbelly, hearing in them voices of power and presence, voices that were uncorrupted and pure.

Understanding the blues revival means untangling that perception, and doing that means looking at James McKune. In the reminiscences of revivalists he looms as a figure of legend: a mysterious loner whose ear for the blues shaped the tastes of a generation, an eccentric iconoclast who wore many faces – a wizard, a prophet, a lunatic. Friends, or rather disciples, clustered around him, but no one knew him very well, and only the barest facts emerge from their stories, many of them hazy and confused. McKune came from Baltimore, or Albany, or North Carolina; he moved to New York City some time in the 1930s, or perhaps it was during World War Two. His personal life was shadowy, at least to his blues acolytes. 'I don't know if this should be mentioned, but he was like a closet homosexual,' remembers his fellow record collector Pete Whelan. 'I didn't know but [another collector] Bill Givens spotted it right away.' What they did spot, all of them, was that he drank, more and more heavily as time went on. By the late 1950s his job as a *New York Times* rewrite man had long been abandoned; for a while he worked as a desk clerk at a men's hostel and sorted letters in a Brooklyn post office, but eventually he lost those jobs too. By 1965 he had moved out of the single room at the Williamsburg YMCA that he had lived in for twenty-five years and could be seen wandering the streets of Lower Manhattan, 'sockless', one collector remembers, 'and seemingly brain-damaged from alcohol'. In September 1971 his unclothed body was found bound and gagged in a welfare hotel on the Lower East Side. Police detectives surmised that he had been killed by a stranger whom he seems to have picked up for sex.

Out of the fog of half-remembered facts of the unconventional life and the ugly death, one thing remains clear in all his friends' minds: the magnificence of his record collection, the pioneering brilliance of his taste in blues. 'There was a guy called Jim McKune who was murdered who was like a grand doyen, if you will, and he was a real mentor,' recalls record collector and blues historian Lawrence Cohn. 'I mean, he was listening to Charley Patton before any of us even knew who Brownie McGhee was.' Pete Whelan remembers: 'He lived in one room in the YMCA and he had all his records in cardboard boxes under his bed. And he would pull out one and say "Here's the greatest blues singer in the world" [and] I'd say "Oh yeah?" cause I had just discovered this guy, Sam Collins, who was great . . . Jim pulls out this Paramount by Charley Patton. I said "Oh yeah, sure", and, of course, he was right!'

No one knows why or how James McKune came to collect blues records. My suggestion that he began with an obsession with old world folk dances, that his first collected disc was a Spanish folk recording, that he discovered the blues through Alan Lomax's list – all of that is simply a plausible story based on speculation and inference. McKune left only scraps of evidence behind him, far too few for any biographer to draw conclusions about his impulses and motives, and far too elliptical for any historian to sustain a narrative with him centre stage. The best we can do is to follow the trail of the discs he pursued with such obsessive intensity. As a neophyte collector in the early 1940s he stepped into the network of trading in disused record-ings that Frederic Ramsey, Charles Edward Smith and William Russell had helped to create in the previous decade, a subterranean world with customs, traditions, even an argot all its own. What made him unique and, in time, influential was the sensibility that he developed, which would ultimately transform the collector's subculture, enveloping the mass-produced disc in an aura of rarefied art. Telling the story of his life means making a virtue of his unknowability. It means imagining him as best we can, a backroom aesthete orches-trating the blues revival from behind the scenes – poring through the bins in used-record stores, trading tips with other collectors, and listening alone in his single room at the Y, conjuring up ghostly, gritty voices from the battered 78s that he stored in a cardboard box under his bed.

The one hundred block of West 47th Street near Times Square in Manhattan is now dominated by an anonymous, glass-fronted office block surrounded by one of those windswept plazas that feel permanently empty of human life. But had you looked in the 1940s, sandwiched between a luggage store and a pipe and tobacco shop you would have found at number 107 an open entranceway giving onto a flight of stairs. To the right of the entrance bold capitals spelled out the legend 'RECORDS', and the stair risers were blazoned with invitations: 'HOT JAZZ RECORDS. RECORDS 4 FOR $1.00. STEP UP SAVE A BUCK'.

This was the Jazz Record Center, or 'Indian Joe's', founded around 1940 by Big Joe Clauberg, a chain-smoking Native American giant and one-time circus strongman who turned to more prosaic work when the Depression hit and the circus trade dried up. In 1938 he and a friend rented the premises near Times Square and set up a used magazine and book store, which they used as a base for publishing the *Hobo News*, a tabloid directed at the growing population of homeless. Since each issue was laden with risqué jokes and cartoons, no regular distributor would take it, so every other week Big Joe loaded copies of the paper into his truck and delivered them to points west and south. One of his customers was a jukebox operator who offered him used records at a very low price. Big Joe hated driving back to Manhattan with an empty truck and, besides, his store had lots of free space. Over time, he increased his stock until those bins of used records took over the shop.

Soon the store was inundated with customers, men (by and large) endowed with obsessive enthusiasms and seemingly endless time to browse. Business peaked on Saturday nights, when collectors squeezed in to rummage for records while rubbing shoulders with Big Joe's colourful cronies – circus performers, grizzled sea captains and a permanently inebriated bookie whose habit of sleeping on the shop floor earned him the nickname of Horizontal Abe. Clauberg's advertisements urged customers to 'come up – play records – chew the fat', and record enthusiasts took him up on the offer. Collector Pete Kaufman remembered: 'We paced about the store, played records, discussed a variety of subjects, and took care to avoid stepping on Horizontal Abe, while Big Joe dozed intermittently at his large desk in the back of the store.' Boasting 'the completest Jazz Stock in the East', 'Everything from Bunk to Monk', the Jazz Record Center soon became the prime resource, hangout and pilgrimage site for record collectors up and down the East Coast.

Setting up the Jazz Record Center with that truckload of jukebox discards, Big Joe stumbled upon what had become, in the ten years since Frederic Ramsey first began collecting, a thriving community. While Ramsey, Smith and their comrades had, by and large, to make up the practise as they went along, the habitués of Indian Joe's found a whole range of institutions available for the enthusiast, to help them find discs, find friends, and cultivate tastes. Secondhand shops were only part of the story. Just as important were the specialist magazines that began springing up in the 1940s, like *Record Changer*, first published in 1942 in which collectors could offer items for sale or trade and put out calls – want lists – for the recordings they sought. Such publications offered neophytes a sense of belonging, along with a wealth of practical tips, from storing and cleaning records, to packing lunches for trips to junk shops ('bananas are the ideal collector's food because they can be peeled and eaten without being touched by the hands'). (Perhaps that practical imperative explains the legendary diet of record collector William Russell, who claimed to subsist only on bananas, raisins, almonds, shredded coconut and the occasional bowl of cornflakes.)

By the mid-1940s, to be a collector was to immerse oneself in a private language rooted in the arcane minutiae of standardisation. Label names and master numbers formed the core of subcultural lingo, echoed by the byzantine system of grading used discs (N, E, VG, G, F, P, with half and quarter stops between) that remains in use to this day. Part of the pleasure of the collector's practise lay in mastering that insider's vocabulary and manipulating the trading resources, developing convoluted webs of exchange. 'Only last night I gave a lady $2.00 for Br. 3457 Melancholy/Wild Man by Dodds, an Okeh Miff Mole, 10 Whitemans with Bix and or Bing on them, 3 Okeh Armstrongs, and about 15 other items of various types,' explained one aficionado in 1945.

Multiply this by 15 or 20 and one has a wonderful batch of trading material . . . I have in my files about 150 want lists so that when I do pick up an item I can always tell just about who I can send it to . . . The guy that has say a Blind Willie Johnson that you want needs only about 12 rare items by Bing Crosby for completion. I dig around in all my correspondence and back issues of record magazines til I find one of those Crosbys for disposition. Then the guy that has it will be interested in nothing I have to offer and will not sell the Crosby except for say $15.00 but will trade it for Lillie Delk Christian's Ok Too Busy. I trade a guy two Bessies for the Lillie Delk and the sailing is easy from then on. Often it is more complicated than this.

Yet merely talking the talk and trading the discs was not enough to place one at the top of the hierarchy – and, by the mid-1940s, this was an intensely hierarchical world. The most prominent members of what had become known as 'the collecting fraternity' – Ramsey, Smith, Russell, Marshall Stearns, John Hammond, Charles Payne Rogers, Steve Smith – made it clear that a genuinely reputable collecting practise raised issues of knowledge, tradition and taste. 'There are collectors, and then there are Collectors,' Rogers explained.

The first-named, lower-case bunch are those who merely collect, seizing upon the current thing in popular music, be it swing, bop, or jukebox, with never a glance at jazz tradition or background . . . They are the blindly crusading devotees, the faddist espousers of 'the latest'. Some may be a little more panoramic in their approach, a little more catholic in their tastes, due to the influence of a slight smattering of jazz history picked up from the trade magazines. But this leads them to collect everything in sight, even the eight bars of Bix embedded in the sticky morass of some mickey-mouse arrangement.

The true Collectors, a relatively small (but expanding) group are far more discriminating. No snobs, they are those whose collections show the selective processes that have been at work in evaluating the whole azimuth of jazz. Your upper-case Collector is himself more musically grounded and is possessed of a more enlightened viewpoint, enabling him to discern the finer jazz performances at will, as they are issued on records. Since his approach is historical, unlike the first group he experiences no particular blush of shame in according some tardily discovered jazz figure his proper proportion of importance.

As Rogers saw it, Collectors distinguished themselves from mere consumers by their rejection of mindless, market-driven buying. Instead, they employed powers of discrimination honed by years of studious listening, immersing themselves in disused recordings that provided a rich sense of the musical past. To be a true Collector, in other words, was to have acquired a sense of history. With that came 'an enlightened viewpoint', a capacity 'to discern the finer jazz perform-ances at will', to serve at once as historian and critic, mapping jazz traditions and hierarchies that flew in the face of popular taste.

At the cutting edge of the collecting fraternity, that sense of discern-ment fused with politics. Men like Hammond, Ramsey and Smith partook of what Michael Denning has characterised as the jazz-inflected imagination of the Popular Front. It was a cosmopolitan, transatlantic community that seized upon recordings of Dixieland jazz as (in Smith's phrase) 'a transcribed history', artefacts full of tantal-ising echoes of the sound of New Orleans in its glory days. To collect those recordings and explore that history was to them a political act. It meant training the spotlight on a distinctly black, defiantly prol-etarian art form in an era when, as they saw it, jazz had been tamed, sweetened and commodified, with white performers like Benny Goodman and Paul Whiteman praised as its consummate practitioners.

Still, for all that the romance of New Orleans jazz guided the tastes of the 'collecting fraternity', by 1950 signs were afoot that its appeal was beginning to wane. The late 1930s had seen the establishment of the first reissue labels – small enterprises, mostly run by collectors (*Jazzmen* contributor Stephen W. Smith was among them), that made deals with the major record companies to issue new pressings of their back catalogues. Once the viability of the experiment was proven, the major labels themselves followed suit. Over the course of the 1940s, the collectors' market was flooded with new pressings of vintage recordings by Joe Oliver, Louis Armstrong and other sought-after New Orleans greats. The result was to send prices of 78s into a nosedive. In 1952, a major auction of choice jazz rarities held by the record trader Francis Wolfe collapsed when the recordings failed to make their minimum bids. While a few collectors held out for the original discs, most were content with the new reproductions and poured scorn on (as one collector put it) 'the jerks who pay ten bucks for an original Louis that's available on a dozen private labels at 79 cents'.

Yet for some, the problem was not reissues but the cult of New Orleans itself. Taking up collecting in New York City, where he moved after World War Two, Pete Whelan felt that the gospel of Dixieland had hardened into an orthodoxy, arid, dogmatic and stultifying, with the collector's bible, *Record Changer*, little more than a 'a propaganda machine'. Though he had loved the music of Morton and Oliver when he heard it on the radio as a boy in New Jersey, he began casting about for music with more lustre about it. Sifting through boxes in junk shops, thumbing through the bins at Indian Joe's, he listened for something singular, something magical, without a clear sense of what that might be.

At some point in the mid-1940s, the oddballs and obsessives who haunted Indian Joe's spotted a new face on the scene, a nondescript man of indeterminate age who turned up in the shop every Saturday night. He was extremely thin, of medium height, with sandy hair greying at the temples, dressed in a white button-down shirt, black trousers, white socks and black shoes, by all appearances his lone set of clothes. Engaging him in conversation was risky. 'He had this way of talking,' one acquaintance remembers, 'he'd make these abrupt gestures, he was very intense, and everybody that he was talking to would be backing up against the wall, because he'd be, not pushing you back, but you'd be afraid of the hands and elbows coming at you.' In his pocket he carried a want list that he distributed to used-record traders: 1,300 78s recorded in the 1920s and 1930s on the most obscure labels by performers of whom no other collectors had heard.

Late in 1943, James McKune ran his first ad in *Record Changer*, and by the end of the decade the singularity of his wants had drawn him a circle of acolytes. Henry Renard, Ron Lubin and Pete Kaufman were intrigued enough to write to him (his advertisements gave his address in Brooklyn), and soon they were meeting regularly, along with Stephen Calt, Lawrence Cohn, Ben Kaplan, Nick Perls, Bernie Klatzko and Pete Whelan, who first encountered McKune in the aisles of Indian Joe's. Most of the men were ten years McKune's junior, and unlike the eminences of the 'collecting fraternity' were not products of the Ivy League. Pete Kaufman ran a liquor store, Pete Whelan wrote ad copy for a railway magazine, Henry Renard clerked for one of Indian Joe's competitors, Ron Lubin drove a truck for a photographer, and none of them had a lot of money to spend. In McKune they found a mentor. He introduced them to the sites of collector's mythology, the places where the *Jazzmen* set got their start: the furniture stores under the subway tracks in Queens where Charles Edward Smith unearthed boxes of untouched Okehs and Vocalions; the Polish Music Shop on 14th Street, where John Hammond found all his Paramounts and Victors; even, incongruously, Bloomingdale's, in whose basement William Russell uncovered a stock of mint condition Paramounts. Saturday afternoons they met at Indian Joe's where, between swigs from the bottles of muscatel that Pete Kaufman brought along from his store, they thumbed through the bins, suspending their searches briefly at three, when a man called Bob turned up with a suitcase of pornographic books. One night each week they convened at each other's apartments and debated the merits of their latest finds. In all of this, McKune took the lead. In July 1950 Kaufman ran an ad in *Record Changer* offering the substantial sum of three dollars, more than most collectors offered for the most prized 78s, for a copy of 'McKune's Comprehensive Want List of 1943'. By then, among a small coterie of aficionados he had developed a reputation as a collector's collector, a connoisseur with an unusually discerning ear.

At the heart of his allure lay the alternative his tastes provided to that of the collecting mainstream, for from the outset the romance of Dixieland appears to have left him cold. Most irritating, as he saw it, was the obsession with the music's history and social significance, the endless speculation about its underworld beginnings, the relentless celebration of its collective improvisations as an inherently progressive form. 'I have read with enthusiasm two books in which you have had a hand, *The Jazz Record Book* and *Jazzmen*,' he wrote to Frederic Ramsey in 1944 from his room at the YMCA. 'But I failed to find in either book information which I had sought therein, namely, how the record collector may find out in what year a particular record was made (or issued), and how he may find out the personnel of the recording group when only the leader's (or vocalist's) name is given on the label.' That Ramsey never replied to the letter only heightened his conviction that the *Jazzmen* cohort had missed the point. For all that they pioneered record collecting, they were weirdly indifferent to the actual recordings, to the mysteries of the recorded disc.

Untangling those mysteries was the self-appointed task of McKune and his circle, who by the mid-1950s had dubbed themselves the Blues Mafia. As that name implied, they were a brotherhood, united by their disaffection for the cult of New Orleans and their devotion to authentic blues, a music known only to cognoscenti, secret, occult and obscure. Having traded away more recordings than most people would hear in a lifetime, McKune was the grand old man of the group, and he surrounded himself with an air of inscrutability that made his

tastes seem all the more pristine and refined. 'On principle', Whelan
recalls, McKune would not pay more than three dollars for any record.
To hand over more substantial sums would tarnish what ought to be
a radical act of salvage, of rummaging through rubbish and finding
treasures ignored by the masses and overlooked by a record-collecting
fraternity whose tastes were too often blinkered and staid. McKune
had nothing but scorn for collectors like used-record trader Jake
Schneider, who became famous among aficionados for amassing nearly
half a million recordings. That McKune's room at the YMCA housed
a comparatively modest collection owed partly to practicalities – only
so many discs could fit under that bed – but more importantly to his
fastidiousness: only 300 discs, Whelan remembers, but 'all of them
choice'. He was contemptuous of the 'treacle fanciers', as he called
them, the bobby-soxers who occasionally ventured into the Jazz Record
Center in search of bargain Glenn Miller, and he had no more time
for the jumped-up sounds of Louis Jordan and Muddy Waters that
were dominating the postwar African American soundscape. Nor did
he enjoy 'people's music', the proletarian folksong purveyed by
Leadbelly and Woody Guthrie under the aegis of the Popular Front.
The recordings that he salvaged came from the bottom of the discard
pile, the dross that everyone else had rejected, records that, as one
collector later put it, were 'considered worthless by everyone but
[McKune] himself'.

It had been in 1944, a year after he took up collecting, that
McKune unearthed his greatest discarded treasure, a scratched,
worn copy of 'Some These Days I'll Be Gone', recorded in 1929 by
Charley Patton, a singer about whom he knew nothing and whom
no other collectors were after. On first hearing, Patton's voice sounded
almost too primitive, but after that initial shock McKune was transfixed. What overwhelmed him was Patton's artistry, his inventive-
ness with his materials, the way his rough-edged voice conveyed a
breathtaking delicacy of technique. 'He tells a story only in part,'
McKune explained, 'singing the same phrases again and again,
varying his voice, almost making the guitar part of his voice.' On

the flip side was the old blues standard 'Frankie And Albert', which he sang 'as it probably has never been sung before . . . His is a tale quietly yet passionately told. At the end you are shaken. You play it again and you forget that anyone else ever sang it.' What McKune heard in Patton's voice was a transcendent, mystical power: 'only the great religious singers have ever effected me similarly.' The only appropriate response to such artistry was to listen 'silently. In awe.'

Patton became McKune's archetypal blues voice, the model that he impressed upon the Blues Mafia, that he had them listening out for in those weekly sessions hunched over the phonograph in each other's apartments. McKune had mixed feelings about those evenings: too often, he complained, they deteriorated into loud boozy chatter, 'conditions not conducive to good listening', when what was needed was the reverent silence in which vocal greatness could make itself heard. Clearly, even in that group of obsessive enthusiasts, McKune distinguished himself by the sheer intensity he brought to the quest. The discographer Dick Spottswood learned as much in 1952, when he was a fifteen-year-old collecting novice and, by some kind of beginner's luck, managed to unearth two Skip James 78s, 'Hard Time Killing Floor Blues' and 'If You Haven't

Any Hay Get On Down The Road', recordings so rare that not even the Blues Mafiosi had been able to find them. Though they were barely acquainted, McKune telephoned him to announce that he would be coming to Spottswood's house to hear them, which meant travelling 250 miles to the suburbs of Washington.

I said, 'Are you sure? That's a long ways,' because he lived
in the Williamsburg section of Brooklyn in New York. And
that's what he did. He got on the Greyhound bus, he came
down to Washington, he took whatever local conveyance he
could – I couldn't help him, because I wasn't old enough to
drive! – and came all the way down to my house in Bethesda.
He listened to those Skip James records once, maybe twice,
I don't know. I know he wasn't there an hour, even. He turned
around and went back home to Brooklyn, having heard the
records that he had come to hear.

The Blues Mafia might have rumbled on forever, honing their tastes,
refining their want lists, had it not been for an upstart collector who
affronted their sensibilities and provoked them to move into the public
eye. The offending party was Samuel Barclay Charters IV, a thirty-year-
old jazz aficionado and aspiring Beat poet who moved to New Orleans
in the early 1950s and began casting around for new sounds when the
Dixieland revival dried up. Equipped with magnetic tape and a contract
from Folkways Records Chief Moses Asch, he spent the next few years
scouring Alabama for skiffle bands, the streets of New Orleans for Mardi
Gras Indians, and the Bahamas for calypso musicians, including the
brilliant guitarist Joseph Spence. In New Orleans he got to know Frederic
Ramsey, who was then undertaking the Southern treks that would result
in *Been Here and Gone*. One glance at Ramsey's photographs fired
Charters's imagination and led in 1959 to a book and an LP issued on
Folkways Records, both entitled *The Country Blues*.

At heart, *The Country Blues* was a work of advocacy. What struck
Charters as important in black music was its sheer emotional intensity. His experiences in New Orleans in the 1950s, as the civil rights
movement intensified, had alienated him from what he saw as a racist,
conformist mainstream, and that sense of disaffection would intensify
in the following decade, when he aligned himself with the New Left,

wrote poetry protesting the Vietnam War, and ultimately left the US altogether. In 1975, he reflected on his motives in writing the book:

> In simple terms I was trying to effect a change in the American consciousness by presenting an alternative consciousness. I felt that much of what was stifling America was its racism, and what it desperately needed was to be forced to see that the hypocrisy of its racial attitudes was warping the nation's outlook on nearly every other major problem it was facing. And I also felt that the black culture itself was a necessary element in the society. The white culture had developed the same kind of defensive hypocrisy toward so many elements of its life, from sexuality to personal mores. In the black expression I found a directness, an openness and an immediacy I didn't find in the white. The texts of the blues were strong and honest, using language in a way the white culture hadn't used it for hundreds of years . . . I found that the awareness of the real sources of power in the society, the consciousness of social inequalities, and the direct expression of sexuality in the black culture was so much closer to the American reality that I felt I somehow had to make people conscious of what these other voices were saying.

To that end, Charters set out to uncover the 'country blues', an intensely personal music that 'became the emotional outlet for Negro singers in every part of the South.' The term itself he appears to have hit upon in consultation with Ramsey, who used it in liner notes in the mid-1950s, but Charters gave it a new kind of prominence, raising it to the level of a brand name. At a fairly late stage in preparing his manuscript, he seems to have met up with Pete Whelan and other members of the Blues Mafia to listen to some of their rare recordings. But he was not really interested in rarities; his aim was to 'keep the focus where the black audience put it', and so he put most of his effort into recovering sales figures from the files of record companies and the industry trade press. The book that resulted barely mentioned Charley Patton, gave a bit more attention to Robert Johnson, but put the spotlight on Lonnie Johnson, Leroy Carr and Big Bill Broonzy, the musicians whose recordings black Americans of the 1930s had bought.

When the book was published to glowing reviews, with Charters lionised for recovering a forgotten art form, McKune was incensed. He contacted Trevor Benwell, publisher of the British-based collectors' magazine *VJM Palaver* (one of the few collectors' magazines to survive the 1950s) and offered to write a riposte. The result was a column pointedly entitled 'The Great Country Blues Singers', which would run intermittently until 1965. Its first instalment is as close as McKune ever got to issuing a manifesto. In its sheer manic fury, it is worth quoting at length.

Collectors of the Negro country blues singers should read this. Or they should have it pinned on them by others who read it.

This essay makes up for what Sam Charters did not say, or did not say fully enough, in his book *The Country Blues*.

At the end of his book Charters acknowledged that he had been helped by listening to the blues records of Pete Whelan, Pete Kaufman, Ben Kaplan. But nowhere did he admit that his book was disappointing to Whelan and to me, or that it might be disappointing to other fanciers of primitive Negro blues.

Do not think me only querulous. What Charters did for the authentic country blues singers, he did well. But he wrote many pages upon the popular blues singers, Blind Lemon Jefferson, Leroy Carr, Lonnie Johnson, Bill Broonzy, Brownie McGhee, Lightning Hopkins.

Jefferson is a country blues singer. He made many Paramount records. I have heard all but five. In my estimation, formed by listening to blues records since 1943,

Jefferson made only one record I can call *great*. That is 'Jack O' Diamonds/Chock House Blues', on Pm 12373.

Lightning Hopkins is a country blues singer today. But I doubt that his most fervent admirers would claim that he was Blind Lemon's equal. The other singers, above, extolled by Charters, *regardless of their sales*, are not country singers.

Charters wrote his book on the basis of record sales. This would, or might, be all right if his book were published for those Negroes, fifty years old or older, who could thereafter read all about the singers they listened to thirty years ago.

Few of these people have bought Charters's book. It has been bought mostly, I should guess, by blues collectors or by students of Negro folkways, *who might become blues collectors.*

This is my important point. I know twenty men who collect the Negro country blues. All of us have been interested in knowing who the *great* country blues singers are, not in who sold best.

On his own basis, best-selling blues singers, Charters may be all right. But I write for those who want a different basis for evaluating blues singers. This basis is their relative greatness, or competence, as country blues singers.

In obvious ways the column was an extended fit of pique. In McKune's eyes Charters was little more than an opportunist, a johnny-come-lately jazz enthusiast with no real knowledge of blues. Not even the visit to Whelan had helped, since (McKune claimed) Charters turned up only once his book was largely written, too late to incorporate anything he might learn. Yet beneath the wounded pride, the aggrieved territoriality, lay McKune's distaste for the whole premise of Charters's project: his decision to use the tastes of African American record buyers as a kind of aesthetic guide. McKune took it as given that the masses could not discriminate, and in his eyes it did not matter whether those masses were white or black. To think otherwise was to resurrect the most philistine brand of left-wing populism, to confuse solidarity with connoisseurship, to pose the appreciation of black music as a political act in itself. While Charters insisted on mining every moan or wail for its social significance ('hours in the hot sun, scraping at the earth, singing to make the hours pass'), the whole point of McKune's *VJM* columns was to evaluate the singers as artists. That, he insisted, was what would-be collectors of country blues needed: advice from experts who had been 'listening to blues records since 1943' and who possessed the training, the cultivation to understand 'greatness', to distinguish the pedestrian from the artful, the ersatz from the real.

To display that training and cultivation (and to expose Charters's mistakes), the Blues Mafia set out to make the truly great voices public. Sometime around 1960, Pete Whelan canvassed his fellow enthusiasts for the least battered copies of their most treasured 78s, hired a tape engineer, a partner with money and set about making taped reproductions. The long-playing albums that resulted began appearing in 1961 on an independent label that Whelan dubbed the Origins Jazz Library. As the name suggested, Whelan envisioned the LPs as a kind of reference collection of primordial sounds, the soil from which jazz sprang, primitive music as an art form in its own right. Just how inadequately Charters had performed his task the label made clear in its first two releases: OJL-1, devoted to Charley Patton, who Charters had wholly neglected; and OJL-2, an anthology of blues greats pointedly titled *Really! The Country Blues*. Wasn't Charters's country blues real? an interviewer asked Whelan twenty years later. 'It was real,' he responded. 'Just not real enough.'

The 'realness' of this 'country blues' lay in its unvarnished sound, its heated, primal emotion and the primitive character of the song form. As one fan of the OJL releases explained: 'The voice is dark and heavy, often thick and congested, with a peculiar crying quality . . . and suffused throughout with an emotional intensity that is all but overpowering (the words seem almost torn from the singer's throat).' These were barely songs at all – more a rhythmic wail of anguish, in which 'monosyllabic cries' expressing 'strong, uncontrollable feelings' often 'carr[ied] far greater meaning than do the song's words'. McKune had spent two decades honing those criteria for blues greatness. Alone in his room at the YMCA, playing his 78s at a low volume so as not to penetrate the building's thin walls, he listened out for spare, sparse music, oblique, poetic lyrics and voices that were unpolished and supercharged with raw emotion. Politics was absent from those recordings, at least on the surface. As he explained, 'After you've listened to the real Negro blues for a long time, you know at once that the protest of the blues is . . . [in the] accompanying piano or guitar,' not in anything as unsubtle as lyrics. 'Real Negro blues' could be recognised by its inimitable vocal: searing, primitive, yet wholly artless, marked by 'an intensity devoid of dramatic effects'. From voices like that McKune assembled a pantheon of 'great country blues singers' – anguished loners and wanderers like Skip James, Son House, Charley Patton and Robert Johnson, their very obscurity testament to their ferocious integrity, the rough, ragged intensity of the songs that they sang.

Issuing these voices on LP could conceivably end that obscurity, but none of the Mafia really expected the albums to sell. Origins Jazz Library was an attempt to preach to the near-converted, to guide the tastes of what they assumed would be a discerning few. Hence the forbidding title for the label, with the word 'Library' guaranteed to scare off the frivolous. Stephen Calt later estimated that about half of OJL's customers were Europeans, the other half a mix of seasoned collectors and young guitarists keen to broaden their repertoires. For OJL-2, *Really! The Country Blues*, Whelan ordered only 500 pressings, and it would take over two years for sales to exhaust that first batch.

Still, it was enough. Almost immediately, the OJL recordings became the bible of new, younger blues enthusiasts like John Fahey, often musicians themselves and entranced by the primitive voices, the scratched, grainy sound and the sense of acquiring secret know-ledge, of eschewing Charters's easy answers and participating in a vanguard. For the future *Deep Blues* author Robert Palmer, who encountered the albums as a musician in Memphis, they were 'the definitive country blues anthologies', a view also held by Jeff Todd Titon, whose exposure to the albums would lead him to study ethno-musicology and write the influential book *Early Downhome Blues*. Other fans included a young historian named Lawrence Levine, just completing his graduate work at Columbia and beginning the inves-tigations into African American folk songs that would result in *Black Culture, Black Consciousness*; Greil Marcus, who discovered the albums at his local record store in Berkeley; and veteran jazz collector Marshall Stearns, a musicologist and director of the Institute for Jazz Studies, which he helped to establish in 1953.

So intense was the country blues mania that even the Library of Congress took notice. In 1962 it released *Negro Blues and Hollers*, an LP compilation of the field recordings made by Alan Lomax, John Work and Lewis Jones in the Mississippi Delta in 1941 and 1942. To write the liner notes, they turned to Stearns, who approached the task with professorial gravitas, an air of establishing scholarly ortho-doxy in a field thick with debate. 'The kind of blues on the present recording, made in the early forties before they disappeared, have come to be called "country" blues – a name which has led to endless argument,' he began. 'Literature on the country blues is hard to come by,' he noted – Samuel Charters, though raising the form's public profile, had made only 'a beginning'. 'To get to the heart of the matter, one has to dig deeper': to the Origins Jazz Library reissues of country blues rarities, and to the 'unique articles' in *VJM Palaver* by 'James McCune [sic], the dean of country-blues fanciers'. The value of McKune's articles lay in dispensing with sociology to focus on the form's 'artistic merits'. Country blues recordings as he defined them were 'archaic in the best sense . . . gnarled, rough-hewn and eminently uncommercial'. In them one heard a music 'fixed in time and space', unaffected by technology or the market, 'tied down to – and unerr-ingly reflect[ing] – the geographic area, the local manners, and the exact vernacular of a specific place'. That specific place was the Mississippi Delta, which thanks to McKune we could now identify as the locus of blues authenticity, the land where the blues was born.

Stearns's liner notes brought McKune momentarily into the lime-light, the closest he would ever come to public recognition as a country blues expert. Yet they also contained the seeds of what would become a rebranding. By the late 1960s, the phrase 'country blues' being, it seems, too tainted by Charters's misapprehensions, aficionados relabelled the music 'Delta blues'. The phrase took on an added lustre in 1963 when Columbia reissued Robert Johnson's recordings on an LP entitled *King of the Delta Blues Singers*. Soon the idea that the Delta was the original home of the blues, that it generated a uniquely pure form of black music, came to seem incontestable; in time, even Samuel Charters agreed. Nowhere else in the South, he wrote in 1965, could have bred a music so raw, so primal, for nowhere else was so cut off from the currents of modern life. And nowhere else did racial oppression rule with such ferocity. In the Delta time had effectively stopped – it remained a quasi-feudal region still stuck in the dynamics of slavery. Those circumstances shaped the blues in its natural state, a music of peculiar power and purity, an intensely emotive, deeply personal song form permeated by alien-ation and pain.

At the heart of this story lay the venerable vision of the pure, uncorrupted black voice. That it could be found uniquely in the Mississippi Delta had never occurred even to as recent a blues enthu-siast as Frederic Ramsey, whose vision of a raw, archaic 'plantation blues' targeted the rural South as a whole. ('Don't know what the Delta along the way will hold,' he wrote to Moses Asch of Folkways Records as he prepared to travel there in 1954. 'Probably at least one good blues singer.') Nor did that tale of a 'Delta blues' emerge readily from what Lomax, Work and Jones found in the region in 1941, three years after the murder of Robert Johnson. Informant after informant attested that the region felt modern to those who lived in it, fast-paced and worldly, particularly in contrast to 'the Hills', the mountainous counties to the east, where families had deep roots in the soil and traditional mores seemed fully in force. In the Delta no one stayed in one place for long, and its young people were flouting tradition – moving around in search of better wages, scorning the church, experimenting with sex, immersing themselves in a mass-marketed world of automobiles, motion pictures and recorded music. Surveying the jukeboxes in the black bars of Clarksdale, Lewis Jones found no recordings by local musicians; the most popular tracks were those by Louis Jordan, Count Basie, Fats Waller, no different from Harlem or the South Side of Chicago. Lomax himself found modernity in the most unlikely places. Late one night outside the small hamlet of Friars Point he stumbled across a juke joint on the edge of a cotton field and opened the door to find a blaring jukebox and a roomful of people jitterbugging to Duke Ellington.

None of those developments could be accommodated in the revivalist vision of Delta blues. Still less could it accommodate Lewis Jones's conclusion that the Delta was home not to a pre-modern 'folk' or a tyrannised 'caste' but a 'rural proletariat'. With its suggestions of black resistance and its echoes of Popular Front radicalism, that phrase had no place in the revival. 'Pure blues', for the likes of McKune, took the form of voices that were searing, personal and apolitical. This would become one of the keynotes of the blues revival: real, authentic blues was not protest music. On this score, in time, even Samuel Charters came round. 'If the blues simply mirrored the protest of the moment they would finally have little more than an historical interest, like the songs of the suffragettes or the Grange movement,' he wrote in the wake of the OJL reissues. Instead, the Negro turned to the blues 'as the expression of his personal and immediate experience'. The result was 'a poetic language' that spoke of 'a larger human reality', timeless truths of alienation and loss.

When James McKune uncovered his forgotten voices, he took it for granted that all these singers were dead. His friend Harry Smith made the same assumption, and so did most of those who bought his *Anthology of American Folk Music*, issued on Folkways Records in

1952. 'All those guys on that Harry Smith Anthology were dead. *Had* to be,' one fan of the anthology remembers believing. Had to be, because those voices had been so fully appropriated, so thoroughly brought back to life. The country bluesman as McKune envisioned him was a man of fierce integrity, an heroic loner. That he could be encountered only on vinyl guaranteed that he would remain uncorrupted. After all, voices on record cannot talk back.

As it happened, however, they could. In June 1964, veteran Mafiosi Nick Perls made an astounding discovery: Son House was alive, aged somewhere in his seventies, living alone in a housing project in Rochester, New York. Within days, three other collectors uncovered the aged Skip James, alive, though not well, in Mississippi. Soon other aged bluesmen emerged from the woodwork and the Blues Mafia swung into action to engineer, publicise and manage their comebacks, setting up dates in the recording studio and tours on the coffee house and folk festival circuit.

In what seemed like an instant, the Delta blues acquired living, breathing embodiments. It is hard to know how to characterise what followed. Record collectors had fleshed out Delta blues as an unvarnished music 'of almost archaeological purity', as one enthusiast put it, and the men they rediscovered cooperated with the fantasy at least to the extent of appearing as old as the music was supposed to be. Most of the musicians welcomed the attention and performed with dignity, and at its best those comebacks succeeded in broadening white musical horizons, drawing new listeners to the blues who might not have taken an interest before.

At its worst, though, the blues revival took on the aura of a circus sideshow. Most of the resurrected heroes were well past their prime – Son House, in particular, was in an advanced stage of alcoholic deterioration – and none of them were prepared for this explosion of white interest in a music that African Americans had rejected long ago. Uneasy with the role they were allocated, they rarely played it as sincerely as their new audience imagined. Skip James, an immensely troubled man, made little effort to conceal his contempt for his new public. Contempt seemed the logical response for an audience that responded reverentially to third-rate performances, that seemed to be applauding not so much his talent but the spectacle of him making it through the song at all.

Skip James died in 1969; Son House, in failing health, retired a few years later, and with their disappearance the blues revival moved back to the disused recordings that first gave it life. By the late 1960s, LP anthologies of blues reissues were released by major industry players like Columbia and small labels like Yazoo, Roots and Arhoolie. No longer did searching for country blues mean relying on trading networks or scavenging in second-hand stores. In a sense it was the story of the New Orleans revival all over again. Yet while reissues of New Orleans jazz rarities in the early 1950s had sent the prices of 78s into a nosedive, in the case of Delta blues reissues, the prices of 78s began to rise. As early as 1963, James McKune was being forced to exceed his three-dollar limit and bid upwards of fifteen dollars per record. By the end of the decade a rare Charley Patton could fetch seventy dollars, and after that into the hundreds and thousands, unimaginably beyond what the likes of McKune could afford.

In a way, this was McKune's own doing, for his approach to collecting had always diverged from that of the *Jazzmen* set. Collecting race records in an era when 78s were still manufactured, Ramsey and Russell had searched for artists, not objects, and if necessary they were content with reissues: their interest lay, by and large, with the music, and they were relatively unconcerned with the medium by which it was conveyed. In contrast, McKune and his acolytes 'cherished the physical symbols' (as one collector put it), the sheer materiality of the original 78s. Already on the wane in the late 1940s, the 78 format vanished altogether by the early 1950s, and for the Blues Mafia that obsolescence was part of the lure. They prized the visible, palpable oddity of what Whelan described as 'the rarest labels in the record collecting fraternity: Autograph (red or light blue with nautical checked border), Black Patti (purple with golden peacock that has a monstrous tail), Electrobeam Gennett (black with Old English lettering), Merrit (purple or black with agonised Greek death masks), Paramount (black, purple, blue; gold eagle holds the world in its talons.' This, he observed, was 'what record collecting intrigue is all about – the music has to be good; beyond that, it is the label and how it LOOKS: the naive 1920s Cheltenham, Broadway, or Gaudy typefaces and 30-year-old colors that would be too expensive to color-match and print today.'

Inextricable from that romance with the obsolescence of the physical object was a sense of the disc as a unique, handcrafted work of art. As the Mafiosi practised it, Whelan once observed, 'record collecting was not like collecting stamps. It was more like collecting paintings'. McKune's passion for the obscure helped erase the discs's standardised, mass-market beginnings: they had effectively dropped out of the commercial nexus, since everyone had rejected them, African Americans and jazz collectors alike. And while they were mechanically recorded, they had something of the handmade about them. Used 78s were dusty, battered and scratched – they had been heavily handled, if not made by hand – and had been recorded on primitive equipment under poor conditions. (Robert Johnson, for example, made his recordings in makeshift studios in a Dallas warehouse and a San Antonio hotel room.) Indeed, part of the appeal of McKune's 'great country blues singers' may have been the very murkiness of the sound quality. In other words, far from destroying the mystery of black singing, recording technology conveyed and conferred it, creating discs whose voices sounded peculiar and striking, muffled and contorted by the machine. It was perhaps no accident that he reserved his highest praise for Charley Patton, whose recordings are virtually unintelligible, owing in part to Patton's slurred delivery but largely to the 'scratches, pops, clicks and hiss' that abound on his surviving 78s. Those layers of surface noise only intensified Patton's aura of mystery, the magic to be found in those blank, black platters whose spiral grooves, once set in motion, released haunting echoes from another world.

In the decades since the blues revival, blues chroniclers have fleshed out the narrative the Mafia first sketched, disentangling the blues from politics, sex, the lore of the city and all suggestions of modernity. Not everyone has approved of the result. 'There is an honest and laudable interest in alleviating Negro suffering or at least mak[ing] it known to the world in every blues book,' the ethnomusicologist Charles Keil remarked. 'Yet I can almost imagine some of these writers helping to set up a "reservation" or Bantustan for old bluesmen; it is often that sort of liberalism.' Revivalists privileged an obsolete form of rural black culture in an era when most African Americans lived in cities, and toward contemporary black music they displayed at best ambivalence, more often hostility. That kind of purism has led some black musicians to a blunt conclusion: whites are prepared to laud black creativity only when it is old and decrepit. As blues singer and guitarist Lonnie Johnson put it when Keil approached him for an interview: 'Are you another one of those guys who wants to put crutches under my ass?'

Yet such scepticism has proven remarkably muted, outweighed by the power of the Delta blues story, a narrative summed up by those hardbitten black faces adorning album covers and book jackets, those unflinching black loners posed before ramshackle cabins, arid fields or empty highways stretching off into nowhere. In the end, that story even won over Alan Lomax. By the time he wrote his magnum opus on African American music, *The Land Where the Blues Began*, in 1993, he had almost wholly discarded the focus on social conflict and change that had once led him to Jelly Roll Morton. If in 1938 Morton's blues had provided 'a rich evocation of underground America', in 1993 they were commercial, superficial, and as such not genuine: 'the blues of the professional jazzman are never quite the real thing'. The real thing was the blues of the Delta, a personal music of torment and pain, a sorrow song that had gained a wide resonance as the bluesman's 'anomie and alienation, orphaning and rootlessness' became key themes of late-twentieth-century life.

Part of the explanation for that story's power lies in the ambiguities that suffused it. If blues revivalists' accounts stressed alienation and anguish, they were not wholly untouched by the erotic. In their celebration of blues poetry's profoundly personal character, its expression of intense inner feeling, enthusiasts infused their romance with the unfettered self with a highly charged sense of the supreme realness of rural black men. A defiant drifter, scorning convention, breaking free from domestic ties, the bluesman embodied the tensions about modern masculinity that from its earliest stirrings in the 1950s simmered beneath the surface of the blues revival. It is surely no accident that so many of the early blues performers that revivalists scorned as inauthentic were women; to them, authenticity had a male voice. In an era of grey flannel suits, backyard barbecues and tract homes in the suburbs, bluesmen were non-conformists par excellence: 'self-made outcasts' as Frederic Ramsey put it in *Been Here and Gone*, 'who prefer this life of impermanence . . . [who] found that the road, which offered adventure, was better than their homes, which offered nothing.' Their authenticity took its power from their stark contrast with the likes of Pat Boone and Bobby Darin dominating the era's bland mass-market pop and with the images of domestic contentment and sober white-collar respectability that pervaded America in the Cold War era.

In that sense, the blues revival stands alongside the Beat movement as an opening salvo of what Barbara Ehrenreich has termed the male 'flight from commitment' that percolated through postwar American culture. What united both movements was their almost exclusively male constituency and their romance with outsider manhood, with defiant black men who seemed to scorn the suburban breadwinner's stifling, soul-destroying routine. For revivalists, that model was the country bluesman, at heart a 'beggar, outcast, near criminal'; for Beats, it was the black urban jazzman, 'a frontiersman in the Wild West of American nightlife' as Norman Mailer described him, who had taken the only route possible if one was to find authenticity in a conformist world: 'to divorce oneself from society, to exist without roots, to set out on that uncharted journey into the rebellious imperatives of the self.'

More than any other commentator, Mailer captured the intensely wrought fantasies that fuelled the Beat romance with black style. For the Beat, the black man was a deeply sexual existential outlaw, a renegade who lived for sex alone.

> Knowing in the cells of his existence that life was war, nothing but war, the Negro (all exceptions admitted) could rarely afford the sophisticated inhibitions of civilisation, and so he kept for his survival the art of the primitive, he lived in the enormous present, he subsisted for his Saturday-night kicks, relinquishing the pleasures of the mind for the more obligatory pleasures of the body, and in his music he gave voice to the character and quality of his existence, to his rage, and the infinite variations of joy, lust, languor, growl, cramp, pinch, scream and despair of his orgasm.

The blues revivalist romance was kinder, gentler, but it was none the less enthralled by the primitive. Revivalists eschewed Mailer's urban underworld for a setting altogether closer to nature. And while they had little taste for music that gave voice to the cramp, pinch and scream of the orgasm, there is no denying the erotic charge of the bluesmen whose portraits dominate blues literature. Look, for example, at the tough, callused black hands minutely detailed in Frederic Ramsey's photographs. Or consider this passage from *The Land Where the Blues Began*, in which Alan Lomax recalls a 1941 session with Son House:

> His voice, guttural and hoarse with passion, ripped apart the surface of the music like his tractor-driven deep plow ripped apart the wet black earth in the springtime, making the sap of the earth song run, while his powerful, work-hard hands snatched strange chords out of the steel strings the way they had snatched so many tons of cotton out of brown thorny cotton bolls in the fall. And with him the sorrow of the blues was

not tentative, or retiring, or ironic. Son's whole body wept, as with his eyes closed, the tendons in his powerful neck standing out with the violence of his feeling and his brown face flushing, he sang in an awesome voice the 'Death Letter Blues'.

But in characterising this romance as primitivist, I do not mean to dismiss it as mere macho posing. As drawn by revivalists, the bluesman could swagger, but he could also be vulnerable, and it was his vulnerability – Son House's weeping body – that drew them most profoundly into his music. Embedded in their search for the authentic was a sensitivity to emotion, a desire to be deeply moved by manifestations of inner feeling. In their hands, the search for authentic black voices was a spiritual quest infused with what for men were forbidden desires: to dissolve boundaries, renounce autonomy, merge with the wellsprings of life. Revivalists channelled that search for life sources into the blues and in the process remade the tradition. At their most positive, they enriched understanding and broadened white horizons. At their worst, they fed on what Luc Sante has described as 'a kind of colonial sentimentalism', an eroticisation of African American despair.

Today the building that once housed the Williamsburg YMCA stands in a state of neglect and decay. On the day I visited, I almost did not find it. The Marcy Avenue BMT stop was closed for repairs, so I got off one stop down the line at Hewes Street and walked back in the opposite direction, past a synagogue, a Muslim community centre, a bakery specialising in matzos, and signs for cheap health care in English and Spanish. On Marcy Avenue I found a sea of unfamiliar street numbers, 179 nowhere among them, so I sought help in a corner grocery, where the cashier told me that the street had been renumbered and pointed me in the right direction. That the building was once a YMCA is discernible only by the crest over the door – the organisation moved out long ago, apparently sometime in the 1980s. What had once been the front entrance is boarded up; through a side door visitors have access to the City of New York Human Resources Administration, the North Brooklyn Food Stamp Center and a branch of the Church of Jesus Christ of the Latter Day Saints. I wandered into the lobby, but it was empty and soulless, so I went back outside and crossed the road and stood on the corner opposite, looking up at the top-floor windows and trying to imagine my way inside.

As much as Son House or Charley Patton, as much as even Robert Johnson, James McKune, in the end, is the enigma at the heart of the Delta blues, enigmatic not least because he falls so abruptly out of its story. Though his protégés succeeded brilliantly at pushing his aesthetic into the spotlight, apart from the columns in *VJM Palaver* McKune himself played no direct part in the process. He wrote no liner notes, managed no artists, set up no record labels, opened no blues clubs. Instead, he seems to have stopped listening to music altogether. His *VJM* columns, always sporadic, ceased in 1965, and sometime that year he moved out of the Williamsburg YMCA for a room in a Manhattan hostel near 34th Street. Eventually he drifted to the Lower East Side and found a room at the Broadway Central Hotel, once an elegant watering hole but now gone to seed. Though the lower floors retained a kind of lowlife glamour – home to the Mercer Arts Center, a gathering place for New York's nascent punk underground, where by 1973 the New York Dolls would be in residence – McKune settled on the floors above, given over to single rooms inhabited by junkies, hookers and derelicts, into whose ranks he quietly slid. Reports of acquaintances who occasionally spotted him suggest that he used his room only infrequently; mostly, he lived on the streets. When police found his body in September 1971, the only clue to his earlier life lay in a letter in the room from Bernie Klatzko, one of the stalwarts of the Blues Mafia. There was no trace of a record collection: McKune had either sold it or given it away.

Perhaps McKune's abandonment of the blues was inevitable. He had always had a fervent sense of his own importance, an unswerving belief in his aesthetic judgements and a taste for enveloping himself in mystery. Making himself elusive was a way of emphasising his maverick status, the singularity of his aesthetic judgements, the cutting-edge character of his musical tastes. In the end, he was a preacher who feared converts, who proselytised passionately for his salvaged recordings but lost interest once others caught on. The pleasures of collecting lie in creating a personal system, an alternative universe of aesthetics and taste. Lose control of that universe and the collector's pride and bravado become envy and frustration; his excitement and euphoria become depression and despair. Perhaps McKune's story illuminates the dark side of collecting, the devastation of the connoisseur who finds that his private passion is private no longer, that his role as a taste-maker has been usurped.

The biographer Hermione Lee has spoken of the writer's temptation, when coming to the end of a work of biography, to try to bring that life to a poetic conclusion, to try to make the death in some way sum it up. Most likely we will never know what propelled McKune into his fascination with blues, but it is hard not to speculate about how his aesthetic resonated with his inner needs. McKune dedicated his life to finding a blues voice that was intense, raw, defiantly marginal, and he ended his days as a homeless, friendless wanderer, dying in circumstances as violent, mysterious and sexually charged as Robert Johnson himself. It is perhaps too pat, but not wholly unjustified, to leave McKune down and out on Skid Row clinging fiercely to his blues vision – living the life of the alienated drifter, scorning the pull of the marketplace, uncorrupted to the very end.

Acknowledgements

This book began in my imagination as a biography of Little Richard. That it became something very different owes a lot to my agent David Godwin, whose readings of my earliest drafts encouraged me to push my ideas to the foreground and follow them where they wanted to lead. My editor at Jonathan Cape, Dan Franklin, believed in this book early on, was patient while I reworked it and made incisive comments in the concluding stages. At Basic Books, Lara Heimert's enthusiasm cheered me through the final revisions.

I was helped in my research by financial assistance from the British Academy, the Leverhulme Trust, and Birkbeck College, and by the knowledge and expertise of the staff of several archives: the Archive of Folk Culture, Library of Congress; the Southern Historical Collection, University of North Carolina at Chapel Hill; the Center for American History, University of Texas at Austin; the Special Collections Library at Baylor University; the Blues Archive, University of Mississippi; the Moorland-Spingarn Research Center, Howard University; the Special Collections Library, Fisk University; the Ralph Rinzler Folklife Archives and Collections at the Smithsonian Center for Folklife and Cultural Heritage; the Beinecke Library, Yale University; the Institute of Jazz Studies, Rutgers University; and the Alan Lomax Archive at Hunter College (much of which is now held at the Library of Congress). Ruth Beecher's research assistance brought me fresh material on Alan Lomax. Mary Frances Odum Schinhan, Anna Lomax Wood, and Alida Ramsey Porter and Martha Ramsey kindly shared their memories of their fathers and allowed me to see unpublished papers. Pete Whelan, Dick Spottswood and Henry Renard gave me wonderful material about blues record collecting and shared their recollections of James McKune.

Alison Light deserves thanks beyond measure for reading every word of this manuscript in its many incarnations. Her imagination, insight and daring shaped it throughout. Hera Cook helped the book to get off the ground and stepped in again in the final stages, and I benefited greatly from her smart, critical readings. At a crucial moment, Barbara Taylor offered to read the whole manuscript; without her help I would probably still be working on it. For debate, suggestions, encouragement and enthusiasm, a thousand thanks too to Paul Anderson, Robert Cantwell, John Carson, Tim Dee, David Feldman, Eric Hobsbawm, Rebecca Lemov, W. T. Lhamon, Peter Mandler, Greil Marcus, Daniel Rodgers, Luc Sante, Matt Seaton, Christine Stansell and Sean Wilentz.

Ken Arnold read endless drafts, wrote up voluminous comments, talked, argued, and listened to more Delta blues than he ever wanted to hear. Jackson Arnold and Lukas Hamilton made the book worth writing, and certainly worth finishing. This is for them, with love.

Notes

Chapter One: The Delta Revisited

1 **the opening years of the blues revival:** Although the
cultural roots of the blues revival have received little attention
from historians, some useful studies of the revival itself have
begun to appear. See Jeff Todd Titon, 'Reconstructing the
Blues: Reflections on the 1960s Blues Revival', in Neil V.
Rosenberg, ed., *Transforming Tradition: Folk Music Revivals
Examined* (Urbana: University of Illinois Press, 1993),
220–40; Jim O'Neal, 'I Once Was Lost, But Now I'm Found:
the Blues Revival of the 1960s', in Lawrence Cohn, ed.,
Nothing But the Blues: the Music and the Musicians (New
York: Abberville Press, 1993), 347–87; Stephen Calt, *I'd
Rather Be the Devil: Skip James and the Blues* (New York: Da
Capo Press, 1994); and Elijah Wald, *Escaping the Delta:
Robert Johnson and the Invention of the Delta Blues* (New
York: Amistad, 2004).

   ninety per cent of the Delta was covered in swamps:
James C. Cobb, *The Most Southern Place on Earth: the
Mississippi Delta and the Roots of Regional Identity* (New
York: Oxford University Press, 1992), viii.

2 **'Nowhere in Mississippi have antebellum conditions of
landholding':** quoted in Cobb, *The Most Southern Place on
Earth*, 98.

   the anthropologists who flocked to the region in the mid-

1930s: John Dollard, *Caste and Class in a Southern Town* (New Haven: Yale University Press, 1937); Hortense Powdermaker, *After Freedom: A Cultural Study in the Deep South* (New York: Atheneum, 1969, originally published 1939); Allison Davis, Burleigh B. Gardner and Mary R. Gardner, *Deep South: A Social Anthropological Study of Caste and Class* (Chicago: University of Chicago Press, 1941).
'Rough, spontaneous, crude and unfinished': Pete Welding, 'Stringin' the Blues: the Art of Folk Blues Guitar', *Down Beat* (1 July 1965), 22. See also Samuel Charters, *The Bluesmen* (New York: Music Sales Corp., 1967), 27-32.

3   **commercial land clearance**: On the Delta as a postbellum, industrial product, see Cobb, *The Most Southern Place on Earth*.

4   **'the very idea of America'**: Greil Marcus, *Mystery Train: Images of America in Rock'n'Roll Music* (London: Penguin Books, 1991, originally published 1975), 39.

5   **'a world without salvation, redemption, or rest'**: ibid., 21.
'made the terrors of the world . . . more real': ibid., 29.
'a two-minute image of doom': ibid., 33.
the release of 'Crazy Blues' by Mamie Smith: See, for example, Francis Davis, *The History of the Blues* (London: Secker and Walberg, 1995), chapter two; William Barlow, *Looking Up at Down: the Emergence of Blues Culture* (Philadelphia: Temple University Press, 1989), chapter five; Lawrence Levine, *Black Culture, Black Consciousness: Afro-American Folk Thought from Slavery to Freedom* (New York: Oxford University Press, 1977), 225–7.

7   **'more vividly and more intensely than any mere poet'**: Leon Litwack, *Trouble in Mind: Black Southerners in the Age of Jim Crow* (New York: Knopf, 1998), 457.

8   **'How much history can be transmitted by pressure on a guitar string?'**: ibid., xvii.
'to touch what the Folk naively touched, to feel what they

felt': Hillel Schwartz, *The Culture of the Copy: Striking Likenesses, Unreasonable Facsimiles* (New York: Zone Books, 1998), 374.

Charley Patton's recordings sold only moderately: Robert Palmer, *Deep Blues: a Musical and Cultural History of the Mississippi Delta* (New York: Penguin, 1981), 123–4.

9   **A Fisk University sociologist:** 'List of records on machines in Clarksdale amusement places', Folder 7 (Lists), Fisk University Mississippi Delta Collection, Archive of Folk Culture, Library of Congress, Washington, DC. The list, compiled by sociologist Lewis Jones, dates from 1941 or 1942.

'almost archaeological purity': *Atlantic Monthly* (1961), quoted in Calt, *I'd Rather Be the Devil*, 218.

'rough, spontaneous, crude and unfinished': Welding, 'Stringin' the Blues', *Down Beat*, 22.

'any distance between the singer and the listener is smashed': Marcus, *Mystery Train*, 32.

11   **'You couldn't get anything on Paramount':** Stephen Calt and Gayle Dean Wardlow, 'The Buying and Selling of Paramounts – Part 3' *78 Quarterly* 1, no. 5 (1990), 8.

what the Edison Corporation had found a few years before: Emily Thompson, 'Machines, Music, and the Quest for Fidelity: Marketing the Edison Phonograph in America, 1877–1925', *The Musical Quarterly* 79 (1995), 131–71.

'the mechanical, nickel phonograph': Quoted in Levine, *Black Culture, Black Consciousness*, 231.

'No, ma'am, they don't make up many songs': Zora Neale Hurston, 'Turpentine', in Pamela Bordelon, ed., *Go Gator and Muddy the Water: Writings by Zora Neale Hurston from the Federal Writers Project* (New York: W. W. Norton, 1999), 129.

12   **'Enclosed find all of the material that I have transcribed into ink':** Hurston to Franz Boas, 29 March 1927, reprinted in Carla Kaplan, ed., *Zora Neale Hurston: a Life in Letters* (New York: Doubleday, 2002), 96–7.

'The bulk of the population spends its leisure': Quoted in
Robert Hemenway, *Zora Neale Hurston: a Literary Biography*
(Urbana: University of Illinois Press, 1977), 92.

'There was a valley . . . with smoke-wreaths during the
day and mist at night': Jean Toomer, 'Autobiographical
Selection', in Toomer, *Cane: An Authoritative Text,
Backgrounds, Criticism*, ed. Darwin T. Turner (New York:
W. W. Norton), 141–2.

'The supreme fact of mechanical civilisation': Toomer to
Waldo Frank, late 1922/early 1923, in Toomer, *Cane: An
Authoritative Text*, 151.

13   'lush glades of primitive imagination': Hurston, 'Go Gator
and Muddy the Water', in Bordelon, *Go Gator and Muddy the
Water*, 69.

the 'aura' of the work of art: Walter Benjamin, 'The Work
of Art in the Age of Mechanical Reproduction' (1936), in
Walter Benjamin, *Illuminations* (New York: Schocken Books,
1969), 221.

'quality of intensity': Miles Orvell, *The Real Thing:
Imitation and Authenticity in American Culture, 1880–1940*
(Chapel Hill: University of North Carolina Press, 1989), xvi.

'There is an enemy at the doors of folk-music': Hubert
Parry, 'Inaugural address to the Folk Song Society', *Journal of
the Folk Song Society* 1 (1899), 2–3, quoted in Richard
Middleton, *Studying Popular Music* (Milton Keynes: Open
University Press, 1990), 131.

14   'Rude and apparently incoherent': Frederick Douglass,
*Narrative of the Life of Frederick Douglass, An American
Slave, Written by Himself* (New York: Signet Books, 1968,
originally published 1845), 31–2.

'that life was joyous to the black slave, careless and
happy': W. E. B. DuBois, *The Souls of Black Folk* (1903), in
John Hope Franklin, ed., *Three Negro Classics* (New York:
Avon Books, 1965), 380.

'death and suffering and unvoiced longing toward a truer
world': ibid., 380.

'men will judge men by their souls and not by their
skins': ibid., 386.

'There is no true American music': ibid., 220.

'All in all, we black men seem the sole oasis of simple
faith': ibid., 220.

15   'a new analytical way of listening to music': Ralph Ellison,
Invisible Man (New York: Vintage Books, 1972, originally
published 1952), 8.

'long, lonely sing-song of the fields': Charles Peabody, 'Notes
on Negro Music', *Journal of American Folklore* 16 (1903), 152.
On the cult of the spirituals, see Jon Cruz, *Culture on the
Margins: the Black Spiritual and the Rise of American Cultural
Interpretation* (Princeton: Princeton University Press, 1999); and
Ronald Radano, 'Denoting Difference: the Writing of Slave
Spirituals', *Critical Inquiry* 22 (1996), 506–54.

'It is difficult to express the entire character': Lucy
McKim, 'Songs of the Port Royal Contrabands', *Dwight's
Journal of Music* XXI, 8 November 1862, reprinted in Bruce
Jackson, ed., *The Negro and his Folklore in Nineteenth-
century Periodicals* (Austin: University of Texas Press, 1967),
62.

16   'The best we can do . . . with paper and types, or even
with voices': William Francis Allen, Charles Pickard Ware
and Lucy McKim Garrison, eds., *Slave Songs of the United
States* (New York: A. Simpson & Co., 1867), iv-v.

'Never, it seems to me, since man first lived and suffered':
Thomas Wentworth Higginson, 'Negro Spirituals', *Atlantic
Monthly* 19 (June 1867), reprinted in Jackson, ed., *The Negro
and his Folklore*, 92.

white listeners could absorb it and experience something
of the sublime: Radano, 'Denoting Difference', 518–19.

17   'the whites of the South to keep *one* bunch of Negroes':

Quoted in Deborah Kodish, *Good Friends and Bad Enemies: Robert Winslow Gordon and the Study of American Folksong* (Urbana: University of Illionis Press, 1986), 140.

'When black takes on the prowlings and pratings of the white race': Review of Howard Odum and Guy Johnson, *The Negro and his Songs*, in *Memphis Commercial Appeal*, undated clipping in file labelled *'Negro and His Songs* (1925): Clippings', in Box 22, Howard Washington Odum Papers, Southern Historical Collection, Wilson Library, University of North Carolina at Chapel Hill.

Chapter Two: Impartial Testimony

19 **'one night in Tutwiler':** W. C. Handy, *Father of the Blues* (New York: Da Capo Press, 1991; originally published 1941), 78.

21 **'Suffering and hard luck were the midwives':** ibid., 76.
    David Evans even speculates: David Evans, *Big Road Blues: Tradition and Creativity in the Folk Blues* (New York: Da Capo Press, 1982), 174–5.

22 **a bespectacled twenty-three-year-old, Howard Odum:** My account of Howard Odum's early life draws on Daniel Joseph Singal, *The War Within: From Victorian to Modernist Thought in the South, 1919–1945* (Chapel Hill: University of North Carolina Press, 1982), 115–52; and Wayne Brazil, *Howard W. Odum: The Building Years* (New York: Taylor & Francis, 1988).

23 **'in and out across swollen streams and backwoods and pinehills'; 'I myself have known Yoknapatawpha':** Howard Odum, 'On Southern Literature and Southern Culture', in Louis D. Rubin Jr, and Robert D. Jacobs, *Southern Renascence: the Literature of the Modern South* (Baltimore: Johns Hopkins Press, 1953), 97.
    Comprising forty-five per cent of the county's population:

On Lafayette County, see Joel Williamson, *William Faulkner and Southern History* (New York: Oxford University Press, 1993), 153. On Reconstruction, see Eric Foner, *Reconstruction: America's Unfinished Revolution, 1863–1877* (New York: Harper & Row, 1988).

24   'If necessary every Negro in the state will be lynched': quoted in Neil McMillen, *Dark Journey: Black Mississippians in the Age of Jim Crow* (Urbana: University of Illinois Press, 1989), 6–7. For life under Jim Crow more generally, see Litwack, *Trouble in Mind*; Joel Williamson, *The Crucible of Race: Black/White Relations in the American South since Emancipation* (New York: Oxford University Press, 1984); C. Van Woodward, *The Strange Career of Jim Crow* (New York: Oxford University Press, 1957).

25   'slipped off and went home': Howard Odum, *An American Epoch: Southern Portraiture in the National Picture* (New York: Henry Holt & Company, 1930), 88.
'his broad forehead moist with perspiration': ibid., 88.

26   'what I designated as AIUP': Howard Odum, untitled address circa 1954, held in 'Odum Manuscripts' file, Box 73, Howard Washington Odum Papers (hereafter HWOP), Manuscripts Department, Library of the University of North Carolina at Chapel Hill.
'Science, and science alone, star-eyed science': Thomas Pearce Bailey, *Race Orthodoxy in the South and Other Aspects of the Negro Question* (New York: The Neale Publishing Company, 1914), 58.
'Does the Negro show potentialities as a race?': ibid., 380.

27   'the physical stock of the higher racial types': ibid., 94.
'Is the Negro really adaptable, or is he parasitic?': ibid., 380–1.
'The Negro has a life and an environment of his own': Howard Odum, *Social and Mental Traits of the Negro* (New York: Columbia University, 1910), 13.

'what he *is* rather than what he appears to be': Howard Odum, 'Religious Folk Songs of the Southern Negroes', *American Journal of Religious Psychology and Education* III (July 1909), reprinted in Katharine Jocher et al, *Folk, Region and Society: Selected Papers of Howard Odum* (Chapel Hill: University of North Carolina Press, 1964), 8.

sociologist William Graham Sumner's 1906 book *Folkways*: For a discussion of the influence of the concept of 'folkways' on Odum's thought, see Daniel T. Rodgers, 'Regionalism and the Burdens of Progress', in J. Morgan Kousser and James M. McPherson, eds., *Region, Race and Reconstruction* (New York: Oxford University Press, 1982), 3–26.

29   'impartial testimony': Odum, 'Religious Folk Songs', 8.

Odum had read the rapturous accounts of the spirituals: Odum discusses the Northern accounts of the spirituals in 'Religious Folk Songs', 6–8. He quotes from the final chapter of *The Souls of Black Folk* in an extraordinary passage in *Social and Mental Traits of the Negro* in which he indicts Negro song for obscenity: 'With the gifted music physicians, musicianers and songsters, a vast throng "swelling with song – instinct with life, tremulous treble and darkening bass", with the "gift of story and song", comes also the inexpressible wilderness of vulgarity and indecency' (166). At no point does he identify the text or the author he is quoting here; clearly, DuBois's book was too threatening to acknowledge by name.

'at all manner of occasions, from funerals to yachting parties': William E. Barton, *Old Plantation Hymns* (New York: AMS Press, 1972; originally published 1899), 3.

'the truest representation of the Negro's real self': Odum, 'Religious Folk Songs', 7.

'have commonly been accepted as the characteristic music of the race': ibid.

30   'We will be able to preserve and hear again': Thomas

Edison, 'The Phonograph and Its Future', *North American Review* 126 (May-June 1878), 530–6.

'I don't want the phonograph sold for amusement purposes, it is not a toy': Quoted in Oliver Read and Walter L. Welch, *From Tin Foil to Stereo: Evolution of the Phonograph* (Indianapolis: Bobbs-Merrill 1976), 55.

the new scholarly disciplines of social science: On the use of the phonograph as an ethnographic tool, see Erika Brady, *A Spiral Way: How the Phonograph Changed Ethnography* (Jackson: University of Mississippi Press, 1999).

31   'The apparatus proves to be a means by which the actual sound itself': Quoted in Brady, *A Spiral Way*, 81.

'notes between the notes': Michael Chanan, *Repeated Takes: A Short History of Recording and its Effects on Music* (London: Verso, 1995), 10.

32   'of high adventure and dedicated scholarship': Mickey Hart, *Songcatchers: In Search of the World's Music* (Washington: National Geographic, 2003), from book jacket blurb.

The purpose of fieldwork, as Boas conceived it: Brady, *A Spiral Way*, 52–88; George W. Stocking, 'Introduction', to Stocking, ed., *A Franz Boas Reader: The Shaping of American Anthropology 1883-1911* (Chicago: University of Chicago Press, 1974), 1–20; George W. Stocking, *The Ethnographer's Magic and Other Essays in the History of Anthropology* (Madison: University of Wisconsin Press, 1992); Richard Handler, 'Boasian Anthropology and the Critique of American Culture', *American Quarterly* 42 (June 1990), 252–73.

black Americans did not have culture patterns: For reflections on this point, see Sidney Mintz, 'Foreword', in Norman E. Whitten Jr and John F. Szwed, eds., *Afro-American Anthropology: Contemporary Perspectives* (New York: The Freee Press 1970), 1–16.

Howard Odum, it seems, was the first: John H. Cowley, 'Don't Leave Me Here: Non-commercial Blues: the Field Trips, 1924-60', in Cohn, ed., *Nothing But the Blues*, 265-311. Certainty on this point is impossible, since few folk-lorists or ethnographers left written accounts of their collection process, and (at least before the 1920s) they were far less concerned than one might have expected with preserving the recordings they made. Cylinder recordings were valued primarily as aids to transcription, as tools for constructing a model of how song, story or narrative forms operated in particular cultures, and once transcription was completed the cylinder's wax surface was often scraped smooth for reuse – no more valuable, writes Erika Brady, than steno pads after a letter has been sent. See Brady, *A Spiral Way*, 62.

33 'music physicianers', 'musicianers' and 'songsters': Howard Odum, 'Folk-Song and Folk-Poetry as Found in the Secular Songs of the Southern Negroes', *Journal of American Folklore* XXIV (July-September 1911), 259.

'I'm po' boy long way from home': ibid., 270.

'coon songs', 'rag times', 'knife songs', 'devil songs', 'breakdowns': ibid., 260.

34 'LINES AND TITLES OF SONGS COLLECTED TWENTY YEARS AGO': Howard Odum and Guy Johnson, *Negro Workaday Songs* (Chapel Hill: University of North Carolina Press, 1926), 24–5.

35 'mind's eye': Mary Frances Odum Schinhan, letter to the author, 15 June 2001.

'We should all try to discharge our duty': Calendar entry for 3 January 1907, found in folder 842, HWOP.

'an independent ethics of vagrancy': Odum, *Social and Mental Traits*, 220.

'The Negro has little home conscience or love of home': ibid., 343.

36   'Filth and uncleanness is everywhere predominant':
     ibid., 160.
     'openly descriptive of the grossest immorality', 'vicious
     and obscene', 'rotten with filth': ibid., 166.
     'The student finds difficulty': ibid., 19.

37   **Odum had an encounter:** Odum first raised the possibility
     of a book on Left Wing Gordon in a letter to H. L. Mencken
     (19 June 1925, HWOP). In *Negro Workaday Songs*, which
     included a brief portrait of Gordon, he described him as 'very
     real', but in time he began to equivocate. After the publica-
     tion of *Rainbow Round My Shoulder*, he claimed that Gordon
     was a composite portrait of several real-life labourers. Nearer
     the end of his life, when asked if Gordon had genuinely
     existed, he replied, 'What difference does it make?' Guy
     Johnson and Guion Griffis Johnson, *Research in Service to
     Society: the First Fifty Years of the Institute for Research in
     Social Science at the University of North Carolina* (Chapel
     Hill: University of North Carolina Press, 1980), 137.
     **the Negro's own story, the autobiography of the Negro
     supertramp':** D. L. Chambers to Odum, 7 January 1928,
     HWOP.
     **'exactly as given', 'all pictures, all concreteness', an
     'untouched phototype':** Odum to Chambers, 6 January 1927
     and 4 January 1928, HWOP.
     dictating in his office for hours at a stretch: Odum's
     stream-of-consciousness method of composition is described
     in Brazil, *The Building Years*, 591.
     'folk blues': Odum and Johnson, *Negro Workaday Songs*,
     17–34.

38   **'Good Lawd, I can't be satisfied':** Howard Odum, *Rainbow
     Round My Shoulder: the Blue Trail of Black Ulysses*
     (Cincinnati: Bobbs-Merrill, 1928), 319–20.
     **'so strange and varied as to reveal a sort of superhuman
     evidence of the folk soul':** ibid., 254.

'There will be the folk blues': Odum and Johnson, *Negro Workaday Songs*, 34.

39 'All manner of "ragtimes", "coon-songs", and the latest "hits"': Odum, 'Folk-Song and Folk-Poetry', 259.

'the young Negro who wished to call out his name': ibid., 262.

'soft, stirring melodies of a folklife': Odum, *Social and Mental Traits*, 167.

Chapter Three: On the Trail of Negro Folk Songs

40 **The moment when her search first came to fruition:** Dorothy Scarborough interviewed John Wyeth in 1921 on a Sunday evening in late April or early May. She did not leave a detailed account of her visit (though she noted Wyeth's cane and his broken hip), so in this first section my account of the interview is drawn from her scattered remarks in *On the Trail*, Wyeth's autobiography *With Sabre and Scalpel* and a letter Scarborough wrote days later to Thomas Nelson Page (one of the only letters from her to be found in her papers at Baylor). The decor of Wyeth's home and his manner in beginning their interview are my invention, drawing on biographical details and photographs included in his autobiography. I do not know whether or not Scarborough ever heard 'Crazy Blues', either from her roof garden or elsewhere, though she notes the noise of her New York neighbours' Victrolas when mentioning her roof garden in *From a Southern Porch*. In both the letter to Page and in *On the Trail*, she describes Wyeth tossing aside his cane and performing a double shuffle and a plantation breakdown. My description of the steps themselves comes from a nineteenth-century manual of plantation dances available online and held at the Library of Congress.

she had an intimate knowledge of Southern patriarchs:

For biographical information on Dorothy Scarborough, see
Sylvia Ann Grider, 'Introduction', in Dorothy Scarborough,
The Wind (Austin: University of Texas Press, 1986; originally
published 1925); Grider, 'Scarborough, Emily Dorothy',
Handbook of Texas Online, http://www.tsha.utexas.edu/
handbook/online/articles/SS/fsc1.html.

41 **'I can see a black woman going by on the road'**: Dorothy
Scarborough, *From a Southern Porch* (New York: G. P. Putnam
& Sons, 1919), 7–8.

42 **'the hurdy-gurdy of the street beyond'**: ibid., 31.
**'I am trying to make as complete a collection of these as
possible'**: Scarborough, letter circa January 1921, Dorothy
Scarborough Papers (hereafter DSP), Texas Collection, Baylor
University Library, Baylor University, Waco, Texas.

43 **'so many of the best people in the South'**: John Allan
Wyeth, *With Sabre and Scapel: the Autobiography of a Soldier
and Surgeon* (New York: Harper & Brothers, 1914), 54.
Wyeth's memoir can be found online at
http://docsouth.unc.edu/wyeth/wyeth.html.
'of fine character': ibid., 53.
'When the boy became more proficient than the old man':
Dorothy Scarborough, *On the Trail of Negro Folk Songs*
(Cambridge: Harvard University Press, 1925), 23.

44 **'low order of development'**: ibid., 99.
'He evoked melodies of wistful gaiety': ibid., 100.
**'This is astounding to anybody who has seen him in the
operating room'**: Scarborough to Thomas Nelson Page, 5 May
1921, DSP.

45 **'I felt transported'**: Scarborough, *On the Trail, 100*
'Hundreds of "race" singers have flooded the market':
Stephen Calt, 'The Anatomy of a "Race" Label, Part II', *78
Quarterly* 1.4 (1989), 11.

46 **'the problem of the color line'**: DuBois, *The Souls of Black
Folk* 221.

'the lighter, happier side of slavery': Scarborough, *On the Trail*, 128.

47   irrational, illogical 'colored mind': ibid., 272.

'the fairy tale of a happy slave civilisation': quoted in Grace Elizabeth Hale, *Making Whiteness: the Culture of Segregation in the South, 1890-1940* (New York: Pantheon Books, 1998), 51.

'Sometimes I wonder iffen de white folks didn't make dat song up': quoted in Eugene Genovese, *Roll, Jordan, Roll: the World the Slaves Made* (New York: Vintage Books, 1972), 618.

the classic blackface dynamic: W. T. Lhamon, *Raising Cain: Blackface Performance from Jim Crow to Hip Hop* (Cambridge, MA: Harvard University Press, 2000); Eric Lott, *Love and Theft: Blackface Minstrelsy and the American Working Class* (New York: Oxford University Press, 1993).

48   self-styled 'darky dialecticians': For an insightful analysis of late-nineteenth century dialect fiction, see Gavin Jones, *Strange Talk: the Politics of Dialect Literature in Gilded Age America* (Berkeley: University of California Press 1999).

the protean nature of 'authenticity' itself: On the concept of authenticity, see Orvell, *The Real Thing*; Regina Bendix, *In Search of Authenticity: the Formation of Folklore Studies* (Madison, 1997); Benjamin Filene, *Romancing the Folk: Public Memory and American Roots Music* (Chapel Hill: University of North Carolina Press, 2000).

49   'a region of uncontaminated beauty and pastoral dreams': R. Emmet Kennedy, *Mellows: A Chronicle of Unknown Singers* (New York: A. and C. Boni, 1925), 144.

most seem to have heard in slave song simply savage wails: Cruz, *Culture on the Margins*, 19–66.

50   'the fast-vanishing remains of folklore in America': William Wells Newell, 'On the Field and Work of a Journal of

American Folklore', *Journal of American Folklore* 1 (1888), 3.

'Many a dear little Southern lady': Quoted in Kodish, *Good Friends and Bad Enemies*, 186.

'a queer combination of bookworm and tomboy': quoted in 'Scarborough, Dorothy', *Biographical Cyclopedia of US Women*: Ancestry.com. http://search.ancestry.com/db-bcaw/P291.aspx.

she attended a religious revival: This episode is described in the first chapter of Scarborough's autobiographical novel *The Unfair Sex*, which was serialised in 1925. The manuscript can be found in DSP at Baylor University.

51 **'readers found them more interesting'**: Scarborough, *On the Trail*, 11.

'How many memories of my childhood and youth': ibid., 6, 9–10.

52 **'highest gift, his spontaneity'**: Robert Littell, Review of Howard Odum and Guy Johnson, *The Negro and his Songs*, *New Republic* (9 September 1926), 74.

'The plantation Master and the plantation Negro stand today': DuBose Heyward, 'The Negro in the Low Country', in Augustine T. Smythe et al, eds., *The Carolina Low Country* (New York: Macmillan, 1932), 185–6.

53 **'I sat in the kitchen and learned songs'**: typescript in folder 209, box 2C114, DSP.

'Once the trusted servant and almost constant companion': J. E. Merrow, 'Negro Folk Songs', Unpublished, undated ms in DSP, 1.

54 **'the Negro is by nature a mimetic creature'**: Scarborough, *On the Trail*, 65.

55 **'I was ploughing when I got the word'**: ibid., 17.

'A Negro man came up to him after supper': ibid., 31.

56 **'our demure, delicate, poised, other-minded Dot'**: quoted in Grider, 'Introduction' to Scarborough, *The Wind*, xiv.

57 **'I have wandered through the colored quarters'**:

Scarborough, unpaginated introduction to manuscript of *On the Trail*, box 2C112, DSP.

58 'with each immersion the excitement grew': Scarborough, *On the Trail*, 15–16.

59 'a cylinder phonograph which can be used for home recording': letter from John A. Sherman of Thomas A. Edison Inc to Scarborough, 28 April 1921.

'I lack entire faith in the [making] of wax records': Natalie Curtis Burlin, *Negro Folk-Songs: Hampton Series* (New York: G. Schirmer, 1919), 3.

61 'crooning sweetness'; 'a racial mother-heart'; 'What other nation of mothers': Scarborough, *On the Trail*, 159–60.

'We wear the mask': Paul Laurence Dunbar, 'We Wear the Mask', in Joanne M. Braxton, ed., *The Collected Poetry of Paul Laurence Dunbar* (Charlottesville: University Press of Virginia, 1993), 71.

'wild shouting voice': Scarborough, *The Wind*, 3.

62 'seemed to me necessary to make the life of the section adequately real': Dorothy Scarborough, *A Song Catcher in Southern Mountains: American Folk Songs of British Ancestry* (New York: Columbia University Press, 1937), ix.

'She told him how on Saturday afternoons': Dorothy Scarborough, *The Stretch-Berry Smile* (Indianapolis: Bobbs-Merrill, 1932), 312–13.

'greatest Negro city in the world': Dorothy Scarborough, 'The New Negro and the Old' (review of Kennedy, *Mellows*, and Alain Locke, ed., *The New Negro*), uncited clipping 1925 in DSP.

63 'White critics, whom "everybody" knows': 'A Negro Renaissance', originally published in *New York Herald Tribune*, reprinted in *Opportunity* (June 1925), 187. On the Harlem Renaissance, see George Hutchinson, *The Harlem Renaissance in Black and White* (Cambridge, MA: Harvard University Press, 1995); David Levering Lewis, *When Harlem*

Was in Vogue (New York: Vintage, 1981); Nathan
I. Huggins, *Harlem Renaissance* (New York: Oxford University
Press, 1973); Paul Allen Anderson, *Deep River: Music and
Memory in Harlem Renaissance Thought* (Durham, NC: Duke
University Press, 2001).

'The day of "aunties", "uncles" and "mammy" is gone':
Alain Locke, 'Enter the New Negro', *Survey Graphic* (March
1925), 631.

'more of a myth than a man': ibid., 631.

64 'the energy and awakening of the Negro scholar and folklorist': Eric Walrond, 'Negro Folk-song', *Saturday Review of
Literature* (11 July 1925), 891.

'I am now struggling with Kennedy's *Mellows*': Locke to
Scarborough, 19 January 1926, DSP.

'I am considered something of an authority': Scarborough
to C. A. Hibbard, 8 August 1925, DSP.

'For the last several years': Scarborough, *On the Trail*, 264.

65 'like a cripple dancing because of some irresistible
impulse'; 'like the whip-crack surprise at the end of an
O. Henry story'; 'to have little relation to authentic folk-
music of the Negroes'; 'to trace it back to its origin';
'taken up by many singers': ibid., 265.

'essentially of our race': ibid., 270.

'Each one of my blues is based on some old Negro song':
ibid., 265.

67 'incredibly arid and difficult'; 'No beauty of Greek
columns here': Scarborough, *A Song Catcher*, 6.

'remote from the centers of commerce': ibid., 3.

'On my trips to collect material'; 'The Dictaphone
records, being of wax': ibid., ix–x.

68 'I was a Southerner born and bred': Scarborough, *On the
Trail*, 30.

'There isn't a radio in the district': Scarborough, undated,
unpaginated ms for *A Song Catcher* in DSP.

69   'floating on the breezes': untitled ms, folder 209, Box
      2C114, DSP.
      'songs I knew but did not know that I knew': 'Radio
      Talks', folder 297, DSP.
      'Why not say that it was typical of all publication offices':
      draft of *On the Trail,* folder 232, DSP.

Chapter Four: Sound Photographs of Negro Songs

71   **Louisiana Highway 66 is one of those meandering
      Southern roads:** John and Alan Lomax described their initial
      meeting with Leadbelly many times, most enduringly in their
      book *Negro Folk Songs as Sung By Leadbelly* (New York:
      Macmillan, 1936). For fresh perspectives on the encounter, as
      well as on John Lomax himself, I am indebted to Nolan
      Porterfield, *Last Cavalier: the Life and Times of John Lomax,
      1867–1948* (Urbana: University of Illinois Press, 1996);
      Filene, *Romancing the Folk;* Charles Wolfe and Kip Lornell,
      The Life and Legend of Leadbelly (New York: HarperCollins,
      1992); and Jerrold Hirsch, 'Modernity, Nostalgia, and
      Southern Folklore Studies: the Case of John Lomax', *Journal
      of American Folklore* 105 (Spring 1992), 183–207. For a
      meticulous chronology of the encounter between Huddie
      Ledbetter and the Lomaxes, see the Alan Lomax Archive
      website, http://www.alan-lomax.com/links_leadbelly.html.

72   **'on the upper crust of the po' white trash':** John Lomax,
      Adventures of a Ballad Hunter (New York: Macmillan, 1947),
      1.

73   **That conviction placed Lomax at odds with a generation
      of scholars:** Hirsch, 'Modernity, Nostalgia and Southern
      Folklore Studies', 189; Filene, *Romancing the Folk,* chapter
      one.

74   **'the down-and-out classes':** John Lomax, 'Some Types of

American Folk-Song', *Journal of American Folklore* 28 (1915), 3.

the archive was the brainchild of Robert Winslow Gordon: See Kodish, *Good Friends and Bad Enemies.*

76 'heard for the first time the wail of the Negro woodsman': John Lomax to Ruby Terrill, 11 July 1933, Box 3D149, Lomax Family Papers (hereafter LFP), Center for American History, University of Texas at Austin.

'the words of enough folk songs': John Lomax to Terrill, 7 July 1933, Box 3D149, LFP.

77 'for his wife objected to his singing': John Lomax to Terrill, 21 July 1933, Box 3D149, LFP.

'how Christ took his persecution': ibid.

78 'Everybody knows the story of how Leadbelly sang his way to freedom': Davis, *The History of the Blues*, 165.

80 'Through the Music Division in the Library of Congress': John Lomax, '"Sinful Songs" of the Southern Negro', *Musical Quarterly* 20 (1934), 181.

81 'The songs would make a sensation in cultured centers': undated letter written in Parchman, Mississippi, in file marked 'General Correspondence, 1933-1939', John Lomax Papers (hereafter JLP), Archive of Folk Culture, Library of Congress.

'Folk songs flourish, grow': John Lomax, 'Report of the Honorary Consultant and Curator', from *Report of the Librarian of Congress for the Fiscal Year Ending June 30, 1934*, reprinted in *Archive of American Folk Song: a History, 1928-1939*, compiled from the Annual Reports of the Librarian of Congress, Washington, 1940, 27.

'contented and carefree as a group of children': John and Alan Lomax, *Negro Folk Songs as Sung by Leadbelly*, 38.

82 'Negro songs in their primitive purity': John Lomax, 'Report of the Honorary Consultant and Curator', from *Report of the Librarian of Congress for the Fiscal Year Ending June*

30, 1933, reprinted in *Archive of American Folk Song: a History*, 24.

'dish 'ere w'at dey calls de fonygraf': Joel Chandler Harris, 'The Phonograph', in Harris, *Uncle Remus – His Songs and His Sayings* (New York: D. Appleton and Company, 1881), accessible online at http://www.uncleremus.com/phonograph.html.

83   *'Title: "Angola, Louisiana"'*: Wolfe and Lornell, *The Life and Legend of Leadbelly*, 164–6.

85   'Dear Sir Just a few lines to let you no iom out': Huddie Ledbetter to John Lomax, undated (but circa 6 September 1934), Box 3D157, LFP.

86   'Dear Mr Lomax': Hurston to John Lomax, 5 January 1935, Box 3D160, LFP.
'impossible to transport Negro folk-singers from the South': John Lomax, 'Sinful Songs', 182.
'Contact with whites soon brings about cheap imitations': undated letter written in Parchman, Mississippi, in file marked 'General Correspondence, 1933–1939', JLP.

87   'I do not think there is a boy in the institution': Grube B. Cornish to John Lomax, 15 January 1935, Box 3D171, LFP.
'After a thorough investigation': Robert J. Booth to John Lomax, 17 January 1935, Box 3D171, LFP.

88   'blinding themselves to the power and beauty': John Lomax to Terrill, 1 August 1933, Box 3D149, LFP.
'amid a people we really know little about': ibid.
'Other singers hearing him became ambitious': John and Alan Lomax, *Negro Folk Songs as Sung by Leadbelly*, 37.
'the reels or so-called "jump-up", "made-up", or "sinful songs" of the blacks': John Lomax, 'Sinful Songs', 181.
'Negro spirituals abound in idioms and phrases': ibid., 183.

89   'We sat at a point in the run-around': John and Alan Lomax, *Negro Folk Songs as Sung by Leadbelly*, 37.

well over 200 disc recordings: John Lomax, 'Report of the Honorary Consultant and Curator', from *Report of the Librarian of Congress for the Fiscal Year Ending June 30, 1935*, reprinted in *Archive of American Folk Song: a History*, 32.

'to "show off" among his own color': John and Alan Lomax, *Negro Folk Songs as Sung by Leadbelly*, 38.

90   'Before we reached the farm': ibid., 36-7.

'I'm tired of lookin' at niggers in the penitentshuh': ibid., 39.

'smacked of sensationalism': ibid., 45.

91   'Lomax Arrives with Leadbelly, Negro Minstrel': *New York Herald Tribune*, 3 January 1935.

'absolute sincerity': *New York Herald Tribune*, 5 January 1935.

92   'My chauffeur, while Alan is sick': uncited clipping circa 1934 in Box 2.325/V62, folder 5, LFP.

93   'Boss, I'se nothin' but a nigger': John and Alan Lomax, *Negro Folk Songs as Sung by Leadbelly*, 41.

'Already the pure nigger in him': *Brooklyn Daily Eagle*, 17 January 1935.

'We (Alan and I) are disturbed and distressed': John Lomax to Terrill, 14 January 1935, Box 3D150, LFP.

'We saw no printed page of music either in his prison cell or in his home': John and Alan Lomax, *Negro Folk Songs as Sung by Leadbelly*, xiii.

94   'I learned by listening to other singers once in a while off phonograph records': quoted in Filene, *Romancing the Folk*, 15.

'the most famous nigger in the world': John Lomax to Terrill, circa 7 January 1935, Box 3D150, LFP.

'natural and sincere as he was while in prison': John Lomax to Terrill, 14 January 1935, Box 3D150, LFP.

95   'a low, dirty back room': John and Alan Lomax, *Negro Folk Songs as Sung by Leadbelly*, 59.

'I ain't goin' to sing no more for you': ibid.

'I wants my money': ibid., 60.

'The experience has shattered my nerves': John Lomax to Terrill, 11 March 1935, Box 3D150, LFP.

'I think the main reason I feel about Huddie as I do': John Lomax to Terrill, 17 March 1935, Box 3D150, LFP.

'The little drama was played out': John and Alan Lomax, *Negro Folk Songs as Sung by Leadbelly*, 63–4.

96   'Among his own kind': John Lomax to Terrill, 16 April 1936, Box 3D151, LFP.

'Tell Alan that I drove': John Lomax to Terrill, 26 May 1936, Box 3D151, LFP.

'If I stay up here very long': John Lomax to Terrill, 22 May 1936, Box 3D151, LFP.

97   'She expressed no interest in Iron Head': John Lomax to Terrill, 29 May 1936, Box 3D151, LFP.

'Because Alan will drive recklessly': John Lomax to Terrill, 29 June 1933, Box 3D149, LFP.

98   'I have no means of knowing . . .': John Lomax to Terrill, 3 July 1933, Box 3D149, LFP.

'music and mystery and wistful sadness': John Lomax to Terrill, 11 July 1933, Box 3D149, LFP.

'the simple directness and power of this primitive music': John Lomax to Terrill, 10 August 1933, Box 3D149, LFP.

'As I think back, and in my dreams': John Lomax to Terrill, 17 August 1933, Box 3D149, LFP.

'of hopeless longing, of remoteness': Undated memo in 'General Correspondence 1933–39' folder, JLP.

'The truest, the most intimate folk music': John and Alan Lomax, *American Ballads and Folk Songs* (New York: Macmillan, 1934), xxxv.

99   the Southern novelist Samuel Derieux: Scarborough, *On the Trail*, 209.

'chain gang songs and jail house blues': Odum, *Rainbow Round my Shoulder*, 283.

'uncontrolled category of perception', 'distinctly pleasurable but definitely unbeautiful': Francis Spufford, *I May be Some Time: Ice and the English Imagination* (London: Faber and Faber, 1996), 18–19.

'drove steadily and silently, his black, black face shining';
100 'I can find no little feeling for beauty in him': John Lomax to Terrill, 26 October 1934, Box 3D150, LFP.

'Penitentiary wardens all tell me that I set no value on my life': uncited clipping circa 1934 in Box 2.325/V62, folder 5, LFP.

Those questions began heating up in March 1931: For a brilliant account of the Scottsboro case, see James Goodman, *Stories of Scottsboro* (New York: Vintage Books, 1995, originally published 1994).

John Spivak investigated prison conditions in Georgia: John L. Spivak, *Georgia Nigger* (New York: Brewer, Warren and Putnam, 1932); see also Spivak's essay 'Flashes from Georgia Chain Gangs' in Nancy Cunard, ed., *Negro Anthology* (London: Wishart and Company 1934).

'The trouble we have had in Georgia': John Lomax to Terrill, 18 December 1934, Box 3D150, LFP.

101 'terrible story of the fear of a Negro': John Lomax to Terrill, 10 August 1933, Box 3D149, LFP.

'when convicts were leased by the State': John Lomax, 'Sinful Songs', 180.

'Negroes who have been convicted on Negro evidence only': John Lomax to Hon. Governor James L. Allred, 29 October 1936, Box 3D171, LFP.

'the Negro's desire, as one said, "to git away f'om here"': John and Alan Lomax, *American Ballads*, xxxii.

'the injustice of the white man': John and Alan Lomax, *Negro Folk Songs as Sung by Leadbelly*, ix.

The comeback began inauspiciously: My account of Leadbelly's return to New York draws on Wolfe and Lornell, *The Life and Legend of Leadbelly*, 178–210.

102 'stayed away in droves': Wolfe and Lornell, *The Life and Legend of Leadbelly*, 188.

'The advance publicity stated that this man': quoted in Wolfe and Lornell, *The Life and Legend of Leadbelly*, 189.

he turned to Mary Elizabeth Barnicle: On Mary Elizabeth Barnicle, see Wolfe and Lornell, *The Life and Legend of Leadbelly*, 189–90; 'Biographical Note', http://cass.etsu.edu/ARCHIVES/afindaid/a347.html#bio%20 note.

103 'to collect, study, and popularise American folk music and its traditions': quoted in Wolfe and Lornell, *The Life and Legend of Leadbelly*, 192. For more on Left folk song in the Popular Front era, see Filene, *Romancing the Folk*, 47–75; Steven Garabedian, 'Lawrence Gellert, "Negro Songs of Protest", and the Left-Wing Folk-Song Revival of the 1930s and 1940s', *American Quarterly* 57 (2005), 179–206; Robbie Lieberman, *'My Song is My Weapon': People's Songs, American Communism, and the Politics of Culture, 1930–1950* (Urbana: University of Illinois Press, 1989).

'Huddie Ledbetter, Famous Negro Folk Artist': *Daily Worker*, 12 August 1937, 7.

104 'The camp was in an uproar': quoted in Filene, *Romancing the Folk*, 72.

105 Lawrence Gellert, an activist and folk-songhunter: On Lawrence Gellert, see Wolfe and Lornell, *The Life and Legend of Leadbelly*, 194; Garabedian, 'Lawrence Gellert, "Negro Songs of Protest"'.

'propaganda', music 'as a weapon': quoted in Garabedian, 'Lawrence Gellert, "Negro Songs of Protest"', 182.

106 'the nonsensical jingles served up for the white man's amusement': *New Masses* 20 November 1934, 19.

'Getting "our niggers" out of difficulties with the Law':
New Masses 11 December 1934, 22.

'Imagine Ben Davis Jr, editor of the *Negro Liberator*':
ibid.

107 the presence of Clarence Norris and Heywood Patterson:
Patterson and Norris were transferred from the Jefferson
County Jail in Birmingham to Kilby Prison on 4 February
1934 and remained there for the rest of the year. See
Goodman, *Stories of Scottsboro*, 233–53.

'embodies the master-slave relationship intact': *New
Masses* 11 December 1934, 22.

'On Southern chain gang and jail': *New Masses* 20
November 1934, 19.

108 'Some time ago when I was recording': John Lomax,
undated memo to Henry J. Alsberg, Box 3D171, LFP.

109 He swaggers through the pages of recent accounts of the
blues: See, for example, Filene, *Romancing the Folk*, 47–75;
Hazel Carby, *Race Men* (Cambridge: Harvard University Press,
1998), 101–9, 115.

'Now Mr Lomax, my god he hated old Roosevelt': James
McNutt, 'John Henry Faulk: an Interview', *Folklore Annual*
(11987), 113, in Alan Lomax files, ALC. See also Porterfield,
Last Cavalier, 431–2.

'Because Lomax was unquestionably a genius': Porterfield,
Last Cavalier, 434.

110 'all I had to do was turn over the records': ibid., 393.

'a hundred Negroes resting in their quarters': John Lomax
to Hon. Burnet R. Maybank, 30 June 1941, Box 3D171, LFP.

'never questioned the system': Porterfield, *Last Cavalier*,
434.

111 'the forgotten ones who have no influential friends': John
Lomax to Hon. Governor James L. Allred, 29 October 1936,
Box 3D171, LFP.

'I heard a washerwoman striding along the road':

Lawrence Gellert, 'Negro Songs of Protest', *New Masses* (November 1930 and January 1931).

'For more than a dozen years': Lawrence Gellert, *Negro Songs of Protest* (New York: American Music League, 1936), 6–7.

112 The historian William Stott has written: William Stott, *Documentary Expression and Thirties America* (New York: Oxford University Press, 1973).

'a portion of unimagined existence': James Agee, 'Preface', in Agee and Walker Evans, *Let Us Now Praise Famous Men* (Boston: Houghton Mifflin, 1988, originally published 1941), xlvi.

left-liberal folklorists like Herbert Halpert and Benjamin Botkin: On the work on Left folklorists, see Jerrold Hirsch, *Portrait of America: a Cultural History of the Federal Writers Project* (Chapel Hill: University of North Carolina Press, 2003); Jerrold Hirsch, 'Folklore in the Making: B. A. Botkin', *Journal of American Folklore* 100 (1987), 3–38.

113 'cut up': John Lomax to Terrill, 12 March 1935, Box 3D150, LFP.

'bare-throated, bearded, rough, but clean inside and out': Porterfield, *Last Cavalier*, 339.

'intensely American and flagrantly and vagrantly modern': ibid., 339.

114 'We did well for so short a stay': John Lomax to Terrill, 3 July 1933, Box 3D149, LFP.

115 'It distressed my father very, very much': My account of the Harvard incident draws on material held in Alan Lomax's FBI file, which came to light in April 2006 when the music historian Ted Gioia publicised the findings of his Freedom of Information Act request. The FBI's surveillance of Alan Lomax seems to have begun in the early 1940s, and in a sense it was a consequence of the family tensions I discuss here. Sometime in the late 1930s, John Lomax attended a

wedding reception and told a few guests of his worries about his son's political leanings. (Alan had allegedly told him: 'I am just as much a Communist as I ever was – if not a stronger one, but don't say anything about it for you will only get me in trouble.') Those remarks were reported to the FBI's St Louis bureau, and in response the Bureau launched an investigation of Alan Lomax that lasted until 1980. Alan Lomax's remarks here were made in 1942, when he was questioned about the demonstration by federal agents. He denied charges that he had distributed Communist literature or made speeches in support of the Party. See Ted Gioia, 'The Red-rumor blues', *Los Angeles Times*, 23 April 2006, accessed online on 4 May 2006 at http://www.calendarlive.com/music/cl-ca-lomax23apr23,0,2933896.

'communistic activities': Filene, *Romancing the Folk*, 48.

'He needs to build himself up physically': John Lomax to Terrill, 17 August 1933, Box 3D149, LFP.

'a ballad in himself': John Lomax to Terrill, 22 March 1935, Box 3D150, LFP.

'generosity to me and mine': John Lomax to Terrill, 18 March 1935, Box 3D150, LFP.

'I am quite satisfied to have Alan under her influence': John Lomax to Terrill, 16 March 1935, Box 3D150, LFP.

'the most exciting field trip I have made': Alan Lomax to Oliver Strunk, 3 August 1935, Alan Lomax Collection (here-after ALC), Archive of Folk Culture, Library of Congress.

116 'My dear Mr Lomax': Hurston to John Lomax, 16 September 1935, Box 3D160, LFP.

118 At the core of Hurston's long, furious letter was an accu-sation: Just how seriously one should take Hurston's account of the events in Georgia and Florida is an open question. Hurston herself was hardly a disinterested party: intensely hostile to the radical Left (whose ranks, by 1935, included many of her one-time kindred spirits in the New Negro intelli-

gentsia); prone to dramatic, acrimonious splits with close
friends (like, for example, Langston Hughes); and sometimes
inclined to embroider her facts. She had been much enam-
oured of Barnicle when she met her the previous spring. 'Will
you invite Miss Barnicle to the tea?' she wrote to her friend
Annie Nathan Meyer in March. 'She teaches the ballad at
NYU. Oh, she is grand!' In later years she would claim that
she left the expedition when Barnicle demanded that she take
a photograph of a black child eating a watermelon. See
Valerie Boyd, *Wrapped in Rainbows: the Life of Zora Neale
Hurston* (New York: Scribner, 2003), 275–7. Hurston's letters
are reprinted in Carla Kaplan, ed., *Zora Neale Hurston: a Life
in Letters* (New York: Doubleday, 2002).

Just how Lomax responded to this is hard to gauge: The
closest thing to a direct comment from Lomax came in a note
that he scribbled on the bottom of a letter Hurston had sent
him on 30 August 1935: 'This is the Negro woman novelist
who was with Miss B and Alan a part of the summer. The two
females "fell out"'. (Box 3D160, LFP.)

Barnicle was still writing him warm and effusive letters:
On 1 October 1935 Barnicle wrote: 'It is I who am owing
Alan – my regret and shame is that I haven't anything to offer
him. In every way I am wholly his debtor – all summer long
he shared everything he had with me and gave me open and
free and beautiful the treasure of himself . . . I am glad that
your pain has let up – I hope permanently – and dreadfully
sorry that you had such a physically miserable summer . . .
When are you coming to NY? Is the Leadbelly book coming
out soon? What are you working on now? Good luck to you in
everything you do and my love to you and Miss Terrell.' (Box
3D160, LFP.)

in the ensuing years he filled the archive's shelves: On
Alan Lomax's activities in the late 1930s, see Ed Kahn,
'1934–1950: the Early Collecting Years' in Ronald D. Cohen,

ed., *Alan Lomax: Selected Writings, 1934-1997* (New York: Routledge, 2003), 1–8.

He even pushed for the accession of commercial recordings: Alan first broached the possibility of the race and hillbilly records survey in 1935, when he included it as part of his father's proposal for funding to the Carnegie Corporation. See the memo (in Alan's handwriting) in file of materials related to Lomax's Carnegie Corporation grants, 1933–5, Box 3D170, LFP.

119 **'The commercial recording companies have done a broader and more interesting job':** Alan Lomax to Spivacke, 8 April 1939, ALC. The list (first made available in 1940) can be found in the ALC.

what his friend Benjamin Botkin termed 'living lore': B. A. Botkin, "Folklore as a Neglected Source of Social History", in Caroline F. Ware, *The Cultural Approach to History* (New York: Columbia University Press, 1940), 311–12.

'folklore in the making': B. A. Botkin, 'WPA and Folklore Research: 'Bread and Song'', in Burt Feintuch, ed., *The Conservation of Culture: Folklorists and the Public Sector* (Lexington, KY: University Press of Kentucky, 1988), 259.

'the blues and reels and the work songs': Botkin, 'Folklore as a Neglected Source of Social History', 312.

a two-year survey of black music in Coahoma County, Mississippi: The genesis of the expedition and Lomax's treatment of his African American colleagues have become the subject of much controversy. See Robert Gordon and Bruce Nemerov, eds., *Lost Delta Found: Rediscovering the Fisk University-Library of Congress Coahoma County Study, 1941-1942* (Nashville: Vanderbilt University Press, 2005); Alan Lomax, *The Land Where the Blues Began* (New York: Pantheon, 1993); and the responses gathered on Lomax's behalf at http://www.alan-lomax.com/media_books_LostDeltaFound.html.

120 'to explore objectively and exhaustively': Alan Lomax,
     memo to Library of Congress, 18 September 1941, ALC.
     'It is a folklorist's illusion': Alan Lomax, field notebook
     dated July 1942, ALC.
     'to record what you find, regardless of its import': John
     Lomax to Alan Lomax, 9 October 1941, cited in Porterfield,
     Last Cavalier, 435.
     'hopelessly involved in the slimy toils of Communism':
     John Lomax to John Lomax Jr, 28 February 1940, cited in
     Porterfield, *Last Cavalier*, 427.
     more often than not he left them unanswered: Porterfield,
     Last Cavalier, 427–8.
121 'a bourgeois Southerner': John Lomax to Alan Lomax,
     9 October 1941, cited in Porterfield, *Last Cavalier*, 435.
     he brought Leadbelly along with him: on Alan's continuing
     work with Leadbelly, see Wolfe and Lornell, *The Life and
     Legend of Leadbelly*, 186–239.
     'an absolute zero on any program at any time': John
     Lomax to Alan Lomax, 25 April 1940, cited in Porterfield,
     Last Cavalier, 421.
     a bruising encounter with Mary Elizabeth Barnicle: John
     Lomax to Alan Lomax, 23 July 1940, cited in Porterfield, *Last
     Cavalier*, 370.
     'Save for being a triple murderer': John Lomax to 'Kathy'
     [no surname supplied], 20 February 1944, Box 3D157, LFP.
122 when he carried him outdoors on hot Texas nights: Alan
     Lomax described this to Zora Neale Hurston while they were
     collecting folk songs in Georgia. See her letter to John Lomax,
     30 August 1935, Box 3D160, LFP.
     he watched Alan fiddle with the controls on the disc
     recorder: John Lomax, *Adventures of a Ballad Hunter*, 114.
     'the core and center of my being': John Lomax to Alan
     Lomax, 2 August 1940, cited in Porterfield, *Last Cavalier*, 428.
123 'an outrageous slander on the Southern white man': John

Lomax to Alan Lomax, 10 October 1941, quoted in
Porterfield, *Last Cavalier*, 434.

His publisher, however, thought its inclusion 'unwise': My
account of this episode draws on Porterfield, *Last Cavalier*,
478-9.

'From Nat I learned my sense of rhythm': John Lomax,
Adventures of a Ballad Hunter, 9–12.

Chapter Five: Been Here and Gone

125 **When they looked back to the beginning:** I don't know
when, or indeed if, William Russell, Charles Edward Smith
and Frederic Ramsey went together to the Jungle Inn to see
and hear Jelly Roll Morton. To imagine this encounter I have
drawn on each man's accounts of their meetings with Morton:
Charles Edward Smith, 'Oh, Mister Jelly!', *The Jazz Record*
(February 1944), 8-10, accessed online at http://www.doctor
jazz.freeserve.co.uk/posth.html#cesmith; Frederic Ramsey Jr,
reminiscence included in William Russell, ed., *'Oh, Mister
Jelly': a Jelly Roll Morton Scrapbook* (Copenhagen: Jazz Media
ApS, 1999), 495–505; William Russell, 'Charles Edward
Smith, 1904-1970', in Russell, *'Oh, Mister Jelly'*, 474–85. For
information on the interior of the Jungle Inn, I drew as well
on Roy Carew, '1211 U Street, Northwest', in Albert J.
McCarthy, ed., *Jazzbook 1955* (London: Cassell, 1955),
109–16, accessed online at
http://www.doctorjazz.freeserve.co.uk/page28.html.
it was William Russell who had heard him first: For information on Russell's experience hearing and collecting race
records, I drew on Bruce Boyd Raeburn, 'The Musical Worlds
of William Russell', *The Southern Quarterly* 36 (Winter 1998),
12–13; William Frederick Wagner, 'A Brother Remembers
William Russell', *The Southern Quarterly* 36 (Winter 1998),

20; and Russell's letters to Frederic Ramsey, which form part of Ramsey's collected papers and manuscripts, the Frederic Ramsey Papers (hereafter FRP). Though at the time of my research, Ramsey's papers were still in the family's possession, they have now been acquired by the Historic New Orleans Collection in New Orleans, Louisiana, where William Russell's Papers are also housed.

126 **The sheer complexity of it was what was most striking:** William Russell and Stephen W. Smith, 'New Orleans Music', in Frederic Ramsey and Charles Edward Smith, eds., *Jazzmen* (New York: Harcourt Brace, 1939), 10.

you could buy them in bulk for as little as twenty-five cents a box: Russell to Ramsey, 14 October 1939, FRP.

127 **'To many who have wondered what has become of "Jelly Roll" Morton':** Andy Andrusia, '"Jelly Roll" Gives Out for Capitol Cats', *Down Beat* (May 1937), 11, accessed online at http://www.doctorjazz.freeserve.co.uk/page10.html.

a coterie gathered around him: Smith, 'Oh, Mister Jelly!', 8–10.

Dear Mr Ripley: Morton's letter, dated 31 March 1938, can be found online at http://www.doctorjazz.freeserve.co.uk/page10bc.html#washdc.

129 **Smith recommended him to Alan Lomax:** Ramsey recalls this in his letter to Smith, 5 April 1954, FRP.

Perhaps Lomax even told him of a book he had been reading: Alan Lomax recalls the influence Odum's book had upon him in his memoir *The Land Where the Blues Began*, 493.

'[Morton] will trace by piano and narrative': Harold Phillips, 'Jelly Roll Charts Jazz', *Washington Daily News*, 19 March 1938, p. 6.

once they heard the copies of the recordings that Lomax dubbed for them: Orrin Keepnews, 'Sweet Papa Jelly Roll: Ten Year History of Morton's Library of Congress Recordings',

Record Changer (February 1948), 6–7, accessed online at
http://www.doctorjazz.freeserve.co.uk/page21.html.

130 **Morton unleashed a flood of melody and anecdote:** My
account of Morton's reminiscences draws on Alan Lomax,
Mister Jelly Roll (London: Virgin Books, 1991: Originally
published 1950), and on the transcribed version of the
Library of Congress session available online at
http://www.doctorjazz.freeserve.co.uk/locspeech1.html. *Jelly
Roll Morton – the Complete Library of Congress Recordings* is
now available on CD from Rounder Records (CDROUN1888).

132 **so obscene in places that some of the sessions remained
buried in the Library vaults:** See, for example, 'Winin' Boy
Blues', described by Morton as 'one of my first tunes in the
blues line down in New Orleans in the very early days', which
includes the line 'I fucked her till her pussy stunk'. The track
can be found on *Winin' Boy Blues: Jelly Roll Morton: The
Library of Congress Recordings, Volume 4* (Rounder 1094) and
on *Jelly Roll Morton – the Complete Library of Congress
Recordings*.

133 **'moldy figs':** See Bernard Gendron, '"Moldy Figs" and
Modernists: Jazz at War (1942–46)', in Krin Gabbard, ed.,
Jazz Among the Discourses (Durham and London: Duke
University Press, 1995), 31–56.
  'the longest lasting movement in jazz': Paul Oliver, Max
Harrison and William Bolcom, *The New Grove Gospel, Blues,
and Jazz* (New York: Grove Publications, 1987), 292, quoted
in Eric Hobsbawm, 'The Caruso of Jazz', in his *Uncommon
People: Resistance, Rebellion, and Jazz* (New York: The New
Press, 1998), 240.

134 **a transatlantic circle of jazz aficionados:** The Popular
Front jazz subculture is discussed in Michael Denning, *The
Cultural Front: the Laboring of American Culture in the
Twentieth Century* (London: Verso, 1997), 328–38; David W.
Stowe, *Swing Changes: Big-Band Jazz in New Deal America*

(Cambridge, MA: Harvard University Press, 1994); and
Gendron, '"Moldy Figs" and Modernists'.
'There is a world of difference between the blues as
collectors know them': *HRS* Rag 1 (1939), 11, quoted in
Paul Lopes, *The Rise of a Jazz Art World* (Cambridge:
Camridge University Press, 2002), 194.

the mass production of popular music generated a vast
amount of waste matter: My thoughts on record collecting
have been influenced by Michael Thompson, *Rubbish Theory:
the Creation and Destruction of Value* (New York: Oxford
University Press, 1979).

135 'looked much like his pictures in the old Victor Race
Catalogues': Kenneth Hulsizer, 'Jelly Roll Morton in
Washington', in Kenneth Williamson, ed., *This is Jazz*
(London: Newnes, 1960), 202–16.
'empires of sound': Andre Millard, *America on Record: a
History of Recorded Sound* (Cambridge: Cambridge University
Press, 1995), chapter 8.

136 Ramsey had grown up in a swirl of art and ideas: For
biographical information on Frederic Ramsey, I learned a
great deal from his daughters Alida Ramsey Porter and
Martha Ramsey, as well as from the materials contained in his
collected papers.

137 'I liked your letter for its emphasis upon the good jazz of
other years': Smith to Ramsey, 31 July 1936, FRP.
'one solid row of junk shops': collector George Hoefer,
quoted in Lopes, *The Rise of a Jazz Art World*, 160.
'Make out a want list': Russell to Ramsey, 17 October 1938,
FRP.

138 'a worthy cultural object of study': 'Country's Hot Clubs
Founded by "Swing" Devotees at Yale', quoted in William
Howland Kenney, *Recorded Music in American Life: the
Phonograph and Popular Memory, 1890-1945* (New York:
Oxford University Press, 1999), 16.

139 'There will always be wayward, instinctive and primitive geniuses': Gilbert Seldes, 'Toujours Jazz', *The Dial* 8 (1923), 160, quoted in Lopes, *The Rise of a Jazz Art World*, 61.
'everyone was talking Bix and Chicago': undated, untitled memo from Ramsey, FRP.

140 Frederic Ramsey was approached by an editor at Harcourt Brace: Pete Whelan, 'Fred Ramsey Speaks Out!', *78 Quarterly* 1, no. 4 (1989), 33.

141 'So eager were they for the "truth"': Peter Goldsmith, *Making People's Music: Moe Asch and Folkways Records* (Washington: Smithsonian Institution Press, 1998, 2000), 171.

142 'folk history': On the 1930s fascination with 'folk history', see James S. Miller, 'Inventing the "Found" Object: Artifactuality, Folk History and the Rise of Capitalist Ethnography in 1930s America', *Journal of American Folklore* 117 (2004), 373–93; Robert Dorman, *Revolt of the Provinces: the Regionalist Movement in America, 1920–1945* (Chapel Hill: University of North Carolina Press, 1998); Michael Kammen, *Mystic Chords of Memory* (New York: Knopf, 1998, 1991); William Stott, *Documentary Expression and Thirties America* (New York: Oxford University Press, 1973); Warren Susman, 'The Culture of the Thirties', in his *Culture as History: the Transformation of American Society in the Twentieth Century* (New York: Pantheon, 1984).
'One or another of the authors': Ramsey and Smith, *Jazzmen*, xiii.
'the most glamorous, as well as the most notorious': ibid., 31.

143 'One of the most popular of these combinations': Herbert Asbury, *The French Quarter: an Informal History of the New Orleans Underworld* (New York: Knopf, 1936), 437–8.

144 the voyeuristic taste for 'slumming': See Lewis, *When Harlem Was In Vogue*; Huggins, *Harlem Renaissance*.

145 'elemental conjure woman': Carl Van Vechten, 'Negro

"Blues" Singers', *Vanity Fair* (March 1926), 67, 106.

'I said we were trying to avoid the Van Vechtian line': Smith to Ramsey, 21 June 1939, FRP.

146 the 'sensation' King Bolden created: E. Belfield Spriggins, 'Excavating Local Jazz, Part One', *Louisiana Weekly*, 22 April 1933, reprinted in Lynn Abbott, 'Remembering Mr E. Belfield Spriggins, First Man of Jazzology', *78 Quarterly* 10 (1999), 14–18.

'that the musicians found no appreciative audience in dives': Smith to Ramsey, 15 February 1940, FRP.

'jammed every night with river rowdies': Ramsey and Smith, *Jazzmen*, 34–5.

'Inside the low, smoky room': ibid., 63.

'hated the long hours, the low pay': Charles Edward Smith, 'Men Who Created Jazz', *Jazz Information*, 26 September 1939.

147 a ribald, plebeian Garden of Eden: See the discussion of *Jazzmen* in Scott DeVeaux, 'Constructing the Jazz Tradition', in Robert O'Meally, ed., *The Jazz Cadence of American Culture* (New York: Columbia University Press, 1998), 489.

'the ideal successor to the throne of King Bolden': Ramsey and Smith, *Jazzmen*, 23.

'a transcribed history': Charles Edward Smith et al, *The Jazz Record Book* (New York: Smith and Durrell, 1942), vii.

148 'shallow emotionalism': Charles Edward Smith, 'Collecting Hot', *Esquire* (February 1934), 96.

Ramsey and Smith kept hearing rumours of a wax cylinder: Charles Edward Smith, 'The Bolden Cylinder', *Saturday Review of Literature* (16 March 1957), 34–5. See also Tim Brooks, *Lost Sounds: Blacks and the Birth of the Recording Industry 1890–1919* (Chicago, 2004), 514–15.

149 'mean and dirty': Ramsey and Smith, *Jazzmen*, 13.

Even as Smith, Ramsey, and Russell were writing: For an account of these events, as well as examples of some of

Russell's photographs, see Al Rose, *Storyville, New Orleans* (Tuscaloosa: University of Alabama Press, 1974), ix–x, 166–83.

150 **'The barrelhouse was the refuge of the tragically destitute':** Rudi Blesh, 'Jazz Begins', in George S. Rosenthal and Frank Zachary, eds. (in collaboration with Frederic Ramsey and Rudi Blesh), *Jazzways* (London: Musicians Press Ltd, 1946), 15.

Johnson's recordings were circulating among a small but ardent group of New Orleans enthusiasts: This phenomenon has been little discussed, though John Hammond's zeal for Johnson has been widely noted (he attempted to book the singer for his 'From Spirituals to Swing' concert at Carnegie Hall in December 1938, not knowing that Johnson had been murdered a few months earlier). See, for example, Wald, *Escaping the Delta*, 228–30.

151 **In 1939, Hammond loaned his copies to Alan Lomax:** Alan Lomax, *The Land Where the Blues Began*, 13. The titles he listed were 'Hellhound on my Trail', 'Crossroads Blues', 'Terraplane Blues', 'The Last Fair Deal Going Down', 'Ramblin' On My Mind', 'Stones In My Passway', '32–20 Blues', and 'Kind Hearted Woman'.

'dry on the ear as some wine may be on the tongue': Rudi Blesh, *Shining Trumpets: a History of Jazz* (New York: Knopf, 1946), 108.

'the object of study in the moment of its emergence': Lott, *Love and Theft*, 55.

'"New Orleans" became a multiple myth and symbol': Hobsbawm, *Uncommon People*, 242.

152 **in 1942 he spent a fruitless afternoon trying to coax stories:** Alan Lomax's interview with Jaybird Jones can be heard on *Field Recordings, volume 3: Mississippi (1936–1942)* (Document DOCD-5577).

'were on the whole ignorant of the songs we wanted': Alan

Lomax. '"Sinful" Songs of the Southern Negro: Experiences Collecting Secular Folk-Music', *Southern Review* 19 (1933–34), 120.

'of protest and of pride': Alan Lomax, *Mister Jelly Roll*, xv.

'streets thronging with pimps, chippies, rotten police, and Babbitts on a binge':, ibid., 100.

'a marvel that has spawned a monster': ibid., xiv.

153 'a rich evocation of underground America': ibid., xv.

'did not draw a color line': Ramsey and Smith, *Jazzmen*, 5.

'Alan Lomax. Author, *Mister Jelly Roll'*: quoted in Kahn, '1934–1950: the Early Collecting Years' in Cohen, *Alan Lomax: Selected Writings, 1934–1997*, 7.

Only William Russell continued to devote himself to the gospel of Dixieland: Russell moved to New Orleans in 1956; in 1958 he was appointed Curator of the Archive of New Orleans Jazz at Tulane University. See Raeburn, 'The Musical Worlds of William Russell', 13–18.

154 Charles Edward Smith retreated from jazz research alto-gether: See Russell, 'Charles Edward Smith', 474–5.

a growing enchantment with the power and purity of rural American cultures: Robert Cantwell, *When We Were Good: the Folk Revival* (Cambridge, MA: Harvard University Press, 1996); Rosenberg, *Transforming Tradition;* Filene, *Romancing the Folk*, 183–232.

'For those of us whose revival began around 1958': Cantwell, *When We Were Good*, 22.

the growth of a virulent critique of black social 'pathology': See Daryl Michael Scott, *Contempt and Pity: Social Policy and the Image of the Damaged Black Psyche, 1880–1996* (Chapel Hill: University of North Carolina Press, 1997).

155 'corrupted by city ways': Blesh, *Shining Trumpets*, 112–13.

'lascivious song': ibid., 100.

he wandered into the Village Vanguard: Frederic Ramsey

Jr, 'Leadbelly's Last Sessions', *High Fidelity* (November-
December 1953), reprinted as liner notes to *Leadbelly's Last
Sessions*, Smithsonian Folkways Recordings SF CD 40068/7.

156 **'was rough and grainy, and some of its raw tones came
up'**: Frederic Ramsey Jr, 'Leadbelly's Legacy', *Saturday
Review* (February 1950).

**'record collector who, with a large library to choose
from'**: Ramsey, 'Leadbelly's Last Sessions'.

**'Rambling,' Ramsey concluded, 'was strong in Leadbelly's
blood.'**: Ramsey, 'Leadbelly's Legacy'.

157 **'Life in the country extremely old'**: Ramsey to Moses Asch,
30 March 1954, FRP. My account of Ramsey's journey comes
from his letters (to his family and to Asch) and from early
drafts of *Been Here and Gone*, all held in FRP.

**At first he kept his cameras and tape recorders in his
bag**: Frederic Ramsey Jr, *Been Here and Gone* (New
Brunswick: Rutgers University Press, 1960), xi.

'here, hands are still striving': ibid., 19.

'men who carried the devil on their backs': ibid., 95.

158 **'I got the blues so bad'**: ibid., 108.

'a personal expression': ibid., 31.

'tractors will replace mules': ibid., xii.

159 **Looking back on his time with Leadbelly**: Frederic
Ramsey, 'Leadbelly: A Great Long Time', *Sing Out!* (March
1965). Interviewed in 1991, four years before his death, and
asked about Leadbelly's links to 'the liberal, progressive
crowd', Ramsey replied: 'In that group there were left wingers
who regarded Leadbelly as their tool and they tried to make
him a spokesman for their political ends. I thought this was
crap. He was an artist, he wasn't a PR vehicle. They totally
misunderstood the guy . . . Leadbelly was not a political
person and I think they abused him'. Sean Killeen, 'Fred
Ramsey (1915-1995)', *Leadbelly Letter* 5 (Winter/Spring
1995), 11.

'I had looked vainly': Ramsey, *Been Here and Gone*, xi.
'The kids down South': *New Yorker* (6 August 1955), 14-15.
'It is beginning to be evident': Ramsey to Asch, 6 June
1954, FRP.

Chapter Six: The Real Negro Blues

161 **If you had been walking past the building:** In this opening
section I have tried to imagine a pivotal event from three
sentences James McKune wrote in 1961: 'I first heard Charley
Patton on a beat [battered] record early in 1944. At first he
seemed too primitive to me. But by the end of that year I told
a few friends that he was the greatest blues singer I have ever
heard'. (James McKune, 'The Great Country Blues Singers
(1)', *VJM Palaver* [April 1961], 3.) In 1944 McKune had not
yet attracted his circle of acolytes, and so far as I know he
never told anyone about how he came to collect race records.
Yet while much of this section is by necessity imagined,
throughout I have tried to build upon facts, playing around
with chronology where necessary.

McKune speaks of his taste for Spanish and South
American folk music in a 1951 letter to his friend Henry
Renard reprinted in Renard's article 'Letters from McKune',
78 Quarterly 1 (3) (1988) 54-62. His years of 'reading up' on
old world folk dances are my invention, though here I'm
alluding to what I've observed about collectors in general –
their ability to careen abruptly between minutely focused and
wildly disparate interests. (I was particularly struck by this
when I interviewed Pete Whelan, whose other obsessions have
included vintage cars, nineteenth century physical anthropology, early Anglo-Saxon languages, crocodiles and dwarf
palm trees.) Stephen W. Smith's article 'Hot Collecting', in
Ramsey and Smith's 1939 *Jazzmen*, filled me in on the growth

of a collector's subculture. The account of McKune's experience clerking in a store selling race records draws on remarks he made to his friend Henry Renard. That he disliked what he heard is my inference, based on how wildly his blues aesthetic would diverge from early 1930s black popular tastes. In a 1969 interview (reprinted in Rani Singh's 1999 edited collection of interviews with Harry Smith, *Think of the Self Speaking*), Harry Smith spoke of receiving a letter from McKune in 1942 in which he enclosed the list of untouched Paramounts found at the Central General Store. (Many of those discs turned up ten years later on Smith's *Anthology of American Folk Music*.) That McKune was chagrined by having sent it is my inference. One year later, McKune began collecting blues recordings himself, and at that point I cannot imagine that he would have let those discs pass him by.

From McKune's early 1960s columns in *VJM Palaver*, a record trader's journal, I knew that he began listening to blues in 1943 and to Patton in 1944, and from Renard's 'Letters from McKune', I learned that he compiled two major 'want lists', one in January 1943 that stretched to sixteen typewritten pages and an expanded edition one year later that encompassed 1,300 titles. (No one that I've spoken to ever laid eyes on either the 1943 or the 1944 list. McKune sent them out to record dealers and kept no copies of either; later, he tried to retrieve them by placing an ad in *Record Changer*, but without success.) For the possibility that he drew on Alan Lomax's 'List of American Folk Songs on Commercial Records', I drew on the reminiscences of Harry Smith, who told several interviewers that by the mid-1940s the list had become a kind of collector's bible. For McKune's reaction to specific recordings and the development of his blues-collecting strategies, I have drawn on McKune's *VJM* columns, Renard's 'Letters from McKune', and my interview with Pete Whelan.

169 only the barest facts emerge from their stories: Henry
     Renard, 'Letters from McKune', *78 Quarterly* 1, number 3,
     1988, 54–62; Bernard Klatzko, 'Postscript to the McKune
     Story', *78 Quarterly* 1, number 4, 1988, p. 93; Calt, *I'd
     Rather Be the Devil*,. 216–17; Joel Slotnikoff, *'Pete Whelan
     Interview'*,
     http://www.bluesworld.com/PeteWhelanInterview.html.
     'I don't know if this should be mentioned': Slotnikoff, 'Pete
     Whelan Interview', 3.
     'sockless', one collector remembers, 'and seemingly brain-
     damaged from alcohol': Calt, *I'd Rather Be the Devil*, 217.
     'There was a guy called Jim McKune': Quoted in O'Neal, 'I
     Once Was Lost,' in Cohn, *Nothing But the Blues*, 376.
     'He lived in one room in the YMCA': Slotnikoff, 'Pete
     Whelan Interview', 3.
171 the Jazz Record Center, or 'Indian Joe's': Henry Renard,
     'The Life and Times of Big Joe Clauberg and his Jazz Record
     Center,' *78 Quarterly* 1 (1989), 62–6.
     'We paced about the store': Pete Kaufman, 'A Recollection
     of Big Joe's . . .', *78 Quarterly* 1, no. 2 (1968).
172 'bananas are the ideal collector's food': Frederic Ramsey,
     'Discollecting: How to Care for Records, Where to Find Them,
     Which are Rare', in Rosenthal and Zachary, *Jazzways*, 91.
     'Only last night I gave a lady $2.00': Emerson Parker to
     Ramsey, 17 April 1945, FRP.
173 'There are collectors, and then there are Collectors':
     Charles Payne Rogers, *Record Changer* (May 1950), 13.
174 the jazz-inflected imagination of the Popular Front:
     Michael Denning, *The Cultural Front*.
     'a transcribed history': Charles Edward Smith et al, *The
     Jazz Record Book* (New York: Smith and Durrell, 1942), vii.
175 a major auction of choice jazz rarities: Pete Whelan,
     'Jacob S. Schneider: 63 Years and 450,000 Records Later', *78
     Quarterly* 1 (1967), 31.

'the jerks who pay ten bucks': Bill Grauer, 'In Defense of Label Collecting', *Record Changer* (May 1950), 7.

'a propaganda machine': Slotnikoff, 'Pete Whelan Interview', 7.

176 'He had this way of talking': Interview with Pete Whelan, 6 July 2003.

the singularity of his wants had drawn him a circle of acolytes: Kaufman , 'A Recollection of Big Joe's . . .'

He introduced them to the sites of collector's mythology: Slotnikoff, 'Pete Whelan Interview', 11–12.

177 'I have read with enthusiasm': McKune to Ramsey, 12 January 1944, file '*Jazzmen* correspondence – misc and fan mail', FRP.

178 'On principle': Interview with Pete Whelan, 6 July 2003.

'all of them choice': ibid.

'treacle fanciers': Undated letter from McKune to Renard, published in Renard, 'Letters from McKune', 58.

'considered worthless by everyone but [McKune] himself': Calt, *I'd Rather Be the Devil*, 216.

'He tells a story only in part': James McKune, 'The Great Country Blues Singers (2)', *VJM Palaver* (June 1961), 3.

179 'conditions not conducive to good listening': Letter from McKune to Renard, 27 August 1952, published in Renard, 'Letters from McKune', 61.

180 I said, 'Are you sure? That's a long ways': Interview with Dick Spottswood, July 2003, broadcast 12 October 2003 as part of 'The Room Where the Blues Was Born', BBC Radio 3, written and presented by Marybeth Hamilton, produced by Tim Dee.

Samuel Barclay Charters IV: For information on Charters, see Goldsmith, *Making People's Music*, 255–6, 267–8.

181 In simple terms I was trying: Samuel Charters, *The Country Blues* (New York: Da Capo Press, 1975, originally published 1959), ix.

'became the emotional outlet for Negro singers': ibid., 19.
'keep the focus where the black audience put it': ibid.,
xviii.

182 'Collectors of the Negro country blues singers should
read this': McKune, 'The Great Country Blues Singers (1)',
3–4.

184 'hours in the hot sun': Charters, *Country Blues*, 266.
'It was real': Slotnikoff, 'Pete Whelan Interview', 2.
'The voice is dark and heavy': Pete Welding, 'Stringin' the
Blues,' *Down Beat*, 1 July 1965, 22.

185 'After you've listened to the real Negro blues for a long
time': James McKune, 'The Great Country Blues Singers (3),'
VJM Palaver, September 1961, 7.
'an intensity devoid of dramatic effects': ibid., 7.
Stephen Calt later estimated: Calt, *I'd Rather Be the Devil*,
249. In 1967 Pete Whelan sold the OJL label to his partner
Bill Givens, who moved the company to Berkeley. More information on its releases can be found at
http://www.originjazz.com/ and
http://www.wirz.de/music/ojlfrm.htm.

186 'the definitive country blues anthologies': Palmer, *Deep
Blues*, 281.
a view also held by Jeff Todd Titon: Titon,
'Reconstructing the Blues', in Rosenberg, *Transforming
Tradition*, 224.
a young historian named Lawrence Levine: See Levine,
Black Culture, Black Consciousness, 478, 16n, and 483, 85n,
87n, where Levine draws on the OJL reissues.
'The kind of blues on the present recording': Marshall
Stearns, liner notes to *Negro Blues and Hollers*, originally
published 1962, reissued in 1997 on Rounder Records (CD
1501).

187 even Samuel Charters agreed: Charters, *The Bluesmen*,
27–32.

'Don't know what the Delta along the way will hold': Ramsey to Asch, 28 June 1954, FRP.

Informant after informant attested that the region felt modern: See the report of fieldworker Samuel Adams, 'Changing Negro Life in the *Delta*', included in Gordon and Nemerov, *Lost Delta Found*, 225–90. For more on the study and its portrait of the Delta, see Marybeth Hamilton, 'The blues, the folk, and African American history', *Transactions of the Royal Historical Society* XI (2001), 17–36.

188 Lewis Jones found no recordings by local musicians: 'List of records on machines in Clarksdale amusement places', Folder 7 (Lists), Fisk University Mississippi Delta Collection, Archive of Folk Culture, Library of Congress, Washington, DC.

he stumbled across a juke joint on the edge of a cotton field: Alan Lomax field notes, July 1942, Coahoma County Survey materials, Alan Lomax Archives, Hunter College.

'rural proletariat': Lewis Jones's reflections on the study's findings appear in Charles S. Johnson and associates, *To Stem This Tide: a Survey of Racial Tension Areas in the US* (Boston: The Pilgrim Press, 1943), 28.

'If the blues simply mirrored the protest of the moment': Samuel Charters, *The Poetry of the Blues* (New York, 1963), 17, 173.

189 'All those guys on that Harry Smith Anthology were dead': Greil Marcus, *Invisible Republic: Bob Dylan's Basement Tapes* (London: Picador, 1997), 94.

It is hard to know how to characterise what followed: For a scathing account of the revival by a McKune protégé, see Calt, *I'd Rather Be the Devil*.

'of almost archaeological purity': *Atlantic Monthly* (1961), quoted in Calt, *I'd Rather Be the Devil*, 218.

Skip James, an immensely troubled man: Calt, *I'd Rather Be the Devil*, 239–346.

190 'cherished the physical symbols': Grauer, 'In Defense of Label Collecting', 7.

'the rarest labels in the record collecting fraternity': Whelan, 'Jacob S. Schneider', 29.

191 'record collecting was not like collecting stamps': Interview with Pete Whelan, 6 July 2003.

'scratches, pops, clicks and hiss': Robert Santelli, *The Best of the Blues: the 101 Essential Albums* (London: Penguin, 1997), 57.

192 'There is an honest and laudable interest': Charles Keil, *Urban Blues* (Chicago: University of Chicago Press, 1966), 38.

'Are you another one of those guys': ibid., 35.

'a rich evocation of underground America': Alan Lomax, *Mister Jelly Roll*, xv.

'the blues of the professional jazzmen are never quite the real thing': Alan Lomax, *The Land Where the Blues Began*, 440.

'anomie and alienation, orphaning and rootlessness': ibid., ix.

193 'self-made outcasts': Ramsey, *Been Here and Gone*, 97–8, 122.

'flight from commitment': Barbara Ehrenreich, *The Hearts of Men: American Dreams and the Flight from Commitment* (New York: Random House, 1983).

'beggar, outcast, near criminal': Frederic Ramsey, '"The Country Blues" in Word and Song', *Saturday Review* 43 (16 January 1960), 78–9.

'a frontiersman in the Wild West': Norman Mailer, 'The White Negro', in Mailer, *Advertisements for Myself* (New York: Putnam, 1959), 339.

194 'Knowing in the cells of his existence': ibid., 341.

'His voice, guttural and hoarse': Alan Lomax, *The Land Where the Blues Began*, 18.

195 **to dissolve boundaries, renounce autonomy:** For a suggestive analysis of gender and primitivism, see Marianna
Torgovnick, *Primitive Passions: Men, Women, and the Quest
for Ecstasy* (Chicago: University of Chicago Press, 1996).
'a kind of colonial sentimentalism': Luc Sante, "The Genius
of Blues", *New York Review of Books* (11 August 1994), 52.

196 **the lower floors retained a kind of lowlife glamour:**
Thanks to Luc Sante for information about the history of the
Broadway Central. The building burned down in 1973; the
site now houses a New York University dormitory.
When police found his body in September 1971: Klatzko,
'Postscript to the McKune Story', 9.

197 **Hermione Lee has spoken of the writer's temptation:**
Hermione Lee, 'How to end it all: biography and death', paper
delivered at the *History Workshop Journal* conference on
Biography and History held at Birkbeck College, London, 28
October 2000.